Presidents and Mass Incarceration

Choices at the Top, Repercussions at the Bottom

Linda K. Mancillas

 PRAEGER ™

An Imprint of ABC-CLIO, LLC

Santa Barbara, California • Denver, Colorado

Library of Congress Cataloging-in-Publication Data

Names: Mancillas, Linda K., author.
Title: Presidents and mass incarceration : choices at the top, repercussions at the bottom / Linda K. Mancillas.
Description: Santa Barbara, California : Praeger, [2018] | Includes bibliographical references and index.
Identifiers: LCCN 2017038844 (print) | LCCN 2017048486 (ebook) | ISBN 9781440859472 (eBook) | ISBN 9781440859465 (hardcopy : alk. paper)
Subjects: LCSH: Criminal justice, Administration of—Political aspects—United States—History. | Imprisonment—Government policy—United States—History. | Crime—Government policy—United States—History. | United States—Politics and government.
Classification: LCC HV9950 (ebook) | LCC HV9950 .M25 2018 (print) | DDC 365/.973—dc23
LC record available at https://lccn.loc.gov/2017038844

ISBN: 978-1-4408-5946-5 (print)
        978-1-4408-5947-2 (ebook)

22 21 20 19 18   1 2 3 4 5

This book is also available as an eBook.

Praeger
An Imprint of ABC-CLIO, LLC

ABC-CLIO, LLC
130 Cremona Drive, P.O. Box 1911
Santa Barbara, California 93116-1911
www.abc-clio.com

This book is printed on acid-free paper ∞

Manufactured in the United States of America

For my students, from whom I learn something new every day

and

For the descendants of our grandmothers,
Lois Lowery McLeod and Paz Escarsiga Mancillas,
from which we came

Contents

Preface

This exploration into U.S. mass incarceration began in 2006 when I first looked at the increasing number of women in prisons but discovered that mass confinement was much larger than a gender issue. In 2009, during my time at American University, Washington, D.C., I completed work on the *Law and Order Movement: Politics, Crime and Mass Incarceration in the United States.* I was gifted with many outstanding political science and criminal justice professors at American, including Karen O'Connor, Richard Bennett, Robert Johnson, and Bette Dickerson. In 2010, I was fortunate to serve under the guiding hand of Susan Scanlan as part of a Women's Research and Education Institute Fellowship, working in the position of an education legislative assistant for U.S. Representative Bobby Scott (D-VA 3rd). Mr. Scott had introduced the Youth Promise (Prison Reduction through Opportunities, Mentoring, Intervention, Support, and Education) Act, a comprehensive policy directed toward reducing youth violence through a coordinated prevention and intervention response. Mr. Scott's knowledge and dedication to this cause helped inspire this book.

My work on the Hill with Team Scott was an invaluable asset for understanding over-imprisonment and the repercussions on communities of color and in America. Representative Scott and his staff were visionaries in understanding the consequences of the school-to-prison pipeline and of mass incarceration. Most significant, they were producing solutions to institutional and systemic criminal justice policy problems. All these experiences provided me with a solid academic and practical knowledge base for my research into the circumstances surrounding presidential decision-making and mass incarceration.

At the 2015 annual conference of the American Political Science Association held in Philadelphia, I was sitting in the downtown Marriott lobby. I was perplexed and tired. The conference had not been easy; I was overwhelmed with my new duties as chair of the Committee on the Status of Latinos and

Latinas in the Profession, and two of my political science colleagues that I most wanted to spend time with were no-shows. Also, I had met with Jessica Gribble, acquisitions editor for Praeger/ABC-CLIO, whom I held in the highest regard. We had worked together previously, and it was delightful to renew our relationship. Ms. Gribble wanted to know if I had ever done anything with my dissertation research—a disturbing and haunting question that I did not want to answer. Oh, sure, I had looked every day (for it seemed like a lifetime) at that huge pile of papers sitting on my floor, which I had moved from three different apartments. However, the material hadn't yet evolved into a published work. All that blood, sweat, and tears had gone nowhere.

However, with a warm smile and encouraging demeanor, Ms. Jessica Gribble did her job. She talked about the value and importance of my work and reassured me that—with some work, in a revised format—it was publishable. While I had a fleeting moment of joy and some of my confidence was restored, I was hesitant to go back into the belly of the beast. I had to think about this after I got home, when I was rested and had the energy to think clearly. Yet the travesty of mass incarceration would not leave me alone, and it began to wreak havoc on my brain. For the rest of the conference, I was consumed. On Saturday, I took a break from the meetings and was sitting in the noisy and crowded Marriott lobby when a distinguished gentleman asked me what I was working on. He must have noticed the anguish on my face.

I began my "elevator" speech, but as I was speaking to him, new thoughts were weirdly coming forth. I found myself saying—"Johnson did this, Nixon did that, and, oh yes! It was Reagan and Clinton too, and this is what they did to increase mass incarceration." Little did I know that I was sitting next to and pontificating away to Professor Irwin F. Gellman, author of *The Contender: Richard Nixon: The Congress Years, 1946–1952* (1999). I noticed that he had begun to smile and then said, "Linda, there you go, you have your book. No one has looked at what presidents have done to cause mass incarceration." I was appreciative that Dr. Gellman was so gracious and willing to share a scholarly moment with me. It was a divine experience that carried remnants of predestined fate. Thank you, Professor Gellman, for paying attention and for your inspiration and expert wisdom.

Acknowledgments

Many individuals facilitated the completion of this endeavor. My warmest affection goes to my baby sister, Connie Mancillas Byrd, for her endless proofreading and loyal support of my restless soul. My offspring, my grandchildren, and others in my family deserve all my gratitude; they have had to endure the ups and downs of my never-ending educational pursuits and professional ambitions. I must thank my wonderful feminist professors Wendy Gunther-Canada, Ada Long, and Beverly Hawk of the University of Alabama at Birmingham who tried to teach me what they knew. I am also thankful for Professors Karen O'Connor, Richard Bennett, Robert Johnson, and Betty Dickerson of American University for the political science, criminal justice, and social justice knowledge they imparted upon me. I am grateful to my "bestie," Lucie Magus, for her enlightening and loving friendship throughout the years. And to all my other chicas and amigos, you know who you are and what you have done—I am forever indebted to each of you. Thank you, Robbie, for your "beautiful" daily morning texts. I remain deeply appreciative to Susan Scalan, former director of the Women's Research and Education Institute (WREI) for offering me the amazing opportunity to work with Representative Bobby Scott (D-VA) and his remarkable Team Scott staff. Special affection goes to Senior Legislative Assistant David Daily, my like-minded fellow American University graduate, and Carrie Hughes, fellow WREI associate. My Hill experience provided me with the understanding and practical knowledge of the real-life workings of our federal government in Washington. This unique endeavor will forever enhance and inform my academic and scholarly practice. It is my hope that maybe one day I can return to the Hill.

CHAPTER ONE

Introduction: The Politics of U.S. Mass Incarceration

In my research on U.S. over-imprisonment, I found that the present-day prison boom has been accomplished by the actions of officials in both political parties, all three branches of government, plus the bureaucracy, special interest groups, the media, and the public. Although this is a situation in which responsibility is diffused, much of the blame can be traced to presidents: conservative presidents pushing for harsher penalties, and some liberal presidents trying to manage a backlash against progressive civil rights gains. This over-imprisonment was fueled by the law-and-order rhetoric, with the aftermath of punitive and draconian laws being enacted by Congress. In the end, the persistent and tenacious presidential leadership carried out from President Lyndon Johnson to President Barack Obama has accomplished this disaster. And although it is early, all indications point toward President Donald Trump (with his appointment of Attorney General Jefferson Beauregard Sessions) being the ultimate law-and-order chief executive—pro-prosecution, pro-incarceration, pro-detention, and pro-detainment.

Subsequently, the "lock them up and throw away the key" mentality of presidents from both political parties has produced the highest incarceration rate in the world, with over 2 million people behind bars in 2017. A vital part of stopping the U.S. carceral state is to examine how this miscarriage of justice occurred and how it continues to materialize. We need to know how and why there has been an increase of 550 percent in incarceration over the last 40 years, with nonviolent crimes and relatively minor drug possession offenses accounting for most of the escalation since the mid-1980s. Investigation and analysis is crucial in understanding why over 60 percent of prisoners are racial and ethnic minorities, which has fueled more social resegregation and furthered racial and gender inequality. Attitudes and treatment toward undocumented immigrants as the new federally targeted imprisoned group is central to scrutinizing criminal justice policy alongside the bloated profit-making prison industrial complex. Well before the current situation, President Eisenhower had the foresight to warn about the growing menus of money-making imprisonment known as the prison industrial complex (American Constitutional Society 2009).

Moreover, criminal justice strategy aimed at minorities and the poor has cost over $270 billion, growing by more than 70 percent in the last two decades, with 11 states spending more on corrections than on higher education (Executive Office of the President 2016). This public policy fiasco has triggered destructive and disturbing effects on communities of color. In the United States, 1 in 35 adult Americans are under some form of criminal supervision, and 1 in 9 African American children has a parent in prison or jail (Glaze and Kaeble 2014). Mass incarceration destroys future employment chances, family relations, and neighborhoods and contributes to generational inequality and to the cycles of poverty (McLeod 2015). If the United States is truly dedicated to becoming a more equable society, needless mass imprisonment must stop.

It is important to note that presidents, although fundamentally important, are only one of the factors that contribute to the increasing size of the federal prison population. Crime rates, law enforcement practices, and judicial sentencing patterns also play a role. For example, crime rates sharply increased in the 1980s, and "tough on crime" presidents and Congress continually responded by initiating law-and-order programs and policies. When crime rates began to fall, neither presidents nor Congress discontinued the war on drugs, and crime crusades flourished for political gain. While presidents facilitated harsh federal criminal justice policies, Congress created these laws, the bureaucracy enforced them, and the courts interpreted them constitutionally: all of these factors influenced the prison populations.

Nevertheless, the leadership choices made by President Johnson to President Trump continue to inflict severe repercussions for the citizens at the frayed edges of our communities. Condemned by the United Nations, the human rights catastrophe of super-incarceration needs to end now. It is time to stop this political insanity and societal suicide. The struggle for human rights has resulted in a checkered past, and the fight for "civil rights ain't always civil" (Melfi and Schroeder 2016). However, courageous leaders can make a difference. It is time for our nation's presidents and congressional leaders to do the right thing and demonstrate persuasive social justice leadership in supporting the reduction of mass incarceration of low-level offenders. Passing such reform measures as the Safe, Accountable, Fair, and Effective (SAFE) Justice Act of 2015 that was introduced by Representatives Bobby Scott (D-VA) and Jim Sensenbrenner (R-WI) will safely reduce the size and cost of the federal criminal prison system. It is time for our government to halt the destructive repercussions for those caught in the snare of the unjust American penal system.

The United States has a persistently stubborn history of mass incarceration since the 1960s, when presidential initiatives expanded federal intervention into crime control. Since that time, presidents have used the War on Crime, the War on Drugs, the War on Gangs, and "tough on crime" rhetoric to enact extremely punitive criminal justice policy. As a result, compared to other advanced Western industrial countries, the "United States imprisons at least five times more of its citizens per capita" (Weaver 2007). Consequently, law-and-order politics caused significant unfair and unjust changes in the criminal justice system. This book maps the criminal justice policy initiatives introduced and supported by presidents and their administrations, as well as legislative steps taken by Congress that exploded the growth of our prison population. This book also addresses the media's reaction to crime and the provocation of public fear by highly publicized crime events.

These changes began with the social upheaval of the 1960s and 1970s, including the "rights revolutions," the anti-war movement, and civil disobedience, which prompted reactionary, punitive criminal justice politics. In 1970 Attorney General Ramsey Clark recognized the growing problem by stating that "fear seeks repressiveness as a source of safety" (Bowman 2014, 389). The fear of crime is an emotional response shaped by a sense of danger and produced by the perceived threat of harm. A large number of people report that they have done something in response to the fear of crime, such as avoidance, protective behavior, or sharing information (Garofalo 1981). Jonathan Simon described the crime circumstances more precisely, arguing that the United States "created a new political order and mode of governance that is structured around crime and the fear of crime; crime has become a, if not the, defining problem of governments. Governing through crime has become the dominant mode—whether in managing crime risk, valorizing the victim in political discourse, or in using crime as a legitimate reason for action in other domains" (2008).

Beginning in the 1960s, presidents and their administrations began using executive power to build the institutional scaffolding that created and will maintain mass imprisonment. Years later, Simon continues to argue the importance of "the fears of the 1970s, when day-to-day disorder blended in the public mind with sensationalized media coverage of prison riots and of outliers like the Manson family. In the new conventional wisdom, criminals represented a distinct and internally homogeneous class of determined predators; the only way to contain their threat was to imprison them all for as long as possible" (2014). Governing through crime and the perceived fear of crime unleashed such negative government and social outcomes as the War on Crime and War on Drugs crusades. During these favorable political landscapes, mandatory minimum sentencing and "three strikes and you're out" sentencing tactics were embraced. Little thought was given to the consequences of these reactionary crime-fighting strategies.

Therefore, this work explores one of the most important problems in American politics: why the United States has incarcerated and placed under criminal supervision such an astounding number of its people—over 2 million. A more important question is how we stop this continuing march to law and order and restore social justice in a penal system that is negatively affecting millions of Americans. The answer to this historical puzzle may very well be an "everything causes everything" dilemma. While this may not be a suitable answer for those who demand the running of regressions, descriptive data presents a compelling story of mass incarceration in the United States. Public opinion and fear of crime, interest groups' mobilization, stricter court rulings, and high-profile crime events all contributed to the "governing by crime" environment (Simon 2008). Nonetheless, this book will demonstrate that it took presidential leadership to get the job done, and our presidents are to blame for a great deal of the over-imprisonment predicament the United States is now facing.

History of Law-and-Order Politics

As the civil rights era began, the politics of crime and civil unrest, widely known as the call for "law and order," gained prominence on the United States' political agenda (Flamm 2003, 2005; Gottschalk 2006). The modern political concept of "law and order" is the "guarantee of security for the citizen against violence, crime and disorder" (Garland 2001, 30). Since Thomas Jefferson, many presidents have used the term in reference to domestic security and international defense, and countless scholarly works and much popular attention have been directed to the phenomenon of "law and order." This concept is different from the "rule of law" that requires those in authority to exercise "their power within a constraining framework of public norms, rather than on the basis of their own preferences" (Waldron 2008). In the United States, "law and order" has come to be known as a proactive response to crime from law enforcement and the courts.

Current attention to law and order in the United States started as African Americans and other minorities began their struggle for civil rights (Farber and Roche 2003; Gottschalk 2006). In the liberal tradition of political philosophers like John Locke and Thomas Hobbs, individual freedom includes negative freedom. This freedom is determined by property, wealth, the right to bear arms to defend that property and wealth, as well as mobility and political expression (Davis 2012). For many African Americans, Hispanics, and other marginalized minorities who end up facing the criminal justice system, there is a historical connection between their criminalization and this narrow concept of citizenship rights. American culture harbors vestiges of human enslavement with lingering discriminatory consequences. The organized and mass political participation of the 1960s included successful resistance movements to expand civil liberties by challenging the injustice of legalized racism and discrimination. However, "laws do not produce or guarantee freedom," and the struggle continues as we strive to form a more perfect union for every citizen (Davis 2012, 14). Subsequently, as challenges to the criminal justice system developed in a law-and-order, politically charged environment, presidential leadership and the application of constitutional executive power became a major factor in determining which freedoms applied to which Americans.

In February 1956, during a presidential news conference, reporter Alice Dunnigan of the Associated Negro Press asked President Dwight D. Eisenhower if he felt that the racial violence on the campus of the University of Alabama was a "violation of Federal law and order," and if it was, should the U.S. Department of Justice investigate the situation (President Dwight D. Eisenhower 8 Feb 1956). President Eisenhower was hesitant to order federal intervention and responded that the Justice Department was looking into the matter. He further stressed that he was confident that university, state, and local officials would handle the incident properly. However, as integration intensified, Southern states refused to enforce desegregation laws, and President Eisenhower was forced to use presidential power.

Ultimately, in September 1957 President Eisenhower informed the governor and the people of Arkansas that federal law and orders of a U.S. district court could not "be flouted with impunity by any individual or any mob of extremists." He threatened to use the "full power of the United States," including force, "to prevent obstruction of the law and to carry out the orders of the Federal Court" (President Dwight D. Eisenhower 23 Sep 1957). Thus, in the inchoate stage of the civil rights movement, President Eisenhower took the first step in the government's quest to enforce federal law and maintain local order. Ironically, the law-and-order discourse began with the demand for enforcement of Supreme Court antidiscrimination rulings. However, the call for law-and-order rhetoric quickly took on racist tones. Special attention will be given to the U.S. Supreme Court in this book, because it continues to play a major role in the mass incarceration scenario.

In 1961 President John F. Kennedy, reacting to the FBI's reported increase in crime rates and the sense of growing juvenile delinquency, established the President's Committee on Juvenile Delinquency and Youth Crime. At that time, Gallup opinion polls on "what is the most important problem facing this country" showed that only 1 to 3 percent of the American public indicated concern for juvenile delinquency (Marion 1994, 25). Still, the committee predicted a threat from a growing youth population and an increasing delinquency rate of the baby-boomer generation. The study identified poverty and such substandard urban conditions as deficient housing, family disintegration, racial discrimination, high unemployment, and inadequate education as causes for black juvenile crime. The committee report recommended federal intervention to help large cities cope with and prevent delinquency.

In President Kennedy's 1963 State of the Union Address and Special Message to Congress, he urged investment in the country's youth and stated that "there is no reason why 1 million young Americans, out of school, and out of work, shall all remain unwanted and often untrained on our city streets" (President John F. Kennedy 14 Feb 1963). President Kennedy, like President Johnson to follow, linked lack of opportunity, dropping out of school, and unemployment to crime. Most noticeably, Kennedy's actions in forming the committee and following its recommendations led to federal mobilization around the issue of crime.

Yet a significant blow to the national sense of security occurred when President John F. Kennedy was assassinated on November 22, 1963. Additionally, American-style violence was transmitted into the homes of citizens through television news reports of the fatal day in Dallas, the presidential funeral with First Lady Jacqueline Kennedy and her children, and the live shooting of Lee Harvey Oswald by Jack Ruby. During that time *Newsweek* and *Time* magazines ran three cover stories each on the assassination. Violence again gripped the national stage when the brother of President Kennedy and his former attorney general, Robert Kennedy, was assassinated while running in the 1968 presidential campaign. *Newsweek* and *Time* ran cover stories on Robert Kennedy's death, as well as one story each on guns in the United States.

Following President Kennedy's agenda after his death, President Lyndon B. Johnson and his administration argued that the only effective way to restore law and order was by attacking poverty and unemployment. Under pressure from conservatives to address crime, President Johnson responded to the call for law and order by promoting the War on Poverty as a War on Crime. He set into motion the Great Society, a set of social programs resembling the New Deal's domestic agenda. The Great Society's main goal was to eliminate poverty and racial injustice by tackling such urban problems as education, health care, housing, and transportation. While the problem of black urban crime was used by liberals to support their social agenda to fight poverty, this issue was used by conservatives to attack the civil rights agenda and the expansion of social welfare programs (Flamm 2005).

Race and Crime

In 1968 sociologist Dr. Kenneth B. Clark, whose research was instrumental in demonstrating that separate was not equal in the *Brown v. Board of*

Education (1954) case, stated, "I sense there is a tendency to make crime in the streets synonymous with racial threats or the need to control the urban Negro problem" (Weaver 2007). Conservative Southern politicians favored linking crime to race and blaming the struggle for civil rights on crime in the streets. In 1960 Senator Richard Russell (D-GA), using racially charged language, wrote: "Mr. President, I say that the extremely high incidence of crimes of violence among members of the Negro race is one of the major reasons why the great majority of the white people of the South are irrevocably opposed to efforts to bring about enforced association of the races" (Weaver 2007).

Thus, in the United States, "crime" is often a code word for race (Davis 1996 Davis 2003; Hurwitz and Peffley 1997; Peffley, Hurwitz, and Sniderman 1997). "Race" as a political identity can be defined by the ways an individual is treated by the state. The mass incarceration of African Americans should be analyzed in the context of the civil rights movement and the response to their struggle for expansion of rights.

Traditionally, blacks have suffered under racism through which their basic humanity and rights constantly have been violated under the law. During the late 1950s, black men replaced white ethnic minorities as the new image of urban violence. In 1964 presidential candidate Senator Barry Goldwater (R-AZ) linked black civil disobedience to crime by calling activists and demonstrators "bullies and marauders" and "street mobs" (Murakawa 2008, 235). President Johnson's aides advised him to call a "White House Law-and-Order Conference" to address the issue, and his administration outlined steps for an aggressive crime and delinquency agenda (Weaver 2007).

By late the 1960s, white Americans associated black Americans with street crime and urban riots. This was a successful strategy for those who were against civil rights, as Vesla Weaver (2007) states, "Fusing crime to anxiety about ghetto revolts, racial disorder—initially defined as a problem of minority disenfranchisement—was redefined as a crime problem, which helped shift debate from social reform to punishment." The image of an urban black male as a dangerous criminal is part of the American consciousness and helps support criminalizing such social problems as poverty and drug abuse. This rationale justifies harsh criminal justice policies.

Rising crime rates, riots, and new racial norms may have facilitated the association of crime with black equality (Murakawa 2008). Research provides significant theoretical basis for linking whites who continue to negatively stereotype blacks to substantial support for "get tough" policies (Peffley, Hurwitz, and Sniderman 1997). Therefore, punitive criminal justice policymaking was not only crime fighting in nature but also a response to shift the agenda against racial equality (Weaver 2007). Although these public attitudes are mostly directed at black criminals who commit violent crimes (Hurwitz and Peffley 1997), conservative law-and-order policies resonated with a sympathetic constituency who saw the need for controlling and regulating undeserving and lawless minorities (Yates and Fording 2005). Consequently, detention and imprisonment has increasingly replaced other historic systems of racial control, such as slavery, Jim Crow laws, and ghettoization (Davis 2003).

On January 7, 2008, presidential candidate Hillary Rodham Clinton declared: "Dr. King's dream began to be realized when President Johnson passed the Civil Rights Act . . . It took a president to get it done" (Wheaton 2008). Secretary Clinton was referring to the importance of presidential leadership in assuring the fundamental freedom of the vote was obtained for African Americans. However, while legislative strides were made to end racial discrimination, President Johnson and the Congress were also expanding federal intervention into crime control. In the early 1960s with the civil rights movement, women's rights, and other successful challengers to the status quo, white resentment mounted against newly won gains made by minorities. Many middle-class Americans started harboring animosity against government welfare and affirmative action programs that seemed to cater to the under-served. Also, as apprehension emerged over civil disobedience as racial protest, student demonstrations and violence increased. Moreover, political assassinations, coupled with the rise in street crime, intensified public anxiety. Many Americans felt that the new culture was making it harder to maintain values grounded in religious and moral beliefs (Farber 1994).

Due to the social disruption of the 1960s and 1970s, presidential candidates capitalized on the fear of increasing crime rates. Conservative Arizona Senator Barry Goldwater and Governor of Alabama George Wallace held blacks responsible for crime in the streets and saw the Warren Supreme Court and the Democrats as too lenient on lawbreakers and responsible for a permissive society (Garland 2001). This perceived breakdown of law and order weakened faith in government and left liberals struggling to secure persuasive moral leadership on the crime issue (Flamm 2005). Eventually, both Democrats and Republicans set in motion a "if you do the crime, you'll do the time" movement that had major policy implications for the criminal justice system.

Additionally, the Warren Court's ruling on civil rights cases significantly increased the civil and political rights of minorities, women, and the accused, which radically challenged traditional beliefs. The civil rights movement's efforts to end state-sponsored racial segregation through the judicial, legislative, and executive branches of government drastically changed society. This social revolution threatened long-standing institutional and social structures. The racial violence of the 1960s and 1970s, the Vietnam War, and resulting antiwar student demonstrations heightened the chaos and fueled social tensions.

With reports of increasing crime rates, many blamed the increased leniency of the Warren Court and the criminal justice system for the lack of law and order, and many associated race with crime. The social circumstances of African Americans and Hispanics have led to their overrepresentation as victims of street crime and the subject of law enforcement attention and to their disproportionate numbers in courts, jails, prisons, media reports of crime, and the public fear of crime. The demand for law and order has resulted in approximately 6,741,400 people under some form of adult correctional supervision in the United States at year-end 2016; this includes 1 in 34 adults or 2.7 percent of the adult population (Bureau of Justice Statistics 2016). The 2017 federal budget request for prisons was $7.4 million, with the Bureau of Prisons responsible for over 219,000 federal offenders, both sentenced inmates and detained persons awaiting trial and/or sentencing (Federal Prison System 2016).

According to the Bureau of Justice Statistics, the number of inmates in state and federal prisons decreased by 1.7 percent to an estimated 1,571,013 in 2012 from 1,598,783 in 2011 (Goode 2013). By the end of 2013, persons under the supervision of adult correctional systems had a decline of appropriately 41,500. This was most likely due to decreases in probation and local jail populations (Glaze and Kaeble 2014). However, the decrease can also be attributed to the tightening of state budgets, plummeting crime rates, sentencing law changes, significant shifts in public opinion toward mass incarceration, and overall financial cost (Goode 2013).

Consequently, the United States leads the world in imprisonment rates, and over 5.8 million Americans are denied the right to vote due to felony convictions (Sentencing Project 25 May 2015, update May 2016). The relationship between penalty and citizenship is crucial to understanding the political interactions. Therefore, it is important in a democracy to understand a process that has disenfranchised an extraordinary number of its citizens (Young and Garland 1983, 22). Michael Jacobson, former academic and director of New York City's jail and probation system, suggested that the prison system requires massive reforms, and, since lawmakers have been so slow to act on this issue, he called for a large-scale social movement to stop mass incarceration (2005). Experts have been demanding reform for years; however, over-imprisonment continues, which undermines the legitimacy of the U.S. judicial criminal system process.

After the accusations of police brutality in Baltimore and Ferguson and with law enforcement accused of killing over 136 black people in 2016 (Craven 2016), divisive issues relating to reforming our criminal justice systems have again surfaced on the public agenda. However, these current events only reveal long-standing social justice problems. In the United States, 1 in every 100 adults are behind bars, and nonviolent crimes and relatively minor drug possession offenses account for most of the increase since the mid-1980s (Sentencing Project 2015). Importantly, over 60 percent of the incarcerated are racial and ethnic minorities. In April 2015 incarcerated African Americans numbered 78,219, at 37.5 percent, and incarcerated Hispanics numbered 71,326, at 34.2 percent, mostly due to arrests of illegal immigrants (Federal Bureau of Prisons 2015). From 1980 to 2013 the number of federal offenders incarcerated increased from approximately 24,000 to more than 215,000, making the federal system the largest in the nation. This is nothing new, and we have ignored glaring racial and ethnic inequalities that "permeate every aspect" of the U.S. criminal justice system (Sentencing Project 2013, 25).

Currently, the United States houses around 25 percent of the world's prisoner population (Holland 2013). Prison spending has grown faster than any other state budget item other than Medicaid—the U.S. prison industrial complex is a for-profit business (Tierney 2012; Segura 2013). It costs approximately $30,000 a year to house a prisoner, and $6.7 billion tax dollars were spent on incarceration in 2013 (Pew Charitable Trusts Fact Sheet 2015). Furthermore, approximately 2.7 million children have parents who are in jails or prisons, and evidence shows that inmates who have regular contact with their family fare better upon release. However, due to the privations of state prisons, it is even costly for prisoners to make phone calls.

Looking at the prison industrial complex, *Huffington Post* investigative reporter John W. Whitehead wrote:

> No matter what the politicians or corporate heads might say, prison privatization is neither fiscally responsible nor in keeping with principles of justice. It simply encourages incarceration for the sake of profits, while causing millions of Americans, most of them minor, nonviolent criminals, to be handed over to corporations for lengthy prison sentences which do nothing to protect society or prevent recidivism. This perverse notion of how prisons should be run, that they should be full at all times, and full of minor criminals, is evil. (2012)

The state is the consumer in the prisoner, and the for-profit equation and their financial priorities often run counter to the desires of a humanitarian society—it is making money and the bottom line that counts. This domestic policy is often unjust and unfair and requires social justice reform.

The ineffective, tough-on-crime policy choices made and promoted by presidents and lawmakers, such as expansion of criminal laws, lengthier sentences, and abolishment of parole and probation have contributed to the growing prison population (Gelb 2015). Recently, there was somewhat of a bipartisan push to overhaul the criminal justice system. A few Republican and Democratic 2016 presidential candidates were suggesting ways to reduce incarceration rates while Congress was considering some reforms

(Sensenbrenner and Scott 2015a). Before Donald Trump's candidacy, even some "tough on crime" conservatives were supporters of "smart on crime" reforms that could reduce incarceration in favor of more effective and less costly options. Yet all this has ceased with the election of law-and-order President Trump.

However, due to the tremendous amount of state resources being wasted, states have begun to take action. One early successful state example is Governor Nathan Deal of Georgia's criminal justice "smart on crime" measures. Since 1990 Georgia's prison population has doubled to nearly 56,000 inmates. After two decades of intense growth in Georgia's prison population, corrections spending amounted to more than $1 billion annually, with recidivism rates remaining high. Deal, backed by bipartisan support in the Georgia General Assembly, decided on a "smart on crime," comprehensive, evidence-driven approach that "protect public safety, hold offenders accountable and conserve taxpayer dollars" (Georgia Council on Criminal Justice Reform Report 2015, 3).

First, Governor Deal created the Special Council on Criminal Justice Reform that focused on the adult correctional system. The state of Georgia enacted substantial policy changes regarding violent career criminals, while strengthening probation, drug courts, and other sentencing alternatives for nonviolent offenders. The council moved the juvenile justice system to divert lower-level offenders into programs proven to reduce recidivism. Deal is claiming progress, with Georgia's overall prison population stabilizing in 2015 (Georgia Council on Criminal Justice Reform Report 2015). As of April 2015, the Georgia prison population had dropped to approximately 53,800 inmates, and the percentage of nonviolent offenders had decreased dramatically (Bluestein 2016). This type of calculated criminal justice reform is what each state and the federal government should be doing to reduce imprisonment. On May 9, 2017, Deal signed a bill that strengthened the accountability of the court system, continued to reduce recidivism rates, and provided juvenile court judges with additional resources to help young offenders (Deal 2017).

Presidential Power and Leadership

Politics has been defined as who gets what, when, and how, and presidents must figure out what they want and use their powerful leadership position to get it and keep it (Lasswell 1936). Presidents are national symbols and partisan leaders who must effectively deal with the administration, bureaucracy, Congress, and the public. The renowned political scientist Richard Neustadt defined the power of the American presidency as the power to persuade (1990). He related the president's bargaining advantage to three particular sources: their ability to persuade others that they have a responsibility to do what the president wants them to do; others have expectations regarding the president's ability and will act on these perceived expectations; and how the public views the president and how that public opinion impacts other decision makers. Presidential power resides in their vantage points, reputation, and prestige, as well as in their ability to develop persuasive communication toward their cabinet and Congress and may include persuading the public to make sacrifices (Smith and Smith 1994).

Another notable source of presidential power is in the president's agenda-setting capabilities. Presidents in the modern age employ leadership by "going public" and use television, speeches, including the State of the Union address, appearances with local audiences, and social media like Facebook and Twitter (Kernell 2007). Most presidents have strong personalities, try to influence the media's agenda, and appeal to the public for support of their ideas and proposals. While presidents attempt to mobilize the media in their favor, public awareness and information is inconsistent. In regard to the fear of crime and high-profile crime events, the mass media exerts significant influence on what citizens consider important. Further examination on the impact of current social media will also be presented in the chapter on President Donald Trump's use of fear of crime in his campaign and in his first term.

Presidential success can be measured in how often Congress passes the chief executive's policy initiatives. If Congress is being resistant to a proposal, the president may go directly to the people through the media for backing. For example, in civil rights, presidents have played a critical role in setting the agenda, framing the debate, and formulating policy goals or barriers (Shull 1999). Throughout this book, we will see how presidents have contributed to mass incarceration by utilizing their leadership skills to pass legislation, execute executive orders, work through the bureaucracy, and rally public support.

We have learned that mass incarceration is not the answer to crime. Only evidence-based research will show if new "smart on crime" initiatives will lower the prison population rate (Scott 2015). For understanding mass incarceration, former Senator Clinton's description of presidential power holds markedly true—it took presidents *to get the job done!* From Lyndon Johnson to Barack Obama and now, Donald Trump, U.S. presidents exercised their powerful leadership position to promote and maintain the call to law and order. Presidential leadership has contributed to the United States' overcriminalization phenomenon, but all branches of government have the responsibility to reform the criminal justice system by initiating smart-on-crime policies to reduce our prison population.

CHAPTER TWO

President Johnson's Safe Streets: The First Federal Anti-Crime Entrepreneur

Lyndon Baines Johnson (LBJ) came to the White House after leading the Senate Democrats for the entire eight years of President Eisenhower's administration. First, he was minority leader for two years and then majority leader for six years. While in the Senate, he developed substantial legislative leadership qualities that included unceasing energy, "ambition, attention to detail and an overwhelming personality" (Hatfield 1997). Texas Governor John Connally once described LBJ as being "cruel and kind, generous and greedy, sensitive and insensitive, crafty and naive, ruthless and thoughtful, simple in many ways yet extremely complex, caring and totally not caring; he could overwhelm people with kindness and turn around and be cruel and petty towards those same people; he knew how to use people in politics in the way nobody else could" (Hatfield 1997). Still, the most important quality for presidential leadership was Johnson as the "ultimate compromiser, a broker, and a master of the art of the deal." He possessed the power to persuade with his "sweet talk, threats, and exaggerated facial expressions and body language which was widely known as 'the treatment'" (Hatfield 1997). President Johnson was a tall Texan who wielded his considerable power in a politically artful manner and was known as the "genius legislator" (PBS 2012).

As majority leader, his greatest achievement was the 1957 passage of the first civil rights bill since Reconstruction. Many felt that because of his poor background, Johnson had genuine compassion for African Americans, the poor, and the disadvantaged. This compassion signaled his move away from being a Texas Southerner to being a national leader. Also, in opposition to many of his colleagues, Senator Johnson did not sign the Southern Manifesto against the Supreme Court's ruling in *Brown v. Board of Education* (1954). For many in the Senate, Majority Leader Johnson had been too strong, too difficult, and so tough that many were relieved to have him move to the vice president's office (Hatfield 1997). During his time in the White House, President Johnson would accomplish wonderful victories but face agonizing defeats. Moreover, while it may not have been his intention to begin mass incarceration in the United States, his presidential leadership led him to be the first federal anti-crime entrepreneur.

During the 1960s and early 1970s, many of the United States' white middle class felt that urban unrest and the rise in crime put them in danger. They believed that society was in peril and segregation meant law and order, while integration meant crime. Before this time, crime had not been a salient issue in federal politics, as Castro, the Soviet Union, and communism were the national enemy—not domestic crime and civil unrest (Farber 1994). However, President Johnson was the first chief executive to form a "partnership" between the federal government, states, and local law enforcement for "the preservation of law and order" (Weaver 2007). This federal initiative assisted local law enforcement in strengthening their capabilities toward what was perceived as a growing "national crime problem" (Weaver 2007).

Additionally, the United States' history of slavery and racism contributed to a legacy of linking African Americans with crime. Media images of black youths as protesters or as militant Black Panthers caused fear and anger. At the same time, the discourse surrounding the economic downturn and a growing emphasis on increasing affirmative action and welfare policies resulted in the perceived marginalization of the decent, hard-working middle class. This fostered resentment and hostility toward youth, joblessness, and concentrated poverty. Therefore, as a result of racial bigotry and a white backlash against perceived African American gains, as well as a response to racial violence, there was a demand for more control and law enforcement (Smith, McCarthy, McPhail, and Augustyn 2001). This phenomenon became known as the call for law and order.

Between 1963 and 1968 criminal justice authorities reported that crime had doubled (Flamm 2005). As media coverage of racial violence and student protest intensified, the public grew increasingly concerned about crime. Gallup surveys in response to "the most important problem facing the nation" question reported that juvenile delinquency, coupled with crime, rose to 12 percent. Responses concerning broader crime issues neared 10 percent, college demonstrations neared 4 percent, and lack of respect for the law was around 9 percent (Gallup Poll: Public Opinion 1964–1968, quoted in Marion 1994, 40). Subsequently, the call for law and order developed into a forceful political symbol (Clark 1997).

Consequently, President Lyndon B. Johnson was faced with the tension of violent racial riots and opposition to the Vietnam War, while trying to carry out the Great Society's progressive policies and War on Poverty programs. Simultaneously, the civil rights, anti-war, and women's movements brought new constituencies comprised of minorities and women into the Democratic Party. The demands of these new groups brought change in the political parties (Meyer and Staggenborg 1996).

Lyndon Baines Johnson was a natural politician. Taking office upon President Kennedy's death and following his agenda, President Johnson and his administration argued that the only effective way to restore domestic tranquility was by eliminating poverty and unemployment. However, Johnson was under pressure from conservatives to address crime and responded by promoting the War on Poverty as a War on Crime. He set into motion a set of social programs resembling the New Deal's domestic agenda. The Great Society's main goal was to eliminate poverty and racial injustice by tackling urban problems such as education, health care, housing, and transportation. In signing the Economic Opportunity Act of 1964, Johnson stated that every dollar of funding would result in savings to the local taxpayers in the costs of crime, welfare, and health care, as well as police protection (President Lyndon B. Johnson 20 Aug 1964). In a speech to U.S. Marshals in 1964, President Johnson set the national crime agenda when he declared, "I am determined that we shall use every resource of our Federal Government, in cooperation with State and local authorities, to eradicate organized crime in all of its forms" (President Lyndon B. Johnson 18 Aug 1964). While the Kennedy administration focused on organized crime, President Johnson extended the scope to include delinquency, crime control, and prevention.

In the 1964 campaign, President Johnson gave over 424 speeches, and many addressed the crime issue (Marion 1994, 39). According to him, the Great Society programs would end the social and economic problems that caused crime. The Democratic Party platform stated that lawlessness would not be tolerated and that "lawless disregard for the rights of others is wrong" (President Lyndon B. Johnson 18 Aug 1964). Republican candidate Senator Barry Goldwater (R-AZ) was against expansion of the federal government, labor unions, and many government social programs. He also voted against the 1964 Civil Rights Act. Goldwater's campaign rhetoric claimed that President Johnson and the Democrats had failed to show respect for the law. He and the Republicans demanded that Congress enact legislation to control crime and charged that the Warren Court was too lenient on lawbreakers. As widespread media attention turned to crime and violence, public awareness and anxiety heightened. High-profile crime events kept crime on the public agenda, and the fear of crime became a serious, shared concern with a public expecting a crime-free society.

However, by successfully portraying Senator Goldwater as a racist and a warmonger, Johnson won the election by a landslide. Still, President Johnson was forced to respond to Senator Goldwater to diffuse his accusations of being weak on crime. By introducing and endorsing an anti-crime agenda, he created an environment where the race and crime argument would thrive.

At that time, the Supreme Court was instrumental in promoting the civil rights agenda but was highly opposed by anti-integrationist conservatives. Therefore, during the late 1950s and 1960s, the U.S. Supreme Court had a significant influence on the changing cultural and political environment. Republican President Eisenhower had the opportunity to appoint five members of the Supreme Court, including Chief Justice Earl Warren and Justices John Harlan, William Brennan, Charles Whittaker, and Potter Stewart. Upon his appointment, the president felt that Warren represented the "political, economic, and social thinking" that the Court needed (Fox 2017). But after disagreeing with the Court's liberal civil rights decisions that revolutionized the role of the Court, President Eisenhower believed Warren's appointment had been a miscalculation (Eisler 1997). He stated that it was "the biggest damned-fool mistake I ever made" (Fox 2017). Then, in President John F. Kennedy's short two-year term, he appointed two Democrats to the Supreme Court: Justices Arthur J. Goldberg and Byron R. White.

Consequently, the Warren Court delivered groundbreaking decisions that strengthened the rights of minorities, criminal defendants, and prisoners. As a result of these controversial rulings, there was growing hostility toward the Supreme Court's simultaneously enhancing the rights of minorities and the accused while diminishing law enforcement's authority. Due to the Warren Court rulings, many Republicans and some Democrats believed that the Supreme Court had handcuffed law enforcement. However, history has judged this progressive era differently: "It is to the credit of the Supreme Court that it recognized that the nation was in the midst of a social revolution before this became apparent to most of the elected representatives of the people, and that it sought to eliminate the basic defects in our system for the administration of criminal justice within our present structure" (Pye 1968). Yet several law enforcement organizations such as the Americans for Effective Law Enforcement, Inc. (AELE), the International Association of Chiefs of Police, the National Sheriffs' Association, and the National District Attorneys Association joined in many court cases as friends of the court in support of law enforcement.

In 1967 AELE began their "friend of the court" program and claims to have appeared as amicus curiae over 100 times in the U.S. Supreme Court and over 35 times in federal district courts, the circuit courts of appeal, and various state courts (AELE 2008). Mostly, their arguments focused on the Fourth and Fifth Amendments' search and seizure, the exclusionary rule, and application of Miranda (AELE 2008). For *Brown* (1954) and other desegregation rulings, opposition came from many Southern governors and from the attorneys general from North Carolina, South Carolina, Mississippi, Virginia, Florida, Texas, Alabama, Georgia, and Louisiana. In 1970 a survey that studied white attitudes toward integration since 1942 found that nearly 50 percent of white Southerners approved of school desegregation, while white Northern support was at 80 percent (Costello 1972). However, in October 1971 a Gallup poll found that 76 percent of responding white parents opposed forced busing to achieve integration, while 47 percent of black parents were in opposition (Costello 1972).

Brown v. Board of Education (1954) contributed to a white backlash against integration in several ways (Klarman 1994). First, the ruling was against states' rights and represented federal intervention into Southern race relations. Second, *Brown* was a clear and salient indication that legal segregation was destined to end. Third, the ruling indicated that racial change would take place in schools, where white Southern segregationists were most resistant. Some politicians and the media attempted to draw connections between social unrest and a potential Communist threat. On May 3, 1962, headlines in the *New York Times* exclaimed that Senator James Eastland, Democrat of Mississippi, "Calls Warren Pro-Red" (Eastland 1962). Eastland warned that Chief Justice Warren "decides for the Communists" when there was a "clear-cut" Supreme Court ruling between them and U.S. security. Although Chief Justice Warren had been a vocal anti-Communist, Robert Welch, head of the John Birch Society, started an "Impeach Earl Warren" drive in the 1960s (Farber and Roche 2003).

The media carried negative reports on the Court; for example, on September 10, 1965, the *New York Times* headlines read, "Attack on Court Heard by Warren" (Zion 1965). While attending a panel in Atlantic City with other federal judges, Michael J. Murphy, the former New York City Police commissioner, accused the Supreme Court of "unduly hampering" the administration of criminal justice while "vicious beasts" were loose on the streets. *Time* and *Newsweek* magazines ran four cover stories each on the Court between 1962 and 1967. One story featured Chief Justice Warren, another reported on the activism of Associate Judge Hugo Black, another reviewed the 10-year "momentous" reign of the Warren Court, and the Escobedo decision was the subject of the last story.

In 1968 congressional critics of the Supreme Court argued that the Court was overly concerned with the rights of the accused, leaving police without the latitude needed to investigate crime and interrogate suspects. Congressional hostility toward the Court was clear in the rejection of President Johnson's nomination of Associate Justice Abe Fortas, who was to succeed Chief Justice Earl Warren (Crime and Justice 1969).

Furthermore, public opinion showed discontent with the Supreme Court's position. In 1967, 46 percent of people polled criticized the courts for being too lenient toward criminals. In 1968, 50 to 65 percent blamed the courts for the breakdown in law and order. In 1969, 77 percent and in 1970, 63 to 65 percent of those polled had a problem with the courts being "too soft" on crime (Erskine 1968–1969 and 1974–1975). In 1967, 52 percent of Republicans polled and 42 percent of Democrats gave the Supreme Court a "Fair to Poor" rating. In 1970, 75 percent of Republicans and 61 percent of Democrats who were asked reported that the courts were too easy in dealing with criminals (Erskine 1974–1975). The controversial rulings of the Warren Court fostered the social and political upheaval of the 1960s and 1970s and helped to cultivate the demand for law and order that President Johnson and future presidents were forced to deal with.

In 1964 conservatives continued to define civil disobedience in terms of disrespect for the "hardworking, respectable," and mostly white middle class. They blamed a "permissive culture" for promoting "anti-social behavior" against law and authority (Garland 2001, 97). President Johnson tried to set the agenda by promising to "chart a new course of peace, freedom, morality and constitutional order" (Brennan 2003, 71). He began to dedicate federal government resources to train local law enforcement officers and called for scientific discovery into the causes of crime and investigation into better ways of preventing crime (President Lyndon B. Johnson 4 Jan 1965). Traditionally, law enforcement and crime control were considered a local problem. Until the early 1970s, state and local governments employed more than 10 times as many law enforcement personnel as did the federal government. President Johnson was baffled that the American people blamed the breakdown of local authority on him and the federal government (Flamm 2005). As social unrest increased, demands for order intensified, with white and black Americans experiencing a genuine fear of crime and violence.

When asked about federal expansion into crime control, President Johnson justified federal intervention, indicating that "the Constitution provides that responsibility for law and order should be vested in the States and in the local communities . . . the Federal Government's general police power should be limited to interstate matters and situations where the States' ability to maintain law and order has broken down" (President Lyndon B. Johnson 18 Jul 1964).

At that time, President Johnson considered law enforcement a local matter and thought that the federal government should have limited authority. Feeling pressure to react, he proposed new legislation, established crime commissions and task forces, and held White House conferences. Johnson was the first president to address Congress specifically on the issue of crime, and he submitted four specific messages and speeches on crime to Congress. He took actions to place crime on the national agenda and began the national march to suppress crime with long-lasting criminal justice ramifications.

In his first State of the Union message, President Johnson was concerned more with crime prevention than control. He wanted better trained local police and innovative ways to stop crime (President Lyndon B. Johnson 4 Jan 1965). The president was optimistic that his Great Society programs would curb the crime rate. The President's Committee on Juvenile Delinquency approved a grant of $1 million to fight juvenile delinquency. The money was intended to bring about needed improvements in schools, vocational training, employment services, and crime prevention.

In President Johnson's first major crime address, he stated that crime fighting was no longer a local problem. He proposed the Law Enforcement Assistance Act of 1965 (LEAA) that authorized the U.S. Attorney General to aid state, local, and private groups to improve and broaden crime-control programs. President Johnson also established the President's Commission on Law Enforcement and Administration of Justice, headed by Attorney General Nicholas Katzenbach, to study the crime problem systemically (President Lyndon B. Johnson 8 Mar 1965). At that point in his administration, Johnson was more interested in finding the causes of crime and how to prevent it and wanted alternatives to imprisonment and more emphasis on rehabilitation (Weaver 2007).

In the same month, the news media began addressing the crime problem, and *Newsweek* ran "Crime in the Streets" as a cover story. This piece associated crime with African Americans and contained the first statements regarding a "war on crime" (Barlow 1998). Within a few weeks, *Time* published a cover story on "The Los Angeles Riot," describing the event in terms of crime, disorder, and violence. In September 1965 the president underscored the crime problem and stated that "Crime is a sore on the face of America. It is a menace on our streets. It is a drain on our cities. It is a corrupter of our youth. It is a cause of untold suffering and loss. . . . We must bring it under control, and then we must root out the cause. . . . So let us together spearhead a new war against crime in this country" (President Lyndon B. Johnson 8 Sep 1965). Here, President Johnson wanted to develop a "blueprint" that would "banish crime." But crime control would not be easily accomplished, and his presidential leadership would be constantly compromised.

As a result, the crime commission's recommendations included state and local planning, criminal justice personnel education and training, organization and operation reform of criminal justice agencies, national information systems development, and scientific and technological research and development (Marion 1994, 53). These recommendations provided the Johnson administration with a platform to build criminal justice federal policies. Like President Kennedy's Commission on the Status of Women, which laid the groundwork for the women's rights movement, President Johnson's crime commission acted as the foundational backbone of the advancement toward strict enforcement of the rule of law.

Additionally, due to the rising crime rates in the District of Columbia, President Johnson signed an executive order establishing the President's Commission on Crime in the District of Columbia (President Lyndon B. Johnson 16 Jul 1965). The District of Columbia was under federal control, and President Johnson struggled throughout his presidency to make the nation's capital a safer place to live, work, and visit.

In his March 9, 1966, Special Message to Congress on Crime and Law Enforcement, President Johnson described the seriousness and urgency of the crime problem and tried to engage support by declaring that "Crime—the fact of crime and the fear of crime mark the life of every American. We know its unrelenting pace: a forcible rape every 26 minutes, a robbery every 5 minutes, an aggravated assault every 3 minutes, a car theft every minute, a burglary every 28 seconds. We know its cost in dollars—some $27 billion annually" (President Lyndon B. Johnson 9 Mar 1966). President Johnson urged Congress to pass his comprehensive crime control act. As crime rates increased and Congress debated over proposed legislation, President Johnson's speeches became more intense and his ardent choices more prominent.

In May 1966 President Johnson spoke on efforts to stop organized crime and reported that the Federal Bureau of Investigation, the Intelligence Division of the Internal Revenue Service, the Bureau of Narcotics, and other agencies had been gathering information on organized crime (President Lyndon B. Johnson 5 May 1966). The Task Force on Organized Crime discovered a society of 24 organized crime families or groups involved in gambling and loan-sharking. When almost none of President Johnson's organized crime proposals passed, the Republicans accused the Democrats of not being serious concerning organized crime (Marion 1994).

In November 1966 at the signing of the Narcotic Addict Rehabilitation Act, President Johnson claimed that this act—in conjunction with the Law Enforcement Act of 1965 and a measure to establish a national commission to revise federal criminal statues—would "help us carry on our crusade against crime" (President Lyndon B. Johnson 8 Nov 1966). President Johnson invoked images of war and battle and used this as a tactic in advancing the call for law and order. The Johnson administration had a political critic in candidate Ronald Reagan. Reagan claimed (as did Barry Goldwater and George Wallace) that urban rioters, anti-war protesters, and civil rights activists were the greatest threat to American freedom and civility.

Finding a sympathetic voting bloc, Reagan won the California gubernatorial race, and Republicans gained a charismatic crusader (Schruparra 2003). Ultimately, this rhetoric calmed fear by identifying and targeting the enemy—protesters, rioters, and street criminals. In August 1966 *Newsweek* published a cover story, "Police on the Stop," which indicated that police were in danger due to racial riots. In 1966 polls revealed that a majority of Americans believed the Democrats were failing and that the Republicans would do a better job dealing with urban and racial unrest (Flamm 2005, 82).

Subsequently, President Johnson advocated against the "growing menace of crime and promised to build up law enforcement by 'revitalizing' the entire federal system from crime prevention to corrections" (President Lyndon B. Johnson 12 Jan 1966). As he was faced with the realities of crime in the United States, Johnson effectively used war as a tool to invoke the dread, fear, and terror of crime. He claimed, "We are fighting a war within our own boundaries . . . The enemy is not identified by uniform, but no man, woman, or child is really free from the hostilities . . . This war is a war against crime in America" (President Lyndon B. Johnson 15 Oct 1966). These threatening messages about war, safety, danger, and fear influenced major changes in the criminal justice system (Altheide 2006).

In President Johnson's 1967 State of the Union Address, he told Congress that the crime dilemma was "more massive and profound" than anyone had realized. He contended that the war on crime could not be won in Washington alone, but that crime must be "rooted out in local communities by local authorities." However, he proposed that the national government provide a substantial percentage of the cost (President Lyndon B. Johnson 10 Jan 1967). By supporting major crime legislation and funding, President Johnson expanded federal intervention and acted as a significant anti-crime leader.

In his third special crime speech before Congress, "Message on Crime in America" on February 6, 1967, President Johnson announced the Omnibus Crime Control and Safe Streets Act of 1967, which was based on the crime commission's recommendations. This bill was the first federal program designed as a block grant. It supported the president's belief that the federal government should do more to assist state and local law enforcement agencies. Funds were apportioned to states on a per capita formula to reduce crime. The president worked throughout the year to obtain passage. In 1968 President Johnson delivered his final crime message to Congress, urging passage of the Safe Streets legislation. This bill proposed a 22-point anti-crime program and requested passage of over a dozen separate bills. Interestingly, included in this legislation was the use of court-ordered electronic surveillance of certain specific violations. All of these anti-crime measures made by President Johnson would have serious consequences for those at the bottom of the criminal justice spectrum.

Eventually, Congress followed through with funding for many of these recommendations. For example, Johnson proposed a Federal Judicial Center for analysis, research, and planning to improve the federal court system, and Congress enacted the necessary legislation. Due to changes made in the House and the Senate, President Johnson was not pleased with the final bill. However, it was signed into law on June 19, 1968—a few weeks after Robert Kennedy was assassinated (Marion 1994).

Criminal justice scholar Nancy E. Marion makes the argument that President Johnson's crime-control measures did not have the "ultimate goal of reducing criminal behavior in the United States" (1994, 36). She claims that the Johnson administration's crime policies only provided "a series of symbolic gestures aimed at appeasing the public sentiment about crime control" (1994). However, his leadership enhanced a crime-fighting movement through the manipulation of language that signified the urgency and seriousness of "safe streets."

In 1968, while the Democrats were following President Johnson's crime agenda, the Republican Party platform aimed to address the "Crisis of the Cities" and blamed lawlessness for "crumbling the foundations of American society" (Republican Party Platform of 1968). The Republicans accused President Johnson of failed leadership by ignoring the rising crime rate, failing to implement recommendations of his own National Advisory Commission, opposing legislation that would assist law enforcement, and failing to prosecute effectively those who posed threats to national security. They pledged an all-out crusade against crime. While Republicans railed against a growing federal government, most failed to recognize how the War on Crime would contribute to federal authority's seizure of state law enforcement powers.

Importantly, the conservative Democrat George Wallace provided hope for those who wanted to halt racial progress and who sought retaliation against rioters and criminals. Wallace supporters believed that he stood for "what this country is built on"—"Law and Order" (Hart, J., quoted by Flamm 2005, 166). However, by October 1968, under both Democratic and Republican assault, there was an increase in those who felt that Wallace was an extreme racist. In the end, Wallace support fell significantly from 53 percent to 21 percent, and he received only 13.5 percent of the vote (Harris 1968). Yet Wallace's highly visible law-and-order candidacy guaranteed that crime would play a major role in the campaign.

Furthermore, some conservatives felt that the civil rights movement, the growing welfare state, and the youth culture were evidence of a Soviet conspiracy (Roche 2003). The anti-Communists saw the agitation for rights, social programs, and anti-war efforts as a Soviet-engineered Communist threat. For conservatives, restoration of patriotism and security rested in the national government assuming a major role in the struggle against chaos and communism.

Yet Johnson gave legitimacy to expanding federal intervention into crime control and other criminal justice activities such as illicit drugs. Although he was certainly in opposition to many of the more conservative legislative measures, he shared the goal of reducing crime with both Republicans and Democrats. However, during the Johnson presidency, expansion of civil rights and social justice began to wither while criminal justice policies grew.

Throughout the Johnson presidency, many organizations opposed more progressive criminal justice policies. These special interest groups included professional organizations such as the National Sheriffs' Association; the International Association of Chiefs of Police; corrections officers associations; victims groups; neighborhood associations; local, state, and national crime-prevention organizations; and private prison corporations such as Corrections Corporation of America (Miller 2004). In the 1960s and 1970s, approximately four prisons a year were built in the rural areas of the United States (Merritt 2008). Moreover, these groups worked both separately and together to obtain stricter law enforcement policies and federal funding with little or no insight into the negative repercussions of their actions.

Several scholars claim that the public's growing concern over crime and the drive for more punishment was led by a well-funded cartel of conservatives alarmed over liberal social programs and civil disorder (Austin and Irwin 2001; Beckett 1997; Chambliss 1999). These conservatives argued that poverty was caused by bad choices, and crime was the result of greed. According to the "culture of poverty" theory, individuals were poor because they refused to work hard, opting instead for handouts from the government. For this conservative philosophy, the welfare state undermined self-discipline and promoted crime. Criminalizing the poor transformed their image from a needy population to a dangerous, undeserving underclass (Beckett and Sasson 2004).

Subsequently, crime policy flourished during the Johnson administration. Important to the advancement of law-and-order politics was the array of crime policies passed by Congress. The 89th Congress significantly expanded the federal government's role in crime control under the Safe Streets Act of 1968, which included the Law Enforcement Assistance Administration (LEAA). This act established and created the Bureau of Narcotics and Dangerous Drugs to coordinate national, state, and local anti-drug activities (Beckett and Sasson 2004, 52). With this piece of legislation, the crime agenda was furthered and supported by the federal government. Since the founding of the United States, crime has been a "habitual"—coming up again and again—public policy item (Cobb and Elder 1972). However, beginning in the 1960s, crime reduction gained momentum on the public agenda.

Most importantly, the formation of LEAA was "the 'most tangible mark' of the arrival of crime on the institutional agenda at the federal level" (Bevacqua 2000, 117). The purpose of the LEAA was to encourage innovative and experimental methods for stopping crime and enforcing laws, and served as the central funding agency for local and state criminal justice activities, which included research and training projects (Feeley and Sarat 1980). Yet Congress reshaped President Johnson's Safe Streets Act. Democrats, who wanted to provide federal grants to police for training, equipment, pilot programs, and research, essentially lost control of the crime issue. In opposition, the Republican version of the bill, which was heavily supported by Southern Democrats, provided block grants to the states.

The final version of the Omnibus Crime Control and Safe Streets Act distributed millions of dollars to the states for police riot control—not research and training. The House version added \$25 million to the bill and mandated that the funds be used for riot control, not for training or research. Also, as a result of pressure from the International Association of Chiefs of Police, the Senate followed the House and adopted block grants, with only general provisions on how federal money could be spent instead of categorical grants that required more strict and specific provisions on spending for local departments (Flamm 2005, 133). By that time, the majority of state governors were Republican, and they made appointments to these agencies. Therefore, they could allocate a large share of the funds to towns and suburbs (instead of urban areas) where crime rates were low but where many of their voters lived (Flamm 2005, 134).

Additionally, the LEAA contained new legal provisions directed at civil disorder and set the first criminal penalties for crossing state lines to incite a riot (Rioting 1969). The bill disqualified any person convicted of a felony while participating in a riot from federal employment (Flamm 2005). Enacting the Safe Streets Act of 1968 and the Civil Obedience Act of 1968 criminalized political dissent and attempted to reign in the social turmoil by trying to offset the liberal Warren Court's decisions (Pye and Lowell 1975). The legislation also allowed wiretapping in an assortment of cases and sought to overturn three controversial Warren Court decisions involving the rights of a suspect during police interrogation of federal crimes (President Lyndon B. Johnson 1969).

In the end, Democrats were unable to gain popular support for their more liberal measure, and in March, after President Johnson announced that he would not seek reelection, the Democrats' political leverage was weakened (Flamm 2005). A reluctant President Johnson signed the Omnibus Crime Control and Safe Streets Act of 1968, commenting that he was signing the bill only because it contained "more good than bad" (Feeley and Sarat 1980, 46). Ultimately, however, the bill shifted President Johnson's crime-fighting efforts away from the War on Poverty to stricter enforcement tactics.

It is important to note that Congress did enact several of President Johnson's less draconian measures. These bills included a major juvenile delinquency control program to prevent delinquency and rehabilitate young offenders. In addition, Congress passed the Bail Reform Act of 1968 that was meant to assist accused persons who did not have the means to raise bail. Other legislation addressed drug abuse control, rehabilitation of alcoholics and drug addicts, and the rehabilitation of prisoners (Crime and Justice 1969). As a result of the Johnson administration's broad and sweeping policymaking agenda, political opportunity structures opened as new commissions were formed, new agencies were established, and police departments competed for federal funds in block-grant form.

Although President Johnson recognized that state and local governments were the primary law enforcers, he deemed that the federal government had a special responsibility in addressing organized crime, drug control, gun control, and law enforcement activities in the District of Columbia. President Johnson pledged "not only to reduce crime . . . but . . . to use every single resource of the Federal Government to banish crime from the United States of America" (President Lyndon B. Johnson 8 Sep 1965). Speaking before a meeting of the International Association of Chiefs of Police, he called on the attorney general, the secretary of the Treasury, the Department of Justice, and the other heads of federal law enforcement to enlarge their efforts against crime (President Lyndon B. Johnson 14 Sep 1967).

Importantly, government agencies became important facilitators and supporters for success of the efforts to control crime and restore order (Costain 1992). Executive branch entities included the Department of Justice, Federal Bureau of Investigation, Drug Enforcement Administration, Bureau of Narcotics, Secret Service, Internal Revenue Service, Immigration Service, and the Bureau of Prisons and involved local, state, and federal judges; state attorneys general; state and local police; district attorneys; and state and local prison officials (Miller 2004). These bureaucrats influenced the policy process, legitimated strategies, and supported more stringent policies (Miskel and Song 2004).

In the early 1960s, fighting crime was a relatively new area for which the federal government could concentrate resources, but there was limited knowledge concerning crime control. Therefore, emphasis was placed on research—establishing special commissions and task forces to provide a comprehensive review of the criminal justice system. The new presidential entities included the Commission on Law Enforcement and Administration of Justice, whose mission was to deliver a national strategic plan. This commission instituted seven panels: Public Safety, Administration and Organization of Police Forces, Corruption, Administration of Criminal Justice, Youth Crime, Corrections, and Free Society (Marion 1994, 52). An 18-member Commission on Obscenity and Pornography was also created to study a possible relationship between criminal behavior and obscenity.

Besides the social disorder of the 1960s, specific critical events kept crime on the public agenda. In Chicago, on the night of July 14, 1966, Richard Speck, a drifter and petty criminal, broke into a women's dorm. He brutally murdered eight nursing students, was found guilty after 49 minutes of deliberation, and was sentenced to the electric chair. In 1972, when the U.S. Supreme Court declared the death sentence unconstitutional, Speck was resentenced to hundreds of years in prison and died there in 1991 (Chua-Eoan 2007).

Between July 15, 1966, and June 10, 1967, the *New York Times* ran approximately 56 stories related to the Speck murders (Lexis Nexis ProQuest Historical Newspaper, the *New York Times*). On July 22, 1966, *Time* ran "One by One," a lengthy, detailed story of the gruesome murders. In March 1967 another story concerning press access to the trial, "The Press & Richard

Speck," was printed in *Time*. Movies include *Born for Hell* (1976) by Denis Héroux, which was re-released in 1984, *Speck* (2002) by Keith Walley, and *Chicago Massacre: Richard Speck* (2007) by Michael Feifer. In 2007 *Time* named these murders as one of the "Top 25 Crimes of the Century" (Chua-Eoan 2007). American pop culture has been intrigued with sensational killings, and shocking crimes of this type provide justification for those who believe lawbreakers are evil and who advocate for harsher punishment.

Another spectacular crime event crystallized suspicion and concerns of the counterculture held by most of the country. In early August 1969 Hollywood actrress Sharon Tate, who was married to the director Roman Polanski and who was eight and a half months pregnant, was hanged and stabbed to death in her Los Angeles home. Four of her friends were also found brutally stabbed or shot at the Tate-Polanski mansion (Memmott 1989; Shales 1994).

The killings were committed by a counterculture group called the Charles Manson family. Manson had hoped that the celebrity killings would incite a race war (*Two Nights of Butchery* 1992). After this did not occur, Manson and his followers brutally murdered Rosemary and Leno LaBianca the next evening. This horrendous crime mystified the public, not only because of the shaggy-haired lunatic Manson, but also because of Krenwinkel, Van Houten, and Atkins, who were his female accomplices. Shockingly, these ordinary-looking young women were active participants in the most bizarre murders of the century. Charles Manson and members of his group were put on trial, and all were found guilty in 1970.

Over time, Charles Manson came to represent insane evil and became the symbol of anti-establishment hatred. From 1969 to 2007 *Time* published eight stories that focused mainly on Manson, including naming the Tate murder as one of the "Top 25 Crimes of the Century" (Chua-Eoan 2007). Charles Manson was also in 136 stories for *Time*. Between August 10, 1969, and March 15, 1972, the *New York Times* published approximately 200 stories on the murders, the victims, Charles Manson, and the members of the Manson family (Lexis Nexis ProQuest Historical Newspaper, the *New York Times*). For some, this random and wanton attack served as an appalling example of the precarious 1960s counterculture. Moreover, it provided justification for Middle America's fears regarding the social disorder and violence. In 1992 Sharon Tate's mother, Doris Tate, was recognized by President George Bush as one of his "thousand points of light" for her volunteer victims' rights work. The Doris Tate Crime Victims Foundation was founded in 1995 as a nonprofit organization to support victims of violent crime.

A consequence of the media's treatment of high-profile crime events is that it keeps crime on the public agenda. As the President's Commission on Law Enforcement and Administration of Justice offered, "The most damaging of the effects of violent crime is fear, and that fear must not be belittled" (1967). The Sentencing Project found that media crime coverage fuels racial perceptions of crime and that white Americans more strongly associate crime with racial minorities and support more punitive policies. Whites are more punitive than blacks and Hispanics, even though they experience less crime (Ghandnoosh 2014).

Another critical event influenced the growth of the call for law and order. In March, President Johnson announced that he would not seek reelection. Polls revealed that Johnson's favorability ratings were in the mid-30 percent range, and polls showed only around 23 percent support for his Vietnam War policies (All Politics 1997). President Johnson's announcement produced uncertainty among the anti-war groups. Additionally, during his presidential run against Democrat Hubert Humphrey, candidate Richard Nixon continually referred to the rise in crime and ever-increasing social spending as evidence that the Great Society and the War on Poverty were expensive fiascos.

Candidate for president Hubert Humphrey warned about the fear of crime being linked to the civil rights movement and the Civil Rights Act. He argued:

Segregationists and some white conservatives use the riots as an excuse not to take the action for racial justice that they do not support anyway. They are very much afraid we will "reward the rioters," as they say . . . Ever since Watts, and particularly since Detroit and Newark, the discussion of equal rights has been distorted and sometimes even sidetracked by the very different issues of riots and civil disorders, of "'crime in the streets' and 'law and order.'" . . . It is dangerous nonsense to believe that social progress and a respect for law are somehow in opposition to each other. (quoted by Weaver 2007)

Hubert Humphrey and Attorney General Nicholas Katzenbach displayed a more reasoned approached to the crime hysteria. A few visionaries had the foresight to understand that law-and-order politics differed from social justice. Unfortunately, their concerns fell on deaf ears, and the federal anti-crime entrepreneurs won.

Consequently, with nearly 90 million Americans watching on their television sets, the 1968 Democratic Convention held in Chicago sentenced the Democratic Party and Hubert Humphrey to disastrous failure. The powerful coverage of a Chicago police force out of control and beating protesters, bystanders, and news reporters left the nation with a dire wish for social order (Farber 1994).

Immediately, Nixon responded to the Democrats' misfortune by questioning how a party that failed to keep law and order in its own backyard could bring order to the nation (Flamm 2005). Therefore, Republicans benefited from the Chicago police riot and from the aversion most Americans felt toward the protestors' disorder and the brutal behavior of law enforcement officials. The Chicago debacle and Humphrey's support of racial progress cost him the election. The conservative Republican candidate, Nixon, portrayed himself as a moderate alternative between the belligerent George Wallace and the permissive Humphrey.

*   *   *

This chapter examined the presidential term of Democrat Lyndon B. Johnson from where the call for law and order materialized and the race to incarcerate began. In 1963 Vice President Johnson tragically ascended to the presidency after the young and popular president, John F. Kennedy, was assassinated in Dallas, Texas. President Johnson won the next election with a landslide victory over conservative Republican Senator Barry Goldwater. He engineered both the Civil Rights Act of 1964 and the Voting Rights Act of 1965, two of the most important U.S. laws in the 20th century. And his War on Poverty included social welfare policies that were meant to build a Great Society.

However, President Johnson was faced with a citizenry that was concerned over controversial Warren Court decisions, the civil rights movement and the protests, the disastrous Vietnam War, affirmative action, and growing welfare rolls. Racial and student unrest, increasing drug use, and a rising crime rate threatened the goals of President Johnson's Great Society programs, and he responded accordingly. Ultimately, President Johnson's leadership played a major role in creating and advancing punitive law-and-order politics.

President Johnson hoped that his Great Society programs would control and prevent crime. Yet the turbulent societal atmosphere of the 1960s coupled with the Johnson administration's failure to curb the chaos generated fertile ground for mass imprisonment. As campus unrest continued and drug abuse increased, the mass media helped to keep crime on the national agenda, causing the public to react with fear and embrace the call for more law and order. President Johnson's federal intervention into crime would provide the scaffolding for the building of a massive prison system.

CHAPTER THREE

President Nixon's Crime and Drug Wars: Bleeding-Heart Liberals and Lawlessness

Richard Milhous Nixon was elected the 37th president of the United States after previously serving as a U.S. representative and a U.S. senator from California. He was vice president under President Dwight D. Eisenhower, but in 1960 lost his bid for the presidency to John F. Kennedy. In 1968 he won his party's nomination and defeated Democrat Vice President Hubert H. Humphrey and third-party candidate Governor George C. Wallace of Alabama.

President Nixon's failings, such as his paranoia, his unlikeable personality, and his dysfunctional administration have been well documented. Yet Nixon had gained considerable experience within the federal government. Importantly, while he continually campaigned for other Republicans, he promoted himself and became an expert at turning the vice presidency into a platform for his greater ambitions (Hatfield 1997). Nixon also possessed important leadership traits, such as a smart intellect, "ambition, vision, experience, communication skills, courage and luck" (Couturier 2007). President Nixon ended the Vietnam War and improved international relations with the Soviet Union and China. However, due to the Watergate scandal, he became the only U.S. president ever to resign the office.

Most noteworthy is the fact that despite "personal awkwardness and apparent lack of charisma," President Nixon used law-and-order rhetoric to convince voters to award him with one of the biggest electoral landslides in U.S. history for his second term (Couturier 2007). He showed presidential leadership when he seized the opportunity to run as the law-and-order candidate and claimed to be committed to restoring peace, confidence, and freedom from fear back to the country.

In 1967 Nixon wrote an article published in *Reader's Digest* entitled "What's Happened to America." He framed the civil unrest surrounding the civil rights movement not as a racial one but more a matter of public safety and respect for the law. He wrote, "Certainly racial animosities . . . were the most visible causes. But riots were also the most virulent symptoms to date of another, and in some ways graver, national disorder—the decline in respect for public authority and the rule of law in America. Far from being a great society, ours is becoming a lawless society" (Newell 2013). He portrayed himself in the image of a more moderate Republican candidate and not like Barry Goldwater or George Wallace, who were viewed as racists.

Presidential candidate Richard M. Nixon mounted a powerful media campaign to express his complaints against the Democrats. Nixon saw conservative candidate George Wallace as a significant threat and offered himself as a "standard bearer of the reasonable center" (Farber 1994, 227). He portrayed himself as a calm and collected statesman, effectively using commercial television to capitalize on the public's fear of crime. He successfully described himself as a "defender of law and order," and this distanced him from the more blatant racism of Goldwater and Wallace, while appealing to moderates (Newell 2013).

In a September 1968 Harris poll, results showed that Nixon had a spread of 12 percentage points over Hubert Humphrey on the crime issue and held widespread support for his conservative approach (Loo and Grimes 2004; Lurching off to a Shaky Start 20 Sep 1968). Though Nixon was continually reminding voters of the turmoil of the 1960s, he understood that Americans were in need of reassurance. He based his presidential bid on "freedom from fear," added narcotics to the list of the United States' leading enemies, and declared a national War on Drugs (Flamm 2005, 84).

After winning the election, one of the first actions President Nixon made when he took office was his attempt to deal with the crime problem in Washington, D.C. He was willing to expand executive power, stating, "Crime in America today is both a primary local responsibility and a primary national concern. . . . By searching for new ways of applying the resources of the Federal Government in the war against crime here, we may discover new ways of advancing the war against crime elsewhere" (President Richard M. Nixon 31 Jan 1969). The president was identifying, advocating, and seeking new remedies for political and social dilemmas (Snow and Benford 1988). However, the situation in the nation's capital demonstrated how difficult it was to stop crime. President Johnson was unsuccessful, and President Nixon introduced another government escalation plan.

Starting in the late 1960s, with the Republicans in the White House, the turbulent 1960s and the need for stability set the perfect stage for the burgeoning anti-crime movement. Although crime is often considered a local issue, it continued to be in the forefront of national presidential politics. The 1968 Republican Platform included a section on crime, claiming that "Lawlessness is crumbling the foundations of American society" (Republican Party Platform 15 Aug 1968). Richard Nixon and Spiro Agnew accused the Democrats of being "bleeding heart" and "do-gooder" liberals who irresponsibly squandered taxpayer money on ineffective social programs to control crime. As a candidate Nixon also identified the race issue with lawlessness and stated that it was "all about law and order and the damn Negro-Puerto Rican groups out there" (quoted by Weaver 2007). Nixon's focus was directed at the "silent majority," consisting of socially conservative Americans who were not vocal but were fearful of minority civil rights gains, student anti-war demonstrations, the counterculture, and crime. He declared that the "first civil right" was the "right to be free from violence" (quoted by Weaver 2007). However, it seems that the silent majority supported "law and order" when it favored keeping the status quo of white power in control. Importantly, President Nixon made an impact on the political culture by using war symbols and language to create new pejorative meanings surrounding race and crime.

Unlike the Kennedy and Johnson philosophies, Richard M. Nixon and the Republicans did not hold society responsible for criminal behavior. They held individuals responsible for their behavior, believing that people had alternatives and could choose not to participate in criminal behavior. President Nixon announced that the government could only do so much about crime and that the problem was partly a moral issue. In his acceptance speech for the presidential nomination, he stated:

> The wave of crime is not going to be the wave of the future in the United States of America. . . . We shall re-establish freedom from fear in America so that America can take the lead in re-establishing freedom from fear in the world. . . . And to those who say that law and order is the code word for racism, here is a reply: Our goal is justice for every American. If we are to have respect for law in America, we must have laws that deserve respect. (Richard M. Nixon 1968)

For him, the country needed people who respected the law, and Nixon claimed that this respect did not exist in many areas of the country (President Richard M. Nixon 24 Jun 1970).

In an atmosphere of strict crime control, President Nixon labeled the Johnson era a decade of intensified criminal activity and promised safety by waging a full-blown War on Crime. Demonstrating the power of presidential influence, Nixon criticized the Democrats for being "soft on crime" and stressed mandatory minimum sentences, stricter penalties, and more stringent judges. His "get-tough" approach to crime was aimed at working-class voters and became a vital feature of conservative ideological and political discourse. Republican and Democrat leaders identified crime as the main campaign issue (Harris 1968). In a 1968 television campaign advertisement, Vice President Humphrey retorted that Nixon believed that "the most important thing was to double conviction rates" and that Nixon had "lost his sense of values" (Squier 1968). With remarkable and accurate long-range vision, Humphrey stressed that building more jails would not make the United States a better place and warned that there could not be punishment without justice.

In opposition, President Nixon felt that the convicted deserved swift and harsh punishment, and local and state law enforcement knew best how to solve those criminal problems, not the federal government (Beckett and Sasson 2004). Yet he stepped in and attempted to deal with the crime problem in Washington, D.C., by defining it as a "war" when he said, "Crime in America today is both a primary local responsibility and a primary national concern. . . . By searching for new ways of applying the resources of the Federal Government in the war against crime here, we may discover new ways of advancing the war against crime" (President Richard M. Nixon 31 Jan 1969). The situation in Washington demonstrated how difficult it was to stop crime. President Johnson was unsuccessful, and President Nixon introduced another government escalation plan. He wanted more personnel for the Bureau of Narcotics and Dangerous Drugs (BNDD) for drug enforcement in the District and other troubled cities (President Richard M. Nixon 22 Feb 1969). Nixon's government response to crime expanded the size of the national government and would eventually increase imprisonment.

From January 1969 to May 1969, public concern over crime and civil unrest began to climb in public opinion polls, with a high of 15 percent for college demonstrations (Marion 1994, 74). In April 1969 President Nixon announced another new crime-control package that would make "clear the Federal Government's commitment . . . to assisting local authorities in protecting the lives, rights and property of their citizens" (President Richard M. Nixon 14 Apr 1969). He drew from victims' accounts and emphasized their victimization to justify federal intervention and expansion. Conservatives often talk about support for limited government, and President Johnson certainly started the criminal justice federal intervention. However, Republicans were willing participants as initiators and supporters and did little to resist the growth of incarceration as a result of more stringent and draconian laws.

When President Richard Nixon won the 1968 election, he faced the unpopular Vietnam War, the uncertainty surrounding the Great Society programs, and a contentious citizenry. During the campaign, candidate Nixon had made 17 law-and-order speeches and submitted 20 anti-crime pieces of legislation (Weaver 2007). Demonstrating aggressive and targeted presidential leadership, Nixon blamed President Johnson and his liberal administration for the increase in crime, drugs, and disorder. This election revealed the voters' need for bold promises and substantial results. Nixon's campaign appeased the "law-and-order" majority that voted for him by a considerable margin (Flamm 2003). As a result, the Republicans intensified the march to law and order and to mass incarceration.

Consequently, Nixon had accused President Johnson of ignoring the rising crime rates and of opposing legislation that assisted law enforcement. Moreover, President Nixon felt that the judiciary had failed to interpret the law in a way that would strengthen anti-criminal forces and accused the Supreme Court of "seriously hamstringing" law enforcement to the advantage of criminals (quoted by Maclin 2007). The president's choice of Supreme Court appointments is an important aspect of American governance, and chief executives can insure a tough-on-crime higher court.

In the Nixon era, many of the legal rights and protections handed down by the Warren Court were undermined. Republican conservatives criticized lenient policies and accused the judiciary of promoting criminal behavior. In reaction to the liberal rulings of the Warren Court, President Nixon sponsored legislation that challenged defendants' rights and pledged to appoint "strict constructionist" judges to the Supreme Court. He thought the Supreme Court had gone too far in weakening law enforcement and pledged to nominate justices who would show more respect for the Constitution (Flamm 2005). He claimed that "America has become among the most lawless and violent [nations] in the history of free people because liberal decisions in the courts were 'weakening the peace forces against the criminal forces'" (Epstein 1977, 36). Conservative commentator William F. Buckley blamed much of the civil rights violence on the "lawlessness" caused by the *Brown v. Board of Education* (1954) ruling. Buckley accused the Warren Court of what we would call today judicial activism and thought that the civil rights movement was a threatening conspiracy to weaken the power of white America (Mickens 2014).

Therefore, President Nixon appointed conservative Warren Burger as chief justice. He stated that Justice Burger was a strict constructionist as far as the Constitution was concerned (President Richard M. Nixon 22 May 1969). As a primary leader against progressive gains, Nixon injected the justice system with political vulnerability while creating an atmosphere receptive to fear of the political system (McAdam 1982). But his other constructionist nominees, Clement Haynsworth and G. Harrold Carswell, were rejected by the Democrats in the Senate (Dean 2001).

Importantly, Justice Warren Burger was known as the law-and-order judge, and he was more sympathetic toward the prosecution in criminal procedure cases than Chief Justice Earl Warren (Lamb 1991). In 1969 President Nixon's leadership in this appointment was embraced, as 81 percent of

Americans thought "law and order" had broken down, with a majority blaming "Negroes who start riots" and *Time* magazine reporting that "law and order" had been the number-one issue of the 1968 election (Newell 2013, 15). President Nixon exerted a substantial influence on the Court through his appointments when juxtaposed to the more liberal-leaning Warren Court (Heck 1981). When President Nixon appointed Lewis F. Powell Jr. and William H. Rehnquist as associate justices to the Supreme Court, he claimed they would act as guardians of the Constitution by building respect for the rule of law and justice (President Richard M. Nixon 21 Oct 1971).

In 1969, in response to *Miranda v. Arizona* (1966), William H. Rehnquist, the acting assistant attorney general in charge of the Office of Legal Counsel, who only served for 90 days in the position, wrote a memorandum to the associate deputy attorney general, John Dean. Future Supreme Court Chief Justice Rehnquist charged that the Warren Court was too far in favor of criminal suspects. He suggested that President Nixon establish a national commission "to determine whether the overriding public interest in law enforcement requires a constitutional amendment" (Kamisar 2006). With all of Nixon's appointments to the Supreme Court, he was able to leave a considerable judicial legacy, with some charging the he injected an atmosphere of fear into the justice system (McAdam 1982).

Chief executives have the resources to champion certain causes and use the bully pulpit to seek support from the public and to apply pressure for congressional action. Presidents also create new government entities that promote their goals. According to President Richard Nixon, the convicted deserved swift and harsh punishment, and conservatives believed that local and state law enforcement knew best how to solve those criminal problems, rather than the federal government. Thus, the Nixon administration continued to assert that crime was a local and state problem but addressed the federal government's lack of authority to combat local street crime in several ways (Beckett and Sasson 2004).

In his 1970 State of the Union message, President Nixon noted that there was one area in which he was ordering increases rather than cuts—law enforcement—and declared:

> We have heard a great deal of overblown rhetoric during the sixties in which the word "war" has perhaps too often been used—the war on poverty, the war on misery, the war on disease, the war on hunger. But if there is one area where the word "war" is appropriate it is in the fight against crime. We must declare and win the war against the criminal elements which increasingly threaten our cities, our home and our lives. (President Richard M. Nixon 22 Jan 1970)

Here, President Nixon framed the issue as a war on the problem of crime. This presidential rhetoric helped to justify funding the War on Crime as the

Nixon administration provided the Law Enforcement Assistance Administration (LEAA) with a massive increase to subsidize local police and courts. This aided in the growing government support for more law enforcement and the courts that increased the number of arrests. Still, with the Republican takeover, crime had increased by 25 percent from 1968 to 1970 (Weaver 2007).

Ongoing from the Johnson administration, block grant programs guaranteed the growth of the criminal justice system as police, district attorneys, and corrections and parole officials secured federal funding to expand their law enforcement capabilities. Accordingly, billions of dollars in federal money was appropriated to states and localities through the 1968 Safe Streets Act's LEAA (Marion 1994). Importantly, before the 1960s, the federal government did not spend large sums of money on crime control. However, when crime hit the national agenda, President Nixon and other presidents felt that a federal response was warranted. This program was highly criticized because of the "expenditures of billions of dollars under the Safe Streets Act" (Marion 1994).

With this new federalism, the state-level organizational structures that the Safe Streets Act fostered did not have the "political authority and strategic location to make a difference in the long run" (Feeley and Sarat 1980, 4–5). From the onset, implementation of this program's ambitious and complex agenda was problematic and presented procedural difficulties. As a result, local and state law enforcement agencies, correction facilities, and court systems competed for federal block grant funding administered by the Law Enforcement Assistance Administration. This federal program was responsible for the stunning growth of the U.S. criminal justice system (Feeley and Sarat 1980).

In June 1970 President Nixon condemned Congress for delaying his crime package. Democrats were a majority in the Senate and the House, leading him to complain that not one of his bills had reached his desk for signature (President Richard M. Nixon 11 Jun 1970). Nixon traveled all over the country with his crime message. In Denver, Colorado, he reiterated that his administration wanted to be "more helpful to the States, and the cities, and the counties in waging a winning war against those who have been responsible for the rising crime in this country" (President Richard M. Nixon 3 Aug 1970). In October 1970 President Nixon signed the Omnibus Crime Control Act of 1970, which increased the federal commitment to law enforcement funds from 65 percent to 75 percent (Marion 1994, 80). He remarked that law enforcement would have the tools "to launch a total war" against crime and that the war would be won (President Richard M. Nixon 15 Oct 1970). Incrementally, presidential leadership on the so-called war on crime persistently, actively, and systematically constructed a criminal justice regime that began to criminalize and imprison staggering numbers of young, urban black males (Hinton 2016).

Importantly, President Nixon identified federal drug control as a vital weapon against crime. In spite of problematic evidence, the administration justified the focus on drugs by positing that drug abusers were guilty of committing the majority of street crimes to support their addiction (Beckett and Sasson 2004). By treating and naming drug use as a criminal offense rather than a public health problem, get-tough policies resulted in laws emphasizing law enforcement rather than treatment (Cooper 2000). Nixon did grasp the situation, as he supposed that penalties, in some instances, were not effective and "must be tough for the more severe trafficking offenses and offenders while having sufficient flexibility for dealing with persons possessing for their own use" (President Richard M. Nixon 23 Oct 1969). Initiated by President Nixon, this change in public policy marked a watershed occurrence for increased imprisonment.

Transforming drug abuse from an illness to a crime allowed politicians, criminal justice officials, and the courts to pursue lengthier and more punitive sanctions for drug offenders. It is argued that the War on Crime, and especially the War on Drugs, entailed efforts to direct public policy away from social welfare to social control (Garland 2001). Public officials who depicted crime in terms of poverty, delinquency, and addiction helped shape perceptions about crime and its solution.

In 1970 the Narcotics Treatment Administration was established by the Nixon administration. Furthering the War on Drugs in a surprisingly less punitive manner, his agency expanded Washington, D.C.'s controversial methadone drug treatment program. While conservatives felt that methadone was just a substitute for heroin, liberals saw racist undertones in opposition to the program. Still, a year after the program's initiation, Washington's burglary rate had dropped by 41 percent (Frontline 2006).

On October 27, 1970, Congress passed the Comprehensive Drug Abuse Prevention and Control Act that consolidated federal narcotics laws and reduced sanctions for the possession of marijuana. However, this bill strengthened law enforcement by allowing police to conduct no-knock searches. Also, this included the Controlled Substances Act, which regulated drugs based on their medical value and addiction potential (Peterson 1985). Displaying masterful leadership skills, President Nixon was the initiator of this legislation, and at the signing he stated: "Fifteen months ago I sent an urgent request to the Congress for legislation in this field. I requested it because our survey of the problem of drugs indicated that it was a major cause of street crime in the United States" (President Richard M. Nixon 27 Oct 1970). This act unified many pieces of legislation and set up the different categories or schedules into a fighting force that is used today by the Drug Enforcement Agency (DEA). In that same year, opponents of the drug war showed movement when the National Organization for the Reform of Marijuana Laws (NORML) was founded to decriminalize marijuana (Evans 1978).

Still, consistent with undertones of racial politics, this legislation dealt with two race- and class-based populations. First were the drug users who were young, white, and middle to upper class. They were identified as victims of drug traffickers. Second were the professional drug dealers who were seen as the symbolic enemy and the true source of the drug problem. Legislation brought some protection for the first category, while severe sanctions were levied against the mostly African American latter group (Peterson 1985).

Moreover, in 1970 rape and other violent crimes against women started to become salient issues. The American Bar Association and the Association of American Law Schools formed women's committees. These new groups were made up of attorneys, law students, feminist activists, and lobbyists. One of the major goals of reforming rape laws was to achieve comparable legal treatment between rape and other violent crimes. This reform included "enhancing prosecution and conviction in rape cases" (Bevacqua 2000, 93). The National Organization for Women created their National Rape Task Force in 1973. One of their main objectives was to prepare and recommend a model criminal code guide for state legislatures to adopt (Bevacqua 2000). As a result of this focus, reforms supported a new law-and-order approach to the crime of rape.

In 1971 President Nixon's State of the Union message only mentioned law enforcement in a long list of areas that were included in federal revenue sharing, such as education and transportation (President Richard M. Nixon 22 Jan 1971). However, he announced that in the upcoming budget "the Law Enforcement Assistance Administration would be enabled to vigorously expand its aid to State and local governments." Also, almost one-half billion dollars a year went toward strengthening local efforts to reform court procedures, police methods, correctional action, and other related needs. Nixon pledged that under his special revenue-sharing proposal, law enforcement would receive increased attention and greater funding for states and localities to determine their own priorities (President Richard M. Nixon 11 Mar 1971).

Then in May 1971 an alarming report on the ever-increasing heroin epidemic among the U.S. military in Vietnam was released. In President Richard M. Nixon's Special Message to Congress on Drug Abuse, Prevention, and Control, he called rehabilitation a new priority. He asked for over $155 million in additional funds solely for the treatment and rehabilitation of drug-addicted individuals; this provided a total of $371 million for programs to control drug abuse (President Richard M. Nixon 17 Jun 1971).

In June 1971 President Nixon claimed that drug abuse was America's "public enemy number one," declared a "war on drugs," and created the Special Action Office for Drug Abuse Prevention (President Richard M. Nixon 17 Jun 1971). In his 1972 State of the Union address, Nixon asserted that criminal activity had slowed and predicted that the crime rate would soon decrease (President Richard M. Nixon 20 Jan 1972). Yet he established the Office of Drug Abuse Law Enforcement and created a joint state and federal task force to fight the street-level drug trade (President Richard M Nixon 28 Jan 1972).

The Nixon administration continued to increase the size of government by funding the War on Drugs and creating new government entities intended to deal with the problem.

By 1972 the Republican platform reported that serious crime had only increased by 1 percent and that 80 of the 155 largest cities had reported a decrease in crime. Thus, new statistics were generated to present a more positive representation of the administration's crime-fighting capability (Law Enforcement 1977). The platform hailed the increase in federal funding to state and local law enforcement agencies, which amounted to more than $1.5 billion, on 50,000 crime-control projects. The platform acclaimed raising the Law Enforcement Assistance Administration's budget tenfold, earmarking $575 million in 1973 for upgrading police and courts through revenue sharing (Republican Party Platform of 1972 Aug 1972).

Likewise, the Democrats continued to propagate the crackdown on crime with policy recommendations. The 1972 Democratic Party Platform included U.S. Attorney General Ramsey Clark's hearing statement, "I think we can reduce crime. Society has no more important challenge because crime is human conduct and more than any other activity of people it reflects the moral character of a nation" (Democratic Party Platform of 1972 10 Jul 1972). The platform addressed the issues of crime, law and justice, preventing crime, narcotic drugs, organized and professional crime, rehabilitation of offenders, and quality of justice.

In March 1973 President Nixon's State of the Union message was on law enforcement and drug abuse prevention. He announced that through the combined law enforcement efforts, "the wave of serious crime in the United States is being brought under control . . . our anti-crime program is on the right track . . . the only way to attack crime in America is the way crime attacks our people—without pity" (President Richard M. Nixon 14 Mar 1973). However, crime continued to increase, and Vice President Ford acknowledged that the crime rate was rising despite the billions of dollars in expenditures (Marion 1994). Then Nixon established the Drug Enforcement Agency (DEA) as a "superagency" to coordinate all elements of the War on Drugs (President Richard M. Nixon 28 Mar 1973). Concentrating government resources and marshalling law enforcement power to combat the drug trade remained a trend that both conservatives and liberals embraced. President Nixon played a major role in keeping crime on the national agenda.

Moreover, President Richard Nixon looked at the LEAA as "one vehicle" through which he could carry out his crime-control promises he had made during the campaign (Feeley and Sarat 1980, 84). Placing blame on the Warren Court for coddling criminals, Nixon promised to focus on victims' rights instead of the rights of offenders. Under the LEAA, the Crime Victim Initiative provided critical funding that established hundreds of nationwide victim and witness programs, mostly located in public prosecutors' offices

(Gottschalk 2006). The LEAA also sponsored a number of major conferences to train and educate social service workers and advocates for victims. These actions fostered the emergence of a victims' rights movement. Therefore, through the presidential leadership of the Nixon administration, the LEAA was pivotal in the formation and development of this anti-crime movement and the race to incarcerate.

For President Nixon, the nature of drug addiction and the involvement of Vietnam veterans made it imperative that immediate rehabilitation procedures on a national level be undertaken (Brecher 1972). This was the only time in the history of the War on Drugs that the majority of funding went toward treatment rather than law enforcement (Frontline 2006). In 1970, 58 percent and in 1975, 75 percent of the anti-drug money was allocated to treatment and prevention. In comparison, in 1982 only 21 percent of the anti-drug funding, and in 2003 only 34 percent of the anti-drug funding was allocated for treatment and prevention (Frontline 2006).

Despite President Nixon's promise that all military personnel would be accorded rehabilitation, the U.S. military command in Vietnam discharged thousands of GI addicts (McCoy 1972). After failing the urinalysis test twice, these men were declared of "negligible value" to the U.S. Army (McCoy 1972, 256–58). Although all soldiers were guaranteed the right to declare themselves addicts and volunteer for treatment, the offer was often denied to two-time offenders. Once a commanding officer decided that a two-time user was a hopeless case, the GI addict was flown back home and immediately discharged.

Consequently, President Nixon continued to frame the issue and set the agenda by proclaiming that drug abuse was "public enemy number one in the United States," and this widened the scope of criminal behavior and the federal response (President Richard M. Nixon 4 Oct 1971). Public reaction to drug abuse intensified, with the "concern for drugs" response to the "most important problem facing the country" question rising to a high of 12 percent in May 1972 (Marion 1994, 74).

In October 1973 Vice President Spiro Agnew was forced to resign for income tax evasion and for accepting bribes while governor of Maryland. As a result of the Watergate cover-up, on August 9, 1974, Nixon resigned, temporarily halting the law-and-order momentum. The tough-on-crime crusader who claimed that people must be held responsible and receive swift and harsh punishment had to resign from the presidency due to his and his administration's criminal behavior. The Watergate crimes depict the different treatment for those convicted of street crimes and those convicted of white-collar crimes. While mostly African American offenders of the War on Drugs became subject to mandatory sentences, most white offenders accused of public corruption were less stringently punished by the criminal justice system. President Nixon did not face charges but was given the option to resign from office or face impeachment charges for his high crimes. He was later pardoned for all his crimes by President Gerald R. Ford.

Mandatory Minimum Sentencing

During President Nixon's first term in office, federal incarceration rates fell. Even when rates begin to increase, Nixon's National Advisory Commission on Criminal Justice Standards and Goals recommended a 10-year moratorium on building new prisons, avoided the death penalty debate, and recommended closing juvenile facilities (Gottschalk 2006).

Still, an important development that will continue to have severe implications for the criminal justice system and many Americans took place in 1973. The moderate Republican governor of New York, Nelson Rockefeller, claimed that drug abuse had produced a crisis that threatened the middle-class way of life. He helped establish new national standards for drug offensives by adopting stiff sanctions that included mandatory 15-year prison terms for possessing small amounts of narcotics. President Nixon supported these hard-line policies. Eventually, nearly every state and the federal government followed suit on some form of mandatory sentencing (Farber and Roche 2003; Gottschalk 2006).

Warnings pertaining to the ramifications of get-tough policies were present but ignored. Mandatory minimum sentencing gave prosecutors enormous power. According to former Assistant U.S. Attorney Mark Osler, "Mandatories make it easy to plead a case out, lessening the effort and expense of trial." Now prosecutors fear that removing mandatory penalties might make their jobs more difficult (Haile 2015). The New York mandatory minimum sentences applied to new drug laws and new second-felony legislation. These also increased parole violations, average length of sentences, and expanded inmate populations for decades. It was further warned that the increase in the prison population would increase costs (Benjamin and Rappaport 1974, 213). The United States' attempt to control crime by mass incarceration is a public policy failure. We use terms like the "carceral state" and "Prison America"—clearly, this situation is a disgraceful national disaster.

Several high-profile events kept crime and prisons in the news media. In 1967 there were 5 violent prison riots, and in 1968 there were 15 riots, with many more to follow. However, the most famous prison disturbance took place in September 1971, when New York State's Attica Correctional Facility exploded in a prisoner uprising. After five days of failed negotiations, Governor Rockefeller ordered the state police to seize control of the prison. The armed assault left 29 inmates and 10 guards and prisoner hostages dead (Benjamin and Rappaport 1974; Schlanger 1999). In 1966 Governor Rockefeller's Special Committee on Criminal Offenders recommended total physical and administrative reorganization of the prison system. At the time of the riot, Attica had a strict internal system that demanded absolute obedience and subordination from inmates.

Initially, the Attica tragedy captured popular media and public attention, with both *Newsweek* and *Time* running cover stories concerning Attica. When speaking to Governor Rockefeller on the phone the day of the raid, President Nixon supported the violent operation. Yet the day before the raid, Rockefeller told Nixon that possibly as many as 300 prisoners could be killed. They discussed the racial component of the uprising, calling it "basically a black thing," which played down the multiracial leadership of the uprising (Democracy Now 2011). The mishandling of the uprising generated support for prison reform work and inspired many prisoners' rights lawyers (Schlanger 1999).

In 1972 the American Civil Liberties Union's (ACLU) Prisoners' Rights Project was established. In 1975 journalist Tom Wicker wrote an award-winning book, *A Time to Die: The Attica Prison Revolt*. Yet Attica was the catalyst for other violent prison disturbances. Eventually, prisoners were viewed as out of control, and support for the prisoners' rights movement began to fade (Gottschalk 2006; Jacobs 1980).

This violence produced a situation in which the call for more order overtook correction policy, causing stricter and more punitive measures to be instituted by the legal system and prison officials. A backlash against prisoners' rights ensued, with long-lasting consequences. Penal policies began to swell the penitentiary system with drug-related offenders and severely increased the incarceration rates for minorities and women.

Throughout the 1970s, several other important occurrences facilitated the momentum of violence and crime on the political agenda. In the summer of 1970, in the days following the presidential announcement of the U.S. invasion of Cambodia and Laos, students on university campuses across the United States protested. At Kent State University in Ohio, demonstrators threw rocks and broke windows, and a few attempted to set the Reserve Officer Training Corps building on fire (Bills 1988). On May 3, 1970, Ohio Governor James Rhodes called in the National Guard. On May 4, 28 poorly trained and inexperienced young guardsmen fired over 60 shots directly into the students for 13 seconds. The shots hit unarmed students, injuring 13 and killing 4 (Kent State University Libraries 2007). The guardsmen were never prosecuted, and Vice President Spiro Agnew publicly blamed the students for the incident (Farber 1994).

Then, at Jackson State College in Mississippi on May 14 and 15, 1970, a student demonstration against racial discrimination and the Kent State killings ended in bloodshed (Shootings at Jackson State University 2000). Seventy-five Mississippi State Police armed with automatic weapons, shotguns, and service revolvers fired for more than 30 seconds into the crowd of students. As a result, 2 people were killed and 12 students were injured. FBI investigators estimated that on May 15, the police fired more than "four hundred rounds" and counted "at least one hundred and sixty bullet holes" in the outer walls of the dormitory building stairwell where students had tried to find shelter from the attack (Shootings at Jackson State University 2000, 42–43). After Kent State, Jackson State, and Laos, hundreds of demonstrations were held and more than 500 colleges were temporarily closed. For many conservatives and President Nixon, campus violence would not be tolerated. He wrote, "The university is a precious national asset, a place in American society where the rule of reason and not the rule of force must prevail. Those who cannot accept that rule of reason, those who resort to the rule of force, have no place on a college campus" (President Richard M. Nixon 20 Nov 1970). Although President Nixon established the President's Commission on Campus Unrest to investigate campus unrest and the killings, guardsmen or police were never charged for the killings.

Opinion polls revealed the level of anxiety about student unrest during this time. In August 1970, 17 percent of respondents deemed college demonstrations the "most important problem facing the country," and 13 percent of respondents felt this way in September and October (Marion 1994, 74). From 1968 to 1970 *Newsweek* did eight and *Time* did three cover stories on the campus unrest and Kent State shootings.

In September 1970 the commission concluded that the Ohio National Guard and the Mississippi Police shootings were unjustified. Between May 5, 1970, and November 15, 1971, approximately 150 stories were published concerning Kent State and college campus demonstrations (Lexis Nexis ProQuest Historical Newspaper, *New York Times*, "Kent State shootings"). Arguably, a major aspect of this tragedy was that Kent State was in a conservative region where university students were feared by local residents and vilified by President Nixon, other politicians, and the local media (Bills 1988). The discriminatory rhetoric of political officials and the conservative right described protesters as criminals and dangerous rioters. Additionally, the lack of accountability and punishment for those at fault allowed explosive events to unfold in brutal ways. Due to these two deadly incidences and the decline of the war, only sporadic demonstrations occurred.

In February 1974 another spectacular crime scenario captured the American psyche. Patty Hearst, granddaughter of newspaper magnate William Randolph Hearst, was kidnapped and tortured by an underground terrorist group called the Symbionese Liberation Army (SLA). Hearst became dependent on her captors for survival and became a bank robber. After her capture, even though there was evidence that she had been brainwashed into submission, she was convicted and spent two years in prison for armed bank robbery (Moore 1989). The Hearst affair resonated with the public's fear of black youths, as well as many parents' fears of losing control of their teenage children. Many Americans were unsympathetic to Patty Hearst's plight, and, in the ultimate case of victim blaming, the media and prosecutors unapologetically questioned her about her captivity.

Immediately before Hearst's arrest, a poll revealed that 68 percent of respondents thought she should go to prison, 66 percent believed she had voluntarily joined the SLA, and 50 percent thought she was complicit in her own kidnapping (Moore 1989). For the first six months of 1974, the law-and-order issues of crime, violence, and drugs ranked between 3 and 4 percent for the "most important problem facing the country" (Marion 1994, 74). From February 1974 to June 1975, the *New York Times* ran approximately 15 stories on Patty Hearst (Lexis Nexis ProQuest Historical Newspaper, the *New York Times*, "Patty Hearst"). In 1973 and 1974 *Newsweek* did seven and *Time* did three cover stories on Patty Hearst.

Consequently, the young and affluent Berkeley student developed into "a symbol for a generation who felt that their children had all been kidnapped by counter-culture" (Moore 1989, 42). As many middle-class white parents sought a return to a stable environment in which people respected traditional authority, this situation stoked the fires as the crackdown on crime persisted. In 1976 U.S. District Attorney for North California James Browning Jr. won the case against Patty Hearst for the executive branch. However, in 1979 President Jimmy Carter commuted her sentence, and in 2001 President Bill Clinton granted Ms. Hearst a full pardon (Vulliamy and Arlidge 2001).

During the Nixon law-and-order years, crime rates increased and public concern about crime continued to climb. In response to the Gallup poll's "most important problem facing the country" question, the concern for juvenile delinquency rose to 7 percent, while drugs and drug abuse ranked at up to 12 percent (Marion 1994, 73). Through the leadership of President Nixon, government involvement in crime control was cultivated and grew.

*   *   *

In this chapter, we saw that Richard M. Nixon came into the White House as a seasoned and capable leader. We explored how President Richard Nixon used anti-crime rhetoric by claiming that the Supreme Court and the Democrats were "soft on crime" and blamed liberal social policies for the rising crime rates. He nominated conservative judges to the Supreme Court, and his get-tough approach provided government support for the anti-crime effort by expanding federal law enforcement power through the Law Enforcement Assistance Administration (LEAA).

During Nixon's War on Drugs, the Drug Enforcement Agency (DEA), the Office of Drug Abuse Law Enforcement, and the Bureau of Narcotics and Dangerous Drugs were all established and greatly expanded federal intervention into crime fighting. President Nixon favored mandatory minimum sentencing, and the Democratic-controlled Congress passed his repressive crime bills, making drug abuse a crime.

Additionally, in the early 1970s, the crime of rape became an issue for the women's movement. At this time, women began entering law school in record numbers, and they started advocating for the reform of rape laws. They pressured for a more pro-victim agenda. Therefore, with government support as well as grassroots activism by anti-crime groups, President Nixon ensured growth of the federal government and the U.S. prison population with more laws and with more prisons.

CHAPTER FOUR

President Ford Goes Victims' Rights and President Carter Goes Soft on Crime

President Gerald Ford's zeal toward crime and punishment followed the conservative march to law and order, while President Jimmy Carter's tendency toward punitive law-and-order punishment was less than that displayed by others. President Ford was a conservative and favored harsh punishment for offenders but was also concerned with victims' rights. In contrast, President Carter was the only president who did not increase incarceration while in office and wanted to dismantle the costly and ineffective Law Enforcement Administration Act (LEAA). The Ford administration proposed building four new federal prisons to incarcerate offenders, whereas the Carter administration put more emphasis on drug treatment. During this time, presidential politics and policies focused on victims of crime and government efficiency more than on domestic crime control by over-imprisonment.

During most of 1974, the Watergate scandal dominated media and public attention as congressional hearings and proceedings on the Nixon administration's high crimes were held. President Nixon had refused to surrender tapes and documents subpoenaed by the Senate Watergate Committee. And White House officials were indicted for their part in the break-in and for conspiracy to obstruct justice. Because of this, citizens could not escape the realization that crime had spread to the top tier of government. From 1973 to 1975 *Newsweek* featured 30 cover stories, and *Time* ran 18 on Watergate and President Nixon's criminal involvement. In assessing the "media effects" on the public's opinion during Watergate, scholars Gladys and Kurt Lang claim that "the press was a prime mover in the controversy only in its early phase" and influenced public opinion by reporting on the scandal's unfolding events and by the televising of the Senate's Judiciary hearings. They argue that all of this may have prepared the public for Nixon's ensuing removal, but that it was Congress and not the media that forced him to resign (Feldstein 2004).

With Americans also feeling the pains of an ever-increasing economic downturn, Vice President Gerald Ford assumed the presidency and only served for two and a half years. Ford was a well-liked and respected seasoned politician who served in the U.S. House of Representatives for 25 years. He had a reputation of being honest, loyal, and hardworking and was the Republican House minority leader. President Ford is best known for his "lifelong commitment to principled public service, his integrity, and his ability to reach across the aisle to forge consensus" (The Ford Legacy 2017). However, President Nixon and the Watergate scandal had badly damaged the presidency. As a result, the Democratic-controlled Congress fought Ford on almost every issue. Therefore, he was "reduced to governing by veto," exercising this power 66 times with only 12 overrides (PBS 2017).

After taking office, President Ford established a Public Integrity Section within the Justice Department to discover and prosecute official corruption (President Gerald Ford 29 Oct 1976). Yet President Gerald Ford pardoned Richard Nixon, and the political backlash may have cost him the next election. He justified his decision, stating, "Although I respected the tenet that no man should be above the law, public policy demanded that I put Nixon and Watergate behind us as quickly as possible . . . Being forced to resign the presidency and live with that humiliation the rest of his life was a severe punishment in itself, the equivalent to serving a jail term" (Flanary 2011). Gerald Ford, an unelected president, was the first president to testify before the House Judiciary Committee. He had to defend his pardon of President Richard Nixon; however, he demonstrated keen executive leadership that has had a lasting effect on our government (Curry 2006).

While President Ford served as the U.S. House Republican leader, he led a failed attempt to impeach Justice Douglas for involvement with a foundation partially funded by gambling casinos (Denniston 2006). Representative Ford's action was seen as a deliberate political move in retaliation for the Senate's rejection of two of President Nixon's nominees to the Supreme Court. Critics accused Representative Ford of adding instability to the Court by allowing justices to become targets of political maneuvering (Denniston 2006).

When President Gerald R. Ford took over the presidency, he acknowledged the failure of the Nixon administration to control crime and asserted, "America has been far from successful in dealing with the sort of crime that obsesses America day and night. . . . Despite the strenuous efforts of the recent past, the rate of serious crime in 1974 rose 17 percent above 1973, the largest increase in the last 44 years . . . The fact is that the federal role in the fight against crime, particularly violent crime, is a limited one" (Law Enforcement 1977). President Ford was concerned with two major political positions on crime-related issues: crime prevention and criminal corrections and punishment (Ford Legacy 2017). He was critical of past policy but diagnosed the problem as out of the federal government's reach and a local and state law enforcement problem. However, this did not stop him from attacking the crime problem.

In a news conference, President Ford was confronted with the fact that, although the Republicans had run on a "strong law-and-order platform," crime statistics continued to rise. He refused to take the blame for failed criminal justice policy and responded that crime was not a partisan issue: "The facts of life are that most law enforcement is the local responsibility" (President Gerald Ford 3 Apr 1975). Again in a Special Message to Congress, President Ford admitted that he had failed at crime control and stated that

> America has been far from successful in dealing with the sort of crime that obsesses America day and night—I mean street crime, crime that invades our neighborhoods and our homes—murders, robberies, rapes, muggings, holdups, break-ins—the kind of brutal violence that makes us fearful of strangers and afraid to go out at night. I sense, and I think the American people sense, that we are facing a basic and very serious problem of disregard for the law. Because of crime in our streets and in our homes, we do not have domestic tranquility. (President Gerald Ford 19 Jun 1975)

President Ford introduced mandatory incarceration for (1) offenders who commit offenses under federal jurisdiction using a dangerous weapon; (2) persons committing such extraordinarily serious crimes as aircraft hijacking, kidnapping, and trafficking in hard drugs; and (3) repeat offenders who commit federal crimes—with or without a weapon—that cause, or have a potential to cause, personal injury. Ford also instructed the attorney general to assist Congress in drafting modifications to the sentencing provisions for a mandatory sentencing system. The president believed that too many people guilty of serious, violent crimes did not go to prison and that most victims were the old, poor, or disadvantaged (President Gerald Ford 19 Jun 1975).

However, President Ford believed that Americans found the thought of a federal police force unacceptable and introduced his ways to insure domestic tranquility. He emphasized keeping convicted criminals from committing other crimes by sending them to prison so they could not harm law-abiding citizens (President Gerald Ford 14 Feb 1976). Showing law-and-order presidential leadership, he called for swift and certain lock-them-up punishment. He proposed building new federal facilities, increasing the number of U.S. attorneys and U.S. marshals. All of his policies had the potential of expanding imprisonment and the size of the federal government (President Gerald Ford 19 Jan 1976).

Conversely, the president reiterated that the LEAA had spent around $800 million helping state and local governments upgrade police and sheriffs' departments and the courts. He claimed again, "But the principle responsibility rests at the local level" (President Gerald Ford 3 Apr 1974). President Ford had Congress extend the LEAA, but, due to concerns that federal dollars were being wasted, a lesser amount of $2.5 billion was authorized for a three-year period. He did not display the imprisonment zeal that President Nixon possessed.

On September 8, 1974, President Ford signed his first piece of legislation, the Juvenile Justice and Delinquency Prevention Act of 1974. He argued that federal programs had been fragmented and that the bill represented an effort to consolidate policy direction and coordinate federal programs to assist states and localities in dealing with juvenile delinquency (President Gerald Ford 8 Sep 1974). Like presidents before him, Ford tried to identify problems and solutions with anti-crime policy.

In September 1974 President Gerald Ford told the International Association of Chiefs of Police that the LEAA had increased block grants to the states and stressed that the $880 million in federal funds was simply "seed money." He argued that this was merely 5 percent of the total state and local expenditures on crime. Still, only seven or eight years before, the federal budget for crime had been just $50 million (President Gerald Ford 24 Sep 1974). The growth in funding reveals the involvement of the federal government in trying to reduce crime and increase lending support to mass incarceration.

In his 1975 State of the Union message, President Ford did not even mention crime. He was more concerned with reassuring the public that the Watergate scandal did not include all elected Republican officials (Marion 1994). In a speech about lawbreaking, President Ford went so far as to say that he did not speak in terms of "law and order," but that he went back "to the constitutional phrase—insuring domestic tranquility" (President Gerald Ford 25 Apr 1975). Moving away from the more severe crime rhetoric, he began to direct efforts toward promoting victims' rights and seeking citizen involvement in curbing crime. Although President Ford did continue the expansion of the federal government into crime control through the LEAA, he served less than two years and did not have time to implement a fully developed crime control agenda.

Moreover, in April 1975 President Ford exercised his chief executive pardoning power in a phenomenal way. Upon coming to office, tens of thousands of young men were in prison or being prosecuted for avoiding military service and the Vietnam War. President Ford granted clemency to 13,603 men charged with evading the draft and believed that this executive action would "give these young people a chance to earn their return to the mainstream of American society, so that they can, if they choose, contribute, even though belatedly, to the building and the betterment of our country and the world" (Tolan 2016). The president believed that granting clemency was essential to "bind up the nation's wounds" (Tolan 2016). This was the second time President Ford showed exceptional presidential leadership for the good of the nation's future. The first was when, under intense criticism, he pardoned the highest level of criminality of President Nixon. He acted with authoritative courage because he was convinced that the federal government could not function effectively if Nixon was being dragged through both civil and criminal trials. President Ford's pardoning of the draft dodgers was denounced by many, but history has confirmed that his actions were justified. Gerald Ford was more interested in uniting the country than holding political vendettas or severe punishment for the guilty.

At the Career Criminal Conference, President Ford said that through the LEAA, almost $5 million in grants had gone to equipment, technical assistance, and evaluation. However, he again declared: "With few exceptions, the prosecution of serious crimes in this country is solely within the jurisdiction of State and local authorities. . . . But the day-to-day planning, the conduct, and the decision making are fundamentally yours at the local level. . . . With few exceptions, the prosecution of serious crimes in this country is solely within the jurisdiction of State and local authorities" (President Gerald Ford 26 Sep 1975). President Ford was intending to move the responsibility for crime away from the federal government and toward local government. As was the case in previous administrations, crime increased under President Ford. In 1975 police reported 11.25 million crimes, and in 1976 the number reached 11.3 million (Marion 1994, 105).

During the Ford presidency, as well as during the Carter presidency to follow, some demobilization of mass incarceration occurred. From 1974 to 1976 the public showed ambivalence toward crime, with the crime and drugs category wavering between 1 and 8 percent on Gallup's "most important problem facing the country" question. With President Ford, the victims' rights movement emerged as a spin-off justice movement. President Johnson and the LEAA were the first initiators of victims' rights, but later presidents continued the tradition. As the victims' movement gained momentum, the public and media paid less attention to hard crime issues.

Interestingly, President Ford was the victim of two assassination attempts. On September 5, 1975, Lynette "Squeaky" Fromme, who was a member of the notorious Charles Manson Family, pointed a loaded gun at President Ford as he was walking through a crowd in Sacramento. Fromme moved toward him, and the Secret Service pounced on her and pulled the president to safety. President Ford was the first president to testify in a criminal trial. Fromme was convicted of attempted assassination of a president and sentenced to life in prison. She was paroled in 2009 (Fernandez 2016).

Then, just 17 days after Fromme's assassination attempt on President Ford, Sara Jane Moore fired a loaded gun at the president outside the St.

Francis Hotel in San Francisco. Former Marine Oliver Sipple deflected her arm, and the bullet went over the president's head. Moore pleaded guilty and was sentenced to life. In 2007 she was paroled after spending 32 years in a low-security federal prison for women. Federal parole laws have since been tightened. President Ford in a 2004 interview revealed that he believed both of the would-be assassins were mentally ill (Fernandez 2016).

In President Ford's 1976 State of the Union Address, he again proclaimed that protecting the life and property of citizens was the primary responsibility of local and state law enforcement authorities. Still, he emphasized the protection of the "innocent victims" of crime by keeping convicted criminals in prison (President Gerald Ford 19 Jan 1976). His new budget proposal included funding for building four new federal prison facilities, for increasing prosecution, and for adding more U.S. marshals and federal judges. He stated, "Unbelievably, America still has the same prison capacity as in 1960, although crime has doubled and our population has burgeoned. The need for more prisons is obvious and very, very urgent, and I included in the budget for the next fiscal year four new Federal prisons that are badly needed to meet this problem at the Federal level" (President Gerald Ford 14 Feb 1976). For this president, as well as many others, the only way to insure domestic tranquility was to be swift and certain by putting convicted criminals in prison.

In 1976 President Gerald Ford won the Republican nomination for president. However, California Governor Ronald Reagan challenged Ford by campaigning against what he thought was harmful liberalism. Reagan claimed he would bring decency and order back. Meanwhile, the 1976 Democratic Party Platform criticized the Republicans for a lack of major criminal justice reform but opposed efforts to pass any "repressive and anti-civil libertarian" measures (Democratic Party Platform of 1976 12 Jul 1976).

The 1976 Republican Party Platform focused on the victims of crime and on local and state responsibility for law enforcement with assistance from the federal government through the LEAA (Republican Party Platform of 1976 11 Aug 1976). The Republicans' shift in focus from convicting offenders to taking an interest in the needs and services of crime victims had few repercussions. In a special message to Congress on crime, President Ford proclaimed that for too long the law had centered on the rights of the criminally accused instead of the victims of crime (Gottschalk 2006).

When the LEAA established the Crime Victim Initiative in 1974, it provided funding to victims and witness programs to help enlist citizen support for the War on Crime and to promote awareness of victims and witnesses. Governmental support kept crime on the public agenda. By 1975 the LEAA had invested over $22 million in victims' projects (Schneider and Schneider 1981). In 1975 the National Organization for Victim Assistance (NOVA) was formed. Supported by the Office of Justice Programs' Office for Victims of

Crime (OVC), this organization promoted rights and services for crime victims. According to Gottschalk (2006, 87), NOVA became the "nucleus" of the victims' movement. By 1978 there were nearly 100 programs, including the American Bar Association's Criminal Justice Section establishment of a Victims' Committee. In 1980 there were over 400 victims' programs (Karmen 1984). Federal funding ensured government expansion into the victims' rights arena.

The LEAA continued to be a major source of funding for crime control and for the victims' rights movement. Additionally, President Ford used his leadership in the support of mandatory prison sentencing and strongly favored stricter criminal sentencing. He did not support rehabilitation for offenders and sought harsher punishment, continuing to believe this response would reduce crime. He claimed that he did not seek "vindictive" punishment but protection for victims. He stated:

> People convicted of violent crimes should have to go to jail. I urged the imposition of mandatory sentences for them and for "career "criminals as well. Second, I suggested less delay in bringing those arrested to trial, less plea bargaining and more courtroom determination of guilt or innocence. [We should] amend the Federal code to make more sentences mandatory. We could also supply funds to add judges, prosecutors and public defenders. (President Gerald Ford 25 Apr 1975)

He sought mandatory sentences for repeat federal offenders and for those who used firearms in committing hijackings, for kidnappings, and for trafficking in hard drugs (President Gerald Ford 19 Jun 1975). President Ford remained committed to increasing penalties for criminal behavior. However, Congress failed to pass President Ford's legislative initiatives regarding victim compensation, drug control, or mandatory sentencing. The extension of the LEAA was the only significant bill passed. Still, President Ford showed law-and-order leadership by being in favor of the death penalty. When he was in the U.S. House, he sponsored a bill that established criteria for the mandatory imposition of the sentence of death (On the Issues 2017a).

However, some argue that the most important legacy of President Ford was his appointment of Justice Stevens (Curry 2006). Ford only served two years but appointed Stevens, while Carter severed four years without a Supreme Court appointment. Even years after Ford left the presidency, the United States continues to live under legal rules created by the Supreme Court in which Stevens voted in the majority. These cases include Justice Stevens writing the majority opinion in *Kelo v. New London* (2005), the decision holding that local and state governments could condemn and acquire private property even when it was not to be used for a public purpose, which allowed for government power expansion.

Roper v. Simmons (2005) ruled that convicted murderers under the age of 18 could not get the death penalty. This was a more liberal decision, showing Stevens's moderate and center leanings. *Stenberg v. Carhart* (2004), in which the court struck down a Nebraska law banning so-called partial-birth abortions, also shows Stevens's moderate jurisprudence. President Ford's selection of Justice Stevens is considered an appointment based mostly on merit, rather than on politics: "An example that subsequent presidents have not routinely followed" (Denniston 2006).

Subsequently, the more conservative Burger Court rejected the majority of civil liberty claims (Heck 1981). This Court was more concerned with the institutional consequences of its rulings than protection of individual rights (McFeeley 1979). Unlike the Warren Court, the Burger Court delivered more unfavorable judgments against the rights of criminal defendants (McFeeley 1979). Gradually, the Burger Court permitted exceptions to the strict requirements for arrest and for obtaining a warrant before searches and seizures could occur. Moreover, the Burger Court limited the importance of the *Miranda v. Arizona* (1966) decisions, holding that an uncoerced statement was admissible to impeach a defendant's testimony, even without a Miranda warning, if a defendant testified in his or her own defense case. Jury trial protection was also somewhat compromised when the Burger Court allowed criminal conviction by a jury of less than 12 and with less than a unanimous verdict (McFeeley 1979). When considering civil liberty cases, the Burger Court rejected an overwhelming majority of claims (Heck 1981). These decisions helped shift the Court's ideological composition more to the conservative Right.

President Ford and other political elites began promoting victims' rights, and this perspective began to dominate traditional crime issues. While he did continue to expand the federal government, he took it in a different direction. After the Watergate debacle, President Gerald Ford had the task of reestablishing political legitimacy with the American public. While the nation healed from the Watergate scandal, the Ford administration pulled back somewhat from the Wars on Crime and Drugs. President Ford moved the national discourse away from "law and order" and toward a focus on "domestic tranquility." In the aftermath of Watergate, it would have been hypocritical to stress draconian street crime control while Ford pardoned President Nixon for his part in the Watergate cover-up. Therefore, chief executive and legislative action created favorable policies that enhanced the growth of the federal government through victims' rights.

President Jimmy Carter, "Soft on Crime"

With the Watergate scandal still haunting voters, Democrat Jimmy Carter won the 1976 presidential election against Republican President Gerald Ford.

On September 8, 1974, President Ford pardoned former President Nixon, and this unpopular presidential action may have caused Gerald Ford's defeat. President Jimmy Carter was inaugurated in January 1977, and his campaign platform included decriminalization of marijuana. In the same year, the Senate Judiciary Committee voted to decriminalize possession of up to an ounce of marijuana for personal use. However, like many of Jimmy Carter's visionary ideas, plans to decriminalize marijuana were abandoned as concerns over the high rates of marijuana use by teens intensified (Drug Policy Alliance 2017).

If Jimmy Carter's more progressive ideas toward marijuana use had been adopted and his leadership respected, the United States might not be currently known as Prison Nation. Had past and present presidents had the insight of President Jimmy Carter and not continually promoted and fought the War on Crime, the War on Drugs, and the War on Gangs, perhaps our prisons would not be filled with mostly minority, low-level drug offenders who are costing the United States billions of dollars.

In the 1976 presidential campaign, crime was not a major issue. With the lingering effects of the Watergate affair still inescapable, the Republicans' war rhetoric on crime lessened. Presidential candidate Jimmy Carter condemned the previous administration for ineffective programs and wasteful spending. He suggested abolishing the LEAA because he felt millions of dollars had been misused on failed crime-control measures. The 1976 Democratic Platform held the Republicans responsible for failing to secure their promises (Democratic Party Platform of 1976 12 Jul 1976). Therefore, President Carter sought more efficiency with more controlled spending. Like President Ford, he had other priorities, such as the environment, nuclear arms control, and human rights—not fighting crime (Marion 1994, 128). In addition, the Carter administration was forced to deal with an oil crisis and the Iranian hostage situation.

As President Carter took office, 15 percent of respondents identified crime as the "most important issue facing the country" in March 1977. Yet President Carter was more interested in reforming the LEAA and justice policy than invoking anti-crime rhetoric. With minimal presidential attention and leadership focused on the call for law and order, crime had dropped off the national agenda, and Carter has been accused of being soft on crime—a death sentence for any politician.

In 1976 President Carter proposed reorganization of the LEAA's funding and repeatedly stated that crime-control programs needed to be more cost-effective and efficient. He declared: "The Law Enforcement Assistance Administration funds have been wasted in years gone by. We are trying to bring a more narrow focus on them to prevent crime and to get out of the waste of buying very expensive and fancy machines and . . . actually concentrate in the areas where the crime rate is highest" (President Jimmy Carter 18

Jul 1977). While the Carter administration continued the LEAA's funding, he was also interested in community-based crime prevention and alternatives to incarceration, including supervised-release and work-release programs (Marion 1994).

In 1977 President Carter reported that drug abuse was costing more than $15 billion per year and that he was ordering the attorney general to investigate the connection between organized crime and drug trafficking. He wanted more cooperation "among all law enforcement agencies, and to ensure more certain convictions and quick punishment for those who traffic in drugs" (President Jimmy Carter 2 Aug 1977). Yet Carter wanted to end federal criminal penalties for up to one ounce of marijuana and leave it to the states to adopt their own appropriate drug policies.

Moreover, President Carter was not a hardcore law-and-order leader and had protested that jails were filled with poor people. He stated that, while poor people were not the only ones to commit crimes, they seemed to be the only ones going to prison. He complained that white-collar corporate criminals many times got off with a slap on the wrist. President Carter claimed that this situation caused contempt for the concept of equal justice (President Jimmy Carter 15 Oct 1976). President Carter understood that problems like drug abuse and violence were complicated social issues and could not be solved with strict law-and-order legislation. He stated:

> Problems like drugs, alcohol, unwanted pregnancies, even suicide have reached down to members of a family who are younger and younger. Tragic instances of family violence remind us that the bonds of kinship don't automatically make families a place of nurturing one another. Most violent crimes against a person are committed among those who know each other and often love each other. Some laws, some government policies, tend to disrupt family structures. (President Jimmy Carter 1980)

He also believed that reforming the justice system could make a difference in reducing crime and the number of repeat offenders.

President Carter was sensitive to government waste and wanted to make existing crime-fighting programs more efficient and effective. He believed that a stronger economy and more jobs would lessen crime. The president portrayed strong presidential leadership when he stated: "I think our country's leaders, beginning with the President, can set an example and set a tone that will increase respect for the law and increase the sense of national unity, and that can lessen crime in America" (Carter 1996). President Carter also understood that crime was a societal problem. He criticized the previous administration for abandoning criminal justice rehabilitation in favor of harsher punishment and argued that "Crime reflects sickness in a society. Working together, we can make ours a more healthy society, one in which we need not live our lives in fear. I intend, as President, to provide the leadership that will turn the tide against the scourge of crime" (Carter 1996). Carter was a visionary leader before his time, and one of the few politicians who realized the ramifications of stricter criminal laws and sentences. While governor of Georgia, Carter competed with governors of other states to reduce their prison population. His administration offered reform by trying to prepare inmates with basic education, career training, and psychological rehabilitation while in prison. These incentives were to be followed by early-release and work-release programs (Carter 2005). However, with the race to incarcerate, other politicians abandoned rehabilitation programs.

In August 1977 President Carter told Congress that drug abuse continued to be a serious social problem in the United States. Although he did not promote the War on Drugs, the president claimed that many neighborhoods were unsafe because of drug-related street crime (President Jimmy Carter 2 Aug 1977). During the Carter administration, legislation extended drug treatment to drug addicts but also supported increased funding for the DEA and the Coast Guard for law enforcement.

In President Carter's 1977 Report to the American People, his only remark on crime was that "There are many other areas of domestic policy—housing, health, crime, education, agriculture, and others—that will concern me as President" (President Jimmy Carter 2 Feb 1977). He was much more concerned with the state of the American economy and developing a national energy policy. In March 1977 President Carter stated that federal law enforcement efforts would concentrate on organized crime operations, including curtailing large-scale narcotic traffickers instead of minor offenders (President Jimmy Carter 24 Mar 1977).

In his 1978 State of the Union message, President Carter identified several goals, including reorganizing the federal LEAA, improving criminal research efforts, and developing better law enforcement methods against organized crime, white-collar crime, drug abuse, and public corruption. He also wanted to develop minimum standards for federal correctional institutions (President Jimmy Carter 19 Jan 1978). Although the Office of Drug Abuse Policy was newly established, most of Carter's measures had already been proposed by other presidents.

In President Carter's 1979 State of the Union message, he again emphasized that he wanted to reform the LEAA. This included the creation of a National Institute of Justice to obtain better information and research on crime (President Jimmy Carter 25 Jan 1979). In his 1980 State of the Union message, President Carter was still grappling with LEAA's high expenditures. He signed a bill that incorporated many reforms but reauthorized the LEAA for four more years. He suggested reforms that would stop excessive expenditure for equipment and would permit funding only of innovative programs which had a high probability of success (President Jimmy Carter 23 Jan

1980). Carter's main concern was reducing the cost of the LEAA and lowering crime in the most effective manner. He did not endorse a War on Crime or a War on Drugs. Furthermore, by January 1980 concern for crime was at 0 percent (Marion 1994). The loss of public interest in crime indicates the power of the presidency in promoting national agenda issues. President Carter's progressive vision for the justice system mirrors much of the smart-on-crime philosophy that reformers are trying to enact in 2017.

Previous presidents had also tried to deal with the ineffectual LEAA and Safe Streets Act, described as producing an "overly complex, cumbersome and bureaucratic program" (Feeley and Sarat 1980, 139–41). Still, President Carter provided funding for the construction of more federal correctional institutions. He also added more federal judges and restructured time limits for federal trials under the Justice System Improvement Act of 1979 (Marion 1994). In his last State of the Union message in 1981, President Carter acknowledged that the criminal code still needed major reform. He claimed that by providing treatment and rehabilitation, the Carter administration had reduced the heroin addict population. The number of heroin-related deaths had been reduced by 80 percent and the number of heroin-related injuries had been reduced by 50 percent (President Jimmy Carter 16 Jan 1981).

In the 1980 presidential campaign, the Republican Platform accused the Democrats of being obsessed with special interest demands, preoccupied with expensive "comprehensive" programs, and of "social and fiscal tinkering with our cities and towns." The Republicans claimed that they would address the real problems of neighborhood deterioration, urban blight, dangerous streets, and violent crime (Republican Party Platform of 1980 15 Jul 1980). After the Watergate years and with the defeat of President Gerald Ford, the Republicans took the opportunity to voice grievances and complaints against the Carter administration and the Democrats. Although President Carter opposed the LEAA, the Democratic Platform stated that the new Law Enforcement Assistance Act provided an important framework for close federal cooperation with state and local law enforcement authorities. The Democrats also supported federal assistance to victims of crime, especially for programs that assisted the elderly and victims of rape and domestic violence (Democratic Party Platform of 1980 11 Aug 1980).

The women's liberation movement was perhaps the most radical movement of the 1960s and 1970s, with the greatest enduring societal and political impact (Farber 1994; Gelb and Palley 1996; McGlen et al. 2011). This movement successfully challenged many traditional notions about male dominance and institutionalized male privilege (Ferree and Martin 1995). Beginning in the 1970s, concerned feminists actively worked on behalf of women who had been raped or suffered from domestic violence. The battered women's movement was a sub-movement of the anti-rape movement (Schechter 1982). The success and acceptance of the battered women's and anti-rape movements exposed persistent blaming of the victim and led to the politicization of violence against women (Schechter 1982). Both of these movements appropriately fit into the law-and-order category.

The issue of rape, rooted in male dominance and reinforced by laws, attitudes, and customs, appeared on the feminist agenda as a major problem facing women (Bevacqua 2000). In 1976 the first marital rape law was enacted in Nebraska, making it illegal for husbands to rape their wives. During that time, the LEAA was a major supporter of the anti-rape movement. It funded many of the major studies on women as offenders, victims, and as criminal justice employees (Gottschalk 2006). Due to funding problems, the LEAA and other government agencies began to absorb many of the independent, feminist rape crisis centers.

As time progressed, rape reform became less oriented toward deep social and political problems and instead turned to law enforcement reforms and solutions (Gottschalk 2006). Many feminists pursued law-and-order solutions for rape assaults, including increased law enforcement presence for the protection of women, more stringent enforcement of rape laws, and harsher punishment for convicted offenders. Yet critics of this approach felt it would result in greater numbers of incarcerated black and poor men (Edwards 1976). It is theorized that more black and lower-class men would be jailed for rape because women may be less afraid to press charges against them. Moreover, it is argued that the legal system supports this, as men without resources for proper defense are more likely to be convicted (Bevacqua 2000).

The anti-rape movement was successful in reforming rape laws and helped bring much-needed services to victims of sexual assault and domestic violence. However, focusing on tough law enforcement solutions may have reinforced a more punitive criminal justice environment (Gottschalk 2006). As a result, the anti-rape movement may have been conscripted into the call for law and order by demanding harsher sentences for these offenders instead of offering alternative treatment solutions.

President Carter believed that the LEAA had almost no effect on reducing the crime rate, and he attempted to reduce the agency's funding significantly. In 1977 Carter appointed a Justice Department task force to study the LEAA. The task force report suggested that the LEAA be eliminated. In 1978 President Carter submitted his plan to reorganize the LEAA, but in 1979 Congress passed its own restructuring plan, which authorized $825 million annually through fiscal 1983 (Marion 1994).

Sensational crime events continued to keep the public on edge over crime. In August 1977 David Berkowitz confessed to killing six people and wounding seven others in the course of eight shootings. These crimes terrorized New York City between 1976 and 1977. Berkowitz sent perverse messages to the police and to *New York Daily News* columnist Jimmy Breslin. The killer called himself the Son of Sam in his letters, which spoke of Papa Sam, the master Satanic figure. The Son of Sam's last attack was on July 31, when he killed a young woman and blinded her male companion. That night, a witness saw a man in the neighborhood remove a parking ticket from a Ford Galaxie. The police tracked the car back to 24-year-old David Berkowitz, an employee of the U.S. Postal Service and a trained ex-Army sharpshooter (Chua-Eoan 2007).

This high-profile crime event captured television and mass media attention, introducing Americans to the serial killer phenomenon. *Newsweek* published one cover story on the Son of Sam. Between August 1977 and December 1977, the *New York Times* published approximately 40 stories on David Berkowitz (Lexis Nexis ProQuest Historical Newspaper, *New York Times*, "David Berkowitz"). In 2007 the Son of Sam killings were listed among *Time*'s "Top 25 Crimes of the Century" (Chua-Eoan 2007). All the media attention that serial killers receive may contribute to others seeking the same type of publicity.

Ted Bundy was a handsome and charming American serial killer who strangled and mutilated his victims. He confessed to killing approximately 30 young women across the United States between 1974 and 1978. At trial, he acted as his own defense lawyer in a sensationalized television proceeding. Between December 1978 and February 1989, the *New York Times* published approximately 25 stories on Ted Bundy, his trial, and his execution (Lexis Nexis ProQuest Historical Newspaper, the *New York Times*, "Ted Bundy"). In 2007 the Ted Bundy murders were listed among *Time*'s "Top 25 Crimes of the Century" (Chua-Eoan 2007).

The Son of Sam killings and Ted Bundy's killing spree resulted in middle-class people feeling unsafe in their own homes and communities. However, this was a time of demobilization for the anti-crime movement, with little reaction to crime coming from national government officials. Still, these murders of mostly women reinforced the need for attention to innocent victims of crime. Although President Jimmy Carter was not a zealot crime fighter and tried to reign in the cost of the LEAA, this legislative beast died a slow and complicated death.

President Jimmy Carter did not campaign on issues of crime and was more concerned with human rights. However, his legacy is that he left office with a smaller federal prison population than when he took office. As chief executive, President Carter declared that the LEAA was ineffectual in fighting crime. Reforming federal policy and cutting costs were his major crime concerns. Moreover, the national attention given to victims' rights became the catalyst for the women's movement's anti-rape and domestic violence spin-off movements that addressed crime and grew the government in a different manner. In addition, drug addiction remained a major problem, and the Carter administration responded with funding for treatment, as well as for continued law enforcement measures. During President Carter's term, the crime rate fell, and so did the public's concern for crime. However, the serial killer phenomenon and the media's fascination with several high-profile serial murders kept crime in the public eye.

Neither President Ford nor President Carter was known for his harsh stance on crime and punishment. The Gerald R. Ford Library claims that President Ford cut the growth of crime by 75 percent while he was in office and that the rate of increase went down by 9 percent (President Ford '76 Fact Book). Pew Research Center's analysis of data from the Bureau of Justice Statistics reveals that, although President Jimmy Carter only served four years between 1977 and 1980, there was a more than 34 percent decline in prisoners. This is a reduction of 9,625 inmates and was the largest reduction of inmates of any president on record, both in percentages and in absolute numbers (Gramlich 2017a). Jimmy Carter was a visionary president who demonstrated a more humane and less punitive attitude toward what would later become the problem of mass incarceration.

CHAPTER FIVE

President Reagan Declares All-Out War on Crime and Drugs

In the 1980s the social and political chaos of the two previous decades left the public more hostile toward crime, social disorder, and the welfare state (Garland 2001). Like Nixon and other conservatives, President Ronald Reagan capitalized on the presumed relationship between crime and welfare programs. He demonized and denigrated poor, female welfare recipients and scapegoated them by calling them "Welfare Queens" in a time of increasing inequality and insecurities. He believed that being poor encouraged crime and that the individual was to blame; he aimed to end crime by cutting social services and assistance to the poor. Ronald Reagan's law-and-order presidential legacy is marked by an extended period of "skyrocketing rates of incarceration mostly due to the unprecedented expansion of the drug war. This resulted in the number of people imprisoned for nonviolent drug law offenses increasing from 50,000 in 1980 to over 400,000 by 1997" (Drug Policy Alliance 2017).

Ronald Reagan, the Great Communicator, had a strong and charming personality and a calming leadership demeanor. In the 1980 presidential election, he accused the Carter administration of having more concern for criminal rights than for the victims of crime. While the Democrats defended their record, the 1980 Republican Platform claimed that a vital element to ending crime was fair, firm, and speedy criminal penalties, as well as a strong court system willing to use them (Republican Party Platform of 1980 15 Jul 1980).

In an effort to attract white working-class voters and to appeal to the Southern coalition, the 1980 Republican Platform focused on strict and swift application of justice, including mandatory minimum sentencing. They wanted expanded use of capital punishment and harsher punishment for drug users, dealers, and smugglers (Beckett 1997). Republicans blamed President Carter for enacting ineffective crime policies that had allowed for a "murderous epidemic of drugs" to sweep the nation (Republican Party Platform of 1980 15 Jul 1980).

Although studies demonstrated that increased spending on welfare lowered the crime rate, the conservative get-tough rhetoric blamed the poor, welfare programs, a permissive society, and lenient criminal justice policies for rising crime rates (Beckett and Sasson 2004, 59). Reagan pledged to correct the "welfare mess" and endorsed government assistance directed at the middle-class, including affordable mortgages, tax breaks, social security, and college subsidies (Schuparra 2003, 106). These expensive government welfare programs shunned poor minorities (Garland 2001).

Therefore, conservative politicians rode the wave of law and order into office by capitalizing on white fears over the increased crime rate (Schuparra 2003). Ronald Reagan's leadership increased the opportunity to take advantage of the United States' social climate filled with resentment toward the poor. This situation arose during an economic downturn that left millions of the middle class feeling unsure and vulnerable (Garland 2001). Concerns for keeping the public safe replaced concerns for the welfare of disadvantaged individuals and for civil rights. Expanding law enforcement, conservatives argued, would help the poor more effectively. This association between crime and welfare turned the federal government into more of a "security state" (Beckett and Sasson 2004, 58–59). "The increased growth of the criminal justice system replaced social welfare with social control as the principle of state policy" (Beckett 1997, 106). While the Reagan administration and the Republicans talked of limited government by reducing welfare to the poor, the move toward a carceral state had the opposite effect.

Consequently, President Ronald Reagan successfully appealed to the social conservatism of the largely white middle class by conveying hostility toward government spending on the "shiftless" poor (Garland 2001, 96). He was critical and unsupportive of labor unions and alarmed by the disintegration of family values. Like many Republicans, President Reagan felt there was a breakdown of law and order. This represented a backlash to the progressive rights revolutions of the post–World War II decades. In advancing his law-and-order leadership, President Reagan favored expansion of the exclusionary rule regarding illegally seized evidence. However, groups such as the American Civil Liberties Union and the American Bar Association opposed legislation, for fear of eroding the Fourth Amendment's protection against unreasonable search and seizure.

President Ronald Reagan attempted to cut back federal protections that had been expanded under the Carter administration. Due to Democratic opposition, some of Reagan's proposed legislation never made it through Congress. However, in July 1984, the Supreme Court ruled that police evidence obtained "in good faith" was admissible at trial, even when a search warrant was later ruled invalid. This ruling weakened the exclusionary rule (*Mapp v. Ohio* 1961). The six-to-three decision in *United States v. Leon* (1984) was based on the argument that excluding such evidence created a social cost that was unacceptable (Alschuler 1984).

Most of President Reagan's Supreme Court appointees left a conservative imprint on the Supreme Court. He appointed Justice Sandra Day O'Connor (1981), Chief Justice William Rehnquist (1986), Justice Antonin Scalia (1986), and Justice Anthony M. Kennedy (1988). Justice Scalia proved to be most supportive to the policies of the Reagan presidency (Brisbin 1990). Much of President Reagan's energy was spent trying to appoint conservative justices to Court. First, he nominated the strict constructionist Judge Robert H. Bork, and, after a sustained battle with Democrats, Judge Bork failed to obtain Senate approval (President Ronald Reagan 27 Jan 1988). Then the president nominated Judge Douglas H. Ginsburg, and this appointment also failed. Finally, Judge Kennedy won approval. By 1988 the Court's shift to the right was clear, bearing Chief Justice Rehnquist's imprint (Davis 1991). For the next 15 years, the call for law and order found support in Supreme Court rulings, and many precedents protecting the rights of defendants and prison inmates were overturned (Jost 2005). Supreme Court rulings in favor of the law-and-order policies have helped increased the number of inmates, as well as providing longer and harsher sentences.

The call for law and order had vast government support, substantial special interest group assistance to draw on, and plentiful resources. In April 1981 the FBI and other law enforcement statistics indicated that crime continued to be a very serious national problem. President Reagan declared that for too long the victims of crime had been the "forgotten persons" in the criminal justice system. He proclaimed that the week beginning April 19, 1981, was National Victims' Rights Week (President Ronald Reagan 8 Apr 1981).

In September 1981, speaking at the Annual Meeting of the International Association of Chiefs of Police, President Reagan claimed that the "innocent victims of crime" were too "frequently overlooked" (President Ronald Reagan 28 Sep 1981). He supported legislation that allowed judges to order offenders to make restitution to their victims and ordered U.S. Assistant Attorney General Lois Haight Herrington to evaluate the "numerous proposals" regarding victims.

In President Reagan's 1982 State of the Union Address, he stated that the problem of crime was "real and deadly serious" and demanded "transformation" of the legal system, which he claimed "overly protects the rights of criminals while it leaves society and the innocent victims of crime without justice" (President Ronald Reagan 26 Jan 1982). Standing up for the victims of crime was an issue that President Reagan supported throughout his presidency.

Additionally, in 1982 First Lady Nancy Reagan began the school-run anti-drug "Just Say No" program, which encouraged children and teens to pledge not to experiment with harmful drugs. The first lady traveled over 200,000 miles throughout the United States and internationally. Mrs. Reagan hosted two international conferences on youth drug abuse at the White House and appeared on television talk shows, public service announcements, and wrote guest articles concerning drug prevention (Reagan 2009). Reagan continually promoted the anti-crime, anti-welfare, anti-union agenda. These initiatives were directed at minorities and the underprivileged who were caught up in the criminal justice system.

In 1982, with support from the Reagan administration, Congress let the Law Enforcement Assistance Act (LEAA) "quietly" go out of business (quoted by Marion 1994, 166). Between 1968 and 1981 the federal government spent more than $8 billion on crime through the LEAA (Diegelman 1982, 994–1011). Although the LEAA significantly improved the education and training of law enforcement personnel, implemented new programs, and aided in research, crime was not reduced (Diegelman 1982). Like other presidents before him, Reagan felt that the LEAA was too expensive and lacked creditable results.

Although President Reagan said he supported states' rights, he continued to expand federal authority. In May 1982 he issued a statement on anti-crime legislation proposed by Senator Strom Thurmond (R-SC), chairperson of the Senate Judiciary Committee, and Senator Joseph Biden (D-DE) urging Congress to give it prompt attention. He surmised that, although 97 percent of criminal cases lie primarily with the states, "The Federal Government can set an example for the States by establishing a modern, effective criminal justice system" (President Ronald Reagan 26 May 1982). Reagan admitted that the root cause of the federal government's growth was the crime problem. But he blamed the Democrats because they had mistakenly believed that "government as the chief vehicle of change through educational, health, housing, and other programs" could permanently change the evils of human nature (President Ronald Reagan 28 Sep 1981).

In September 1982 Reagan proposed the Criminal Justice Reform Act and announced strong support for the comprehensive Violent Crime and Drug Enforcement Improvements Act. These two pieces of legislation included items like bail reform, victim-witness protection, strengthened drug penalties, sentencing reform, and expanded criminal forfeiture (President Ronald Reagan 13 Sep 1982). President Reagan continually addressed the issue of crime and drugs. In his 1983 State of the Union message, he reiterated the urgency of the problem: "It's high time that we make our cities safe again. This administration hereby declares an all-out war on big-time organized crime and the drug racketeers who are poisoning our young people" (President Ronald Reagan 25 Jan 1983).

President Reagan declared war on crime and drugs to fulfill his campaign promise that a law-and-order agenda would decrease crime. Like Presidents Johnson and Nixon, he employed the language of war to develop support and justification for his anti-crime policies. His political rhetoric helped shape the sentiment that there was no other choice but to respond in this manner.

In the 1984 State of the Union message, President Reagan focused on crime and victims, saying, " Already our efforts to crack down on career criminals, organized crime, drug pushers, and to enforce tougher sentences and paroles are having effect" (President Ronald Reagan 25 Jan 1984). He claimed that the crime rate had had the biggest decline since 1972 and reiterated that protecting victims was as important as safeguarding the rights of defendants (President Ronald Reagan 25 Jan 1984). Subsequently, tougher sentences and less parole meant more prisoners and the need for more prisons. He further asserted that "numerous" state legislatures had passed "tough" new sentencing laws and that his administration was taking three critically important steps to fight crime. First, Reagan wanted to appoint federal judges that would uphold the "rights of society and the innocent victims as well as the rights of the accused" (President Ronald Reagan 25 Jan 1984). Second was an "all-out assault on the illicit drug trade" (President Ronald Reagan 25 Jan 1984). This included adding more than 1,200 new investigators and prosecutors and establishing 12 regional task forces to combat "big money drug traffickers" (President Ronald Reagan 25 Jan 1984). As a result, the drug task force initiated 620 cases, indicting more than 2,600 individuals. President Reagan proclaimed that 143 indictments were under the "Drug Kingpin" law, which carried a maximum penalty of life in prison without the possibility of parole. These actions had a profound effect on the growth of the criminal justice system. Third, the new Commission on Organized Crime brought "much needed public attention" to organized crime, resulting in a "full-scale offensive" against career criminals (President Ronald Reagan 25 Jan 1984). President Reagan maintained that organized crime arrests had tripled and, of course, increased incarceration (President Ronald Reagan 25 Jan 1984).

To gain public support, President Reagan blamed Democrats and indicated that his administration was representing millions of Americans who were fed up with the fear of crime, lenient judges, and a system that treated criminals better than victims. He argued that Democrats had "stuck to the old; discredited, liberal illusions about crime—illusions that refuse to hold criminals responsible for their actions" (President Ronald Reagan 7 Jul 1984). The Reagan administration continually attacked the courts, liberals, and the failure to accept personal responsibility to enlist backing.

At the 1984 Annual Conference of the National Sheriffs' Association, Reagan called for cooperation among law enforcement, hailed Neighborhood Watch programs, criticized the too-lenient court system, and applauded the tough, new state statutes directed at repeat offenders (President Ronald Reagan 20 Jun 1984). Like President Nixon, President Reagan did not believe that social factors played any part in criminal behavior. He blamed the liberal approach for perpetuating crime and claimed that traditional values, community involvement, and a sense of responsibility would reduce crime.

Therefore, many members of Congress did not want to be seen as "soft on crime" and supported the conservative law-and-order method to fight drugs. In 1984 the House passed HR 522 (S 422), which created a new federal offense for robbery or burglary of controlled substances. The passing of HR 1580 (S 1146) was also intended to reduce the use of airplanes in drug smuggling. Likewise, Congress passed the anti-crime package (PL 98-473), popularly known as the Comprehensive Crime Act of 1984. This major piece of legislation overhauled federal sentencing and reformed bail and forfeiture procedures. The bill increased penalties for major drug offenses and allowed the government to seize assets and profits of drug traffickers. It also politicized criminal law issues, resulting in this draconian legislation that brought procedural and substantive laws that continue to plague the administration of federal criminal justice (Newell 2013).

Some argue that because of President Reagan's tough-on-crime initiatives, lengthy pretrial detentions are common and federal prisons are "filled with pretrial detainees deemed dangerous, or subject to a handful of statutory presumptions that largely result in jailing low-level drug dealers" (Shargel 2004). Additionally, the Reagan administration diluted the insanity defense, enacted oppressive forfeiture laws, abolished parole, and passed mandatory minimum sentences for offenses involving weapons (Newell 2013). President Ronald Reagan shifted drug-control resources from health agencies to the Department of Justice and passed policies that filled U.S. prisons for decades with low-level drug users (Newman 2016).

Notably, President Reagan signing the 1984 Sentencing Reform Act led the way in federal sentencing guidelines. This law increased the maximum prison sentence for defendants who trafficked in large quantities of heroin and cocaine. This bill also increased the first-offense penalty for distributing or making certain illegal drugs (Marion 1994). Importantly, this law abolished much of parole but established the U.S. Sentencing Commission, which writes mandatory federal sentencing guidelines for courts to follow. The elimination of parole had a major impact on the federal prison system. Under the Sentencing Reform Act, parole was eliminated for those federal defendants convicted after November 1, 1987. However, these prisoners could earn reduced terms for good behavior, and judges could grant a period of supervised release to be served at the end of their sentence. They could also be eligible for early release for exemplary behavior, such as making progress toward a high school diploma.

Altering the federal sentencing guidelines that went into effect in 1987 meant that "doing time" was determined by the weight of the drugs involved in the crime. Parole was abolished, and prisoners had to serve at least 85 percent of their sentence. Most often, judges could no longer factor in the defendant's character, the effect of confinement on their family obligations, or the nature and circumstances of the offence. One of the only ways the violator could receive a less severe sentence was to make a deal with the public prosecutor by acting as an informant against others. These guidelines effectively stripped the judiciary of its sentencing discretion and gave it to prosecutors.

Also in 1984 Congress passed the Justice Assistance Act that established the Department of Justice, Office of Justice Programs, which administered grants (O'Bryant 2003). A major victory for the call for law and order was President Reagan's signing of the Comprehensive Crime Control Act of 1984, which overhauled the federal sentencing system and reformed bail policies and forfeiture procedures (O'Bryant 2003). This was of major importance in several respects and had a significant impact on the imprisonment rate. The enactment of the Comprehensive Crime Control Act of 1984, with its many new federal crimes, abolishment of parole, reinstitution of the death penalty, and stringent sentencing guidelines led to substantial growth of mass incarceration (Federal Bureau of Prisons 2011).

This act is one of the three major federal responses to crime control: the others being the Crime Control Act of 1990, which is discussed in the chapter on President George H. W. Bush, and the Violent Crime Control and Law Enforcement Act of 1994, discussed in the chapter on President Clinton's administration (O'Bryant 2003). Creating longer and more severe sentencing is a major factor in the mass incarceration problem that the United States is now facing. There seems to be no political insight into the unintended consequences of the "lock them up and throw away the key" mentality.

In 1984 President Reagan promoted his crime agenda while campaigning for reelection. He pointed out that there was a 7 percent decrease in crime reported in 1983, and this was the "sharpest decrease in the history of the crime statistics" (President Ronald Reagan 7 Jul 1984). Moreover, it marked the "first time the serious crime index has shown a decline two years in a row" (President Ronald Reagan 7 Jul 1984). He claimed that the statistic demonstrated that national, state, and local law enforcement efforts had finally made an impact on crime. President Reagan talked less about the amount of crime and instead started quoting statistics that indicated a drop in serious crime (President Ronald Reagan 7 Jul 1984). Reagan campaigned on the problem of "crime in the streets" and vowed to expand the federal government's role in battling this problem (Beckett 1997, 44–45; Beckett and

Sasson 2004, 63). Since fighting street crime was a state and local responsibility, identifying drugs as a key element of crime helped resolve the federalism dilemma. Street crime (as well as the welfare issue), with its class connotations and racist imagery, was Reagan's niche.

During the 1984 election, while the Democrats mostly ignored the crime issue, Reagan claimed credit for increasing the federal law enforcement budget by 50 percent for the War on Crime (Marion 1994, 144). Praising the Reagan administration for its victories, the 1984 Republican Party Platform described the federal government's expansion into crime control:

> We added 1,900 new investigators and prosecutors to the federal fight against crime. We arrested more offenders and sent more of them to prison. . . . We set up task forces to strike at organized crime and narcotics. In the year since, 3,000 major drug traffickers have been indicted, and nearly 1,000 have already been convicted. We are helping local authorities search for missing children. (Republican Party Platform of 1984 20 Aug 1984)

The campaign and election process allowed the Republicans to chronicle their accomplishments. The additional crime-fighting resources were federally funded and valued putting people in jail to control drug use.

Continually in his candidacy, Reagan accused the courts of being too lenient on criminals. Speaking to the National Sheriffs' Association, the president asserted that the American people had "widespread loss of faith" in their criminal justice system (President Ronald Reagan 20 Jun 1984). He claimed that 85 percent of Americans said "the courts in their home areas weren't tough enough on criminals and 75 percent believed the criminal justice system just wasn't deterring crime" (President Ronald Reagan 20 Jun 1984). While Republicans embraced limiting the size and scope of the federal government, President Ronald Reagan was a popular leader who expanded government and incarceration by advancing the causes of law and order with his get-tough policies.

Importantly, the Organized Crime Drug Enforcement Task Force, headed by Vice President Bush, recommended the establishment of the National Narcotics Border Interdiction System, and this led to the Marijuana Eradication and Suppression Program (Republican Party Platform of 1984 20 Aug 1984). This program gave the FBI authority to investigate drugs and to coordinate with the Drug Enforcement Agency (DEA). In addition, the Reagan administration was supported by professional organizations such as the National Sheriffs' Association and created crime-fighting initiatives such as neighborhood watch programs (President Ronald Reagan 15 Feb 1984). Other government support for the call for law and order came from the Justice Department with its wealth of law enforcement agencies and bureaucrats. Federal, state, and local criminal justice bureaucrats are a powerful interest group that has grown dramatically over the past 30 years. Members of Congress rely on these government experts and criminal justice bureaucrats[1] to act as "dominant actors" in the policy process (Miller 2004, 570).

Notably, President Reagan's appointee Assistant Attorney General Lois Haight Herrington provided substantial support and formed vast and extensive networks. As an example of how executive branch bureaucrats pushed the law-and-order agenda, Herrington had headed the Office of Justice Programs in the Department of Justice and was the president's national correspondent to the United Nations Congress on the Prevention of Crime and the Treatment of Offenders. She was a member of the President's Child Safety Partnership and the National Sheriffs' Association's Standards, Ethics, Education, and Training Committee and on the advisory board of Crime Stoppers International. She served on the Advisory Committee on Rape Prevention and Control and the National Advisory Board on Child Abuse and Neglect. She was a member of the Victims Committee, Criminal Justice Section, of the American Bar Association and served as chairperson of the National Crime Prevention Coalition. Additionally, Herrington was a member of the federal Coordinating Council on Juvenile Justice and Delinquency Prevention and on the Advisory Board of the National Institute of Corrections (White House 5 May 1987). She served as chairperson and executive director of the 1987 White House Conference for a Drug Free America, where she served as one of the law-and-order "bridge leaders" (Robnett 1997). By taking President Reagan's law-and-order message to organizers and leaders, Herrington demonstrated how support was mobilized in the Reagan administration and accomplished gains for the call for law and order.

In the 1985 State of the Union Address, Reagan maintained the tough-on-crime message. He claimed accomplishments but wanted police-friendly laws and more application of the death penalty to control crime. He echoed that the "explosion of violent crime" was due to more attention to protecting the rights of defendants than to the victims of crime. When speaking about crime, President Reagan took on an imperial presidential manner as he expanded federal intervention into law enforcement and imprisonment.

> We do not seek to violate the rights of defendants. But shouldn't we feel more compassion for the victims of crime than for those who commit crime? For the first time in 20 years, the crime index has fallen 2 years in a row. We've convicted over 7,400 drug offenders and put them, as well as leaders of organized crime, behind bars in record numbers. But we must do more. I urge permitting use of all reliable evidence that police officers acquire in good faith. These proposals would also reform the habeas corpus laws and allow, in keeping with the will of the overwhelming majority of Americans, the use of the death penalty where necessary. (President Ronald Reagan 6 Feb 1985)

He restated that to restore domestic tranquility and "in keeping with the will of the overwhelming majority of Americans," the United States should use "the death penalty where necessary" (President Ronald Reagan 6 Feb 1985). In his governing-through-crime strategy, Reagan used fear of crime to gain public support and contributed to more punitive and strident policies (Caplow and Simon 1999). In 1985 Congress passed HR 3132, which banned armor-piercing bullets and was supported by national law enforcement officers (Marion 1994).

In his 1986 State of the Union message, President Reagan claimed that "there had been three straight years of falling crime rates" (President Ronald Reagan 4 Feb 1986). However, after this initial decrease, crime reports increased to 13.9 million in 1988 (Marion 1994, 146). In spite of evidence indicating decreased drug use, the Reagan administration continued its War on Drugs and federal expansion into crime control (Gottschalk 2006). During the Reagan Era, a high of only 11 percent of respondents identified crime and drug abuse as the "most important problem facing the country" (quoted by Marion 1994, 148–49).

Yet Congress interpreted media attention and increased public concern over drugs as a sign to pass tougher anti-drug legislation. President Reagan was in office for eight years, which gave him an extended amount of time to carry out his law-and-order crime agenda. Although crime was decreasing, the public's increased concern kept crime on the public agenda.

In 1986 President Reagan abolished the Treatment Alternatives to Street Crime policy and pushed for enhanced law enforcement and harsher punishment for "choosing wrong over right and evil instead of good" (Beckett 1997, 49). Democrats joined the War on Drugs and supported the fight to reduce drug abuse. Under President Reagan's watch, Congress passed the Anti-Drug Abuse Act, funneling over $2 billion into the anti-drug campaign. According to Families Against Mandatory Minimums (2013), this draconian law created mandatory minimum sentences for drug trafficking crimes, including the especially harsh 100-to-1 crack-powder disparity—5 grams of crack and 500 grams of powder cocaine triggering a 5-year mandatory minimum and 50 grams of crack and 5 kilograms of powder cocaine triggering a 10-year mandatory minimum. The United States Sentencing Commission also adopted the 100-to-1 ratio in the federal sentencing guidelines for crack offenses.

As a result, those convicted of crack cocaine offenses received harsher punishment than powder cocaine due to unsupported fears, including that crack was more dangerous and addictive than powder cocaine. Other unscientific claims were that prenatal crack exposure was more harmful than exposure to other drugs; that crack led to an increase of "crack babies"; and that crack trafficking involved more guns and violence than powder cocaine trafficking. Initially, federal sentences for selling crack cocaine, which was more heavily sold and used by people of color, resulted in a sentence 100 times more severe than for selling the same amount of powder cocaine that was more heavily sold and used by whites (Crutchfield and Weeks 2015).

According to the ACLU the crack-powder disparity meant that offenders faced longer sentences for offenses involving crack cocaine than for offenses involving the same amount of powder cocaine. Under this law, on average, African Americans served as much time for nonviolent drug offenses as whites did for violent offenses (ACLU 2017a). Here, race matters, as the majority of people arrested for crack offenses are African American and resulted in huge racial disparities in the average length of sentences for comparable offenses. It is important to understand that the tough-on-crime movement creates an intersection between crime, race, and politics. The anti-crime movement started during racial upheaval, and Presidents Nixon and Reagan successfully appealed to voters' fears for political incentives. As a candidate, Reagan had used the same derogatory rhetoric as Goldwater and Nixon. He cautioned that "the jungle comes a little closer" and claimed that there was not "a city street that's safe for our women after dark." Reagan, like Nixon, linked race and criminal justice policy, setting up the road to victory in the 1980 presidential election (Newell 2013).

Goldwater's law-and-order presidential campaign led to President Nixon declaring a War on Crime and the call to "clean up the welfare mess" (Schram and Soss Jacobin 2015). President Reagan also successfully employed the political tactic of using harmful stereotypes. As Sanford Schram and Joe Soss Jacobin explain, "The 'welfare queen' and the 'criminal thug'—infamous, gender-stereotyped paragons of a deviant and threatening blackness—do the symbolic lifting for a politics that dares not reveal its own racism. Together, they evoke a potent stew of class, gender, and racial biases, deepening divisions among potential allies as they smooth the way for an ugly assortment of partisan and policy goals" (2015). As we will see, Republican President George W. H. Bush would also use this political maneuver in the Willie Horton case.

Additionally, the Anti-Drug Abuse Act permitted the military to participate in narcotics control, sanctioned capital punishment for some drug offensives, and allowed illegally obtained evidence to be admitted at times in drug trials (Beckett 1997; Beckett and Sasson 2004). President Reagan had the goal of a "drug-free generation" and stated: "The American people want their government to get tough and go on the offensive . . . And that's exactly what we intend, with more ferocity that ever before . . . Our goal in this crusade is nothing less than a drug-free generation" (Boyd 1986). By providing anti-drug funding, the Reagan administration and Congress encouraged the FBI to shift its focus from organized crime to street crime and drug trafficking (Beckett 1997). This Republican president, with Congressional support. gave more power to national law enforcement and expanded the federal government's scope of authority into local and state jurisdiction. Reagan publicly thanked both Republicans and Democrats for their leadership in passing the Anti-Drug Abuse Act of 1986 (President Ronald Reagan 27 Oct 1986). Both political parties were in a battle to be the toughest on drugs and crime. First, House Democrats proposed a comprehensive and costly anti-drug proposal that in a bipartisan effort was followed by a televised appearance by the president and Nancy Reagan. Later, President Reagan offered a less expensive program (Boyd 1986).

Additionally in 1986 President Ronald Reagan's 1986 Immigration Reform and Control Act provided some undocumented immigrants with citizenship. This sweeping reform bill tightened security at the Mexican border and laid stricter penalties on employers that hired undocumented workers. However, the law granted immigrants who entered the United States before 1982 eligibility for amnesty. This is a far cry from what most people understand about the "father of modern conservatism." President Reagan gave authority to "the idea of amnesty for those who have put down roots and lived here, even though some time back they may have entered illegally" (NPR 2010). With his support, Congress granted legal status to around 3 million undocumented immigrants. He also proclaimed that parents of minor children who were granted amnesty should not be subject to deportation without congressional authorization (Chemerinsky 2016). President Reagan's attitude on immigration was more moderate than the attitude later Republican leaders would hold.

Interestingly, Reagan's own diary demonstrated that he found an aggressively controlled border fence hard to support. When meeting with then–Mexican President Jose Lopez Portillo, President Reagan wrote that he wanted to discuss how the two countries could make the border "something other than the location for a fence" (NPR 2010). This reveals the long-standing complexity of the president's legacy surrounding immigration issues. It is unfortunate that other presidents have failed to follow the "Gipper's" leadership and advice.

In the 1987 State of the Union Address, President Ronald Reagan does not reference crime or incarceration (President Ronald Reagan 27 Jan 1987). But in March he was forced to address the nation on the Iran-Contra Affair (President Ronald Reagan 4 Mar 1987). While at first Reagan denied knowledge of the illegal affair, he later admitted that several of his top officials had violated the law in covert efforts to sell arms to Iran for the release of American hostages. These Reaganites, including Lieutenant Colonel Oliver North, lied to Congress and the public about breaking the law. Yet unlike other nonviolent offenders of the law, those involved eventually escaped criminal punishment by presidential pardons granted by President George H. W. Bush. This is another clear example of how government officials are not held accountable for their criminal activity, while people guilty of much lesser crimes languish in American prisons.

In the 1988 State of the Union message, only the War on Drugs was discussed. President Reagan also gave the first lady credit for her "Just Say No" program: "Nancy, much credit belongs to you, and I want to express to you your husband's pride and your country's thanks" (President Ronald Reagan 25 Jan 1988). He claimed that cocaine and marijuana use were declining among high school students. The War on Drugs was a major part of President Reagan's law-and-order agenda (President Ronald Reagan 8 Mar 1988). In 1988, after holding a White House Conference for a Drug Free America, President Reagan held a briefing for media executives and asked for their continued support for the War on Drugs. President Reagan was an excellent communicator and used media support to get his anti-crime message to the public.

Parental groups opposed to marijuana helped spark the Reagan Revolution. For conservatives, marijuana use signified the permissive liberal society. President Reagan's first drug czar, Carlton Turner, blamed marijuana for "the present young-adult generation's involvement in anti-military, anti-nuclear power, anti-big business, anti-authority demonstrations" (Merritt 2004). The Reagan administration ended the public health model of drug control and replaced it with strict law enforcement. In a major change from the past, drug abuse was no longer considered an illness and was deemed immoral. With President Reagan's moral leadership, it was thought that punishing drug users was "more important than getting them off drugs" (Blum 1997). This approach was a bipartisan effort supported by Democrats as well as Republicans, because there was no political gain in defending drug abusers from excessive punishment (Blum 1997).

In November 1988 President Reagan signed landmark anti-drug legislation, calling it a "new sword and shield" in the battle against the epidemic of illegal drug use. Congress approved the $2.7 billion Omnibus Anti-Drug Abuse Act, which created the cabinet-level office of "drug czar" and allocated over $700 million to support customs agents in halting smuggling and "narco-traffickers" (Marion 1994, 154; Beckett 1997, 54). This legislation placed harsher penalties on casual users with fines of up to $10,000, and courts were allowed to reduce federal benefits, such as student loans, federally guaranteed mortgages, and small business loans to people convicted of drug possession (May 1988).

Importantly, the 1988 Anti-Drug Abuse Act was vital to mass incarceration with the increased mandatory minimum-sentencing laws. This consisted of a five-year minimum punishment for first-time offenders found guilty of possessing five or more grams of crack cocaine. Since crack cocaine was—and continues to be—used mostly by blacks and not preferred by whites, many considered this law to be racist. At the signing ceremony, Reagan reported statistics asserting that cocaine use among high school seniors had dropped by one-third from the previous year, from 6.2 percent in 1986 to 4.3 percent last year. He said that this legislation "helps us close rank on those who continue to provide drugs" (May 1988).

In 1986 the passing of mandatory minimum drug sentences was the first time Congress had passed this type of law since the Boggs Act in 1951 (Merritt 2004). President Reagan's flawed drug policies (continued by most of the future presidents) helped quadruple the United States' incarceration rate to over 2 million. Criminal justice developments like mandatory minimum-sentencing laws were created in response to racial tensions and have unwarranted negative effects on African American communities. The criminal justice system does not represent social justice policies that cause increasing U.S. racial equality. Experts argue that current laws "fail[ing] to regulate criminal record based discrimination are destructive and unsavory on their own merits" (Newell 2013). Advocacy groups like Families Against Mandatory Minimums continue to fight these draconian policies that have been a large contributor to the race to incarcerate, especially people of color.

Subsequently in the 1980s, special interest groups formed to gain favorable legislation on behalf of the victims' rights agenda, including Mothers Against Drunk Driving (MADD), Victims of Child Abuse Laws (VOCAL), and Parents of Murdered Children (POMC). Both MADD and POMC accept government grants to supplement charitable donations and are private watchdog organizations that monitor and comment on official policy. Accordingly, these victim-advocate organizations achieved national recognition through "an aggressive law-and-order campaigning approach, demanding rights for specific types of victims, including compensation, a say in prosecution and parole decisions, and heavier sentences for offenders" (Maguire 1991, 372). MADD claims victory in changing over 400 drunk-driving laws (Davis and Henley 1990).

Other vital players in the victims' rights movement were John and Reve Walsh. In 1981 their six-year-old son, Adam, was abducted from a Sears store and later found murdered. Public pressure from the Walshes fostered the passage of the Missing Children Act of 1982 and the Missing Children's Assistance Act of 1984. In May 1983 Ronald Reagan proclaimed a National Missing Children Day, suggesting that "the solution to this problem demands the attention and cooperation of all our law enforcement agencies, city, State, and local" (President Ronald Reagan 25 May 1983). Victims' rights special interest groups have also contributed to more stringent criminal justice politics, which have increased the incarceration rate.

In 1988 John Walsh's TV show *America's Most Wanted* claimed to have captured over 800 fugitives (CNN 2005). Furthermore, figures from the National Organization for Victim Assistance (NOVA) and the National Association of Victim Support Schemes ("Victim Support"), the two leading victims' organizations in the United States, reveal the tremendous growth of the victims' movement during President Reagan's era. In the late 1980s, NOVA reported the growth of about 5,000 different victim-assistance programs. At this same time, NOVA estimated that over 5,000 pieces of local or federal legislation afforded rights or benefits to victims of crime. Victim compensation programs were also created in 43 states (Maguire 1991). Other advocates for crime victims included feminists, conservative law-and-order groups, public officials, attorneys, psychologists, psychiatrists, social workers, religious organizations, groups of ex-victims, criminal justice agencies, and academics from many disciplines (Maguire 1991).

Therefore, these advocates contributed to the discourse and activity surrounding victims' rights and were active participants in demanding more "restrictive penal policies cast in the name of victim rights" (Barker 2007, 620). Importantly, the victims' rights issue offered agencies the strategy for protecting and increasing their budgets through federal monetary incentives to the states (Maguire 1991). As part of law and order, the victims' movement succeeded in putting victims on the public and political agenda and gained positive public policy through major legislation.

During the Reagan presidency, the law-and-order politics included both elite and grassroots mobilization. The president, political parties, Congress, interest groups, mass media, and the public in varying degrees supported the law-and-order agenda. Federal intervention into crime and drugs resulted in harsher punishment for offenders. Public policies were adopted that ensured longer sentences and have attributed to the high incarceration rates of the current criminal justice system.

Importantly, high-profile crimes provided President Reagan and Congress with reasons to expand federal crime control. First, right before President Reagan took office in December 1980, Mark David Chapman gunned down ex-Beatle John Lennon in New York City. Many felt "a profound sense of collective loss" that was conveyed through the extensive media news coverage (Elliott 1988). From December 1980 to August 1981, the *New York Times* ran over 40 stories on John Lennon, Chapman, and the trial (Lexis Nexis Pro-Quest Historical Newspaper, the *New York Times*). *Newsweek* and *Time* ran a cover story on Lennon's murder. It was shocking to the public that a celebrity who had advocated peace could die in such a violent manner.

When President-Elect Ronald Reagan was asked for his reaction, he said, "We have to stop tragedies of this sort . . . I think the whole overall thing of violence in our streets is something that has to be dealt with . . . We have to find an answer" (McLellan et al. 1980). However, Reagan remained against any new gun control measures. And in February 1981, in response to the "most important problem facing the nation" question, public concern for crime rose only to 4 percent (Marion 1994, 148–49).

Then on March 30, 1981, President Reagan was leaving the Washington Hilton Hotel when John W. Hinckley Jr. fired six bullets into his entourage. The first shot went through the brain of press secretary James Brady, the second bullet hit a police officer in the back, and the third bullet hit the building. A secret service agent was hit in the chest by the fourth bullet. The fifth shot ricocheted off the president's limousine, hit President Reagan in the chest, and lodged in his lung. Subsequently, the president underwent a two-hour operation at George Washington Hospital that saved his life (Linder 2000). Later, it was learned that Hinckley had stalked President Carter during the 1980 general election campaign and had been arrested at the Nashville airport in October 1980 for carrying several weapons. However, the FBI failed to inform the Secret Service of these events.

As presidential assassination attempts and serious presidential illnesses are often "unifying, dramatic, and directly affect the president," it is not surprising that Reagan's popularity jumped over the 60 percent mark after the attempt (Lanoue 1989). *Newsweek* and *Time* published one cover story each on the Reagan assassination attempt, and the *New York Times* ran five stories from March 1981 to May 1981 (Lexis Nexis ProQuest Historical Newspaper, the *New York Times*). Months after the assassination attempt, Reagan stated that controlling crime was "not simply a question of more money, more police, more courts, more prosecutors" and that it was a moral dilemma that needed a moral and a spiritual solution (President Ronald Reagan 28 Sep 1981). Reagan believed that crime and the fear of crime had diminished public confidence in the government. He worked to restore that confidence by employing the law-and-order approach to crime, while the assassination attempt made First Lady Nancy Reagan call for more security.

Highly publicized events continually kept crime in the national spotlight. Between July 1979 and May 1981, Atlanta, Georgia, received national and international media attention when at least 29 young African Americans ranging in age from 7 to 28 were the victims of a bizarre series of killings. These black children were placed on the Atlanta special police task force's list of missing and murdered children, which identified them as victims of serial murder. In October 1980 ABC News did a *20/20* segment devoted to the unsolved child slayings and disappearances. Black celebrities and politicians, such as Jesse Jackson, Marion Barry, and Dick Gregory and authors James Baldwin and Toni Cade Bambara criticized Atlanta's black political establishment for the controversial racial overtones of the police investigation and the later trial. Neither *Time* nor *Newsweek* did cover stories on the Atlanta child murders. Eventually, in 1999, Cade Bambara authored a book about the murders titled *Those Bones Are Not My Child*. Some wondered whether the response would have been different had the murdered children been white.

In March 1981 President Reagan announced that Vice President Bush had been "deeply involved" with the Atlanta task force. In support of Mayor Maynard Jackson, an additional $979,000 in federal funding was allocated to the Justice Department and other federal agencies for investigative and community services related to the murders (President Ronald Reagan 5 Mar 1981). In the same year, a black suspect, Wayne Williams, was arrested and convicted of two of the murders and presumed guilty of the others (Headley 1988; Anderson 2007).

Then on December 22, 1984, engineer Bernhard Hugo Goetz felt threatened by their behavior and shot four young men in a Manhattan subway car. An angry and disgruntled public rallied behind the gunman when it was learned that his victims all had criminal records. In January 1985, when President Reagan was asked about the Goetz shootings, he responded that people were frustrated with the threat of crime, felt that law and order was not protecting them, and felt that this breakdown of civilization resulted in some taking the law into their own hands (President Ronald Reagan 9 Jan 1985). Awkwardly, Reagan displayed empathy toward Goetz's frustration while condemning the lawlessness of his criminal behavior.

In the early 1980s, subway violence was rampant; even token clerks had been firebombed in their booths (Kates 2004). Mayor Ed Koch claimed that the city was entwined in an "OK Corral mentality." New York tabloids dubbed Goetz the "Subway Vigilante," and he became the symbol of New York City's frustrations with a high crime rate (Kates 2004). The Subway Vigilante was front-page news for many months, and *Time* ran one story on this subject. The *New York Times* published over 150 stories on the shootings from December 1984 to March 1985 (Lexis Nexis ProQuest Historical Newspaper, the *New York Times*). Many saw Goetz as defending himself in a situation in which police were ineffective in combating street crime.

At that time, a relatively unknown black preacher, Rev. Al Sharpton, expressed the sentiment that if Goetz were to go unpunished, it would give a license to bigots "to go hunting for blacks" (Kates 2004). After one grand jury decided not to indict Goetz, a second brought him to trial in 1987. Goetz's defense was that he believed he was about to be robbed after one of the teens hassled him for five dollars. This theme struck a chord with a fearful public, and a predominantly white jury acquitted Goetz of all charges but illegal weapons possession. He served only 250 days at Rikers Island (Shipp 1987; Johnson 1987; Spence 1993; Kates 2004).

In 1986 the high-profile overdose deaths of two popular athletes—Len Bias on June 19 and Don Rogers on June 27—as well as the mass media's attention to drug-related stories, helped escalate the War on Drugs (Beckett 1997; Gottschalk 2006). These deaths led Congress to pass harsher punishment laws in an attempt to end the crack epidemic in urban centers.

From 1986 to 1990 the drug problem was one of the most publicized national issues (Beckett 1997; Beckett and Sasson 2004). From 1988 to 1990, *Newsweek* and *Time* ran 11 cover stories each on the drug issue. From June 1986 to September 1986, the *New York Times* ran over 100 stories on Len Bias, Don Rogers, drug use in sports, and drug policy (Lexis Nexis ProQuest

Historical Newspaper, the *New York Times*, key words "Len Bias" and "Don Rogers"). The explosion of media attention toward crime events and drugs fueled the public's awareness and fear. This led to President Reagan and Congress responding with more punitive law-and-order policies.

President Ronald Reagan was a compelling, energetic, and charismatic leader who utilized fear of crime to gain public support for his get-tough justice policies. During President Reagan's eight-year tenure, the federal inmate population rose 78 percent (or 16,539), which was the largest percentage increase for any presidential administration (Gramlich 2017a).

According to the present-day Drug Reform Coordination Network:

> Tens of millions of people have been arrested under the drug laws, millions have been sent to prison, and hundreds of billions of dollars have been incinerated in a program that epitomizes big, intrusive government in one of its most violent forms . . . It was during the presidency of Ronald Reagan that narcotics law enforcement morphed into drug war overdrive with a series of ever more draconian drug laws and an attitude of repressive "zero tolerance" emanating from the White House. (Drug War Chronicle 2004)

Moreover, according to Timothy Lynch, president of the Cato Institute, "When it comes to the drug war, there's just not much good that can be said about Reagan's policy . . . It was bad, no doubt about it" (Drug Reform Coordination Network 2004). President Reagan had stated that his legislation was not intended to fill our jails with drug users (Boyd 1986), but that is exactly what it ended up accomplishing.

Like Republican president Richard M. Nixon, President Reagan placed the blame of increased crime on Democrats' liberal policies and on the lenient Supreme Court. His administration finally phased out the Law Enforcement Assistances Administration (LEAA), while other legislation continued to fund anti-crime programs and victims' rights. This encouraged the formation of active interest groups that propelled the victims' right movement. In addition, media attention highlighted the impact of violence and supplied the platform for protecting the innocent from lawlessness. President Reagan continued the War on Crime with a conservative, hard-line approach. His attack of the welfare system, and linking welfare culture with crime, attracted both Republican and Democratic support. With President Reagan's defense of victims' rights and through his continued War on Drugs, the call for incarceration was revitalized from a decline in the Carter and Ford years. From Johnson to Reagan, presidents promoted anti-crime and anti-drug initiatives that, with congressional support, imprisoned more and more people. Systematically, these policies produced the United States' mass incarceration problem.

Note

1. Criminal justice government officials and interest groups: federal, state, and local agents of the criminal justice system including the FBI, DEA, U.S. Marshal's Office, Bureau of Prisons, federal judges, state attorneys general, state police, state judges, state and local prison officials, state and local police chiefs, county sheriffs, district attorneys, National Sheriffs' Association, International Association of Chiefs of Police (Miller 2004, 575).

CHAPTER SIX

President George H. W. Bush Follows President Reagan's Lead

George H. W. Bush, who served as vice president for eight years, ran a presidential campaign that created a politically and racially charged environment. In July 1988, after the Democratic National Convention, Massachusetts governor Michael Dukakis was beating Republican George H. W. Bush by 17 points in the polls (PBS 216). Dukakis won out of a crowded Democratic field, promising to end the Reagan era and to defeat Vice President George Bush. However, the Bush campaign used the Willie Horton incident to alarm the public and accused the Democratic challenger of being soft on crime for furloughing convicted criminals. In campaign television advertisements, Bush showed how William R. Horton, a black inmate who was convicted of murder and did not return from a Massachusetts weekend furlough program, kidnapped a Maryland couple and raped the woman (Beckett and Sasson 2004; Katel 2008b). Even though the prison furlough temporary release program had been enacted under a former Republican governor and Horton had served a large portion of his sentence, Bush effectively used this race-baiting to win the presidency.

Since Bush had battled the image of being wimpy, he had to seem "tough enough to get down and dirty in the trenches of electoral politics" (Knott 2017). Bush's team successfully portrayed Governor Dukakis as being soft on crime and criminal justice issues. The governor refused to respond to the attacks and carried only 10 states, losing to the law-and-order Bush by around 7 million votes (PBS 2016).

A 2016 *New York Times* letter to the editor on President Bush's legacy claimed that the 1988 Bush campaign "set a new low for racist pandering, with its focus on the blackness of Willie Horton and its dog-whistle reassurances to its deplorable plurality of racist voters" (Mahoney 2016). The letter pointed out "that Poppy Bush was more than happy to profit from these vile racist tactics" (Mahoney 2016). Presidential leadership takes many forms and can have long-lasting implications. Historically, candidates have used race to capitalize on prejudices of voters and to "fan the fires of racial division" as a winning campaign strategy (Johnson and Wright Rigueur 2015). The Willie Horton incident marked the legacy of George H. W. Bush's presidency in a substantial, negative manner.

Consequently, Vice President Bush successfully portrayed presidential candidate Governor Dukakis as weak on crime and placed blame on the Democrats for allowing criminals to go free (Dowd 1988). Although Jesse Jackson and other Democrats accused the Bush campaign of inciting racial fears, this racially charged tactic fostered the law-and-order environment and made it political suicide to appear "soft on crime." Bush played on "racially loaded stereotypes" in using the Horton furlough incident (quoted in Glazer 1996, 185). Additionally, Republican law-and-order rhetoric, as well as the Republican Party's welfare-abuse and wasteful social program messages, employed the same racial theme (Edsall and Edsall 1991; Glaser 1996). While these race-coded strategies may not mean that Bush was a racist, they demonstrated presidential leadership that was willing to exploit the societal ill of racism for political gains (Johnson and Wright Rigueur 2015).

Between 1985 and 1987 the Iran-Contra Affair developed. Senior Reagan-Bush officials secretly sold military arms to Iran, which was under a congressional arms embargo. These officials tried to secure the release of several U.S. hostages and to provide funds to the Contras in Nicaragua. Fourteen administration officials were indicted with 11 convictions including then Secretary of Defense Caspar Weinberger. Some of these convictions were cleared on appeal, and all others were pardoned by President George H. W. Bush, who was vice president during this scandal. Although the Reagan and Bush administrations talked tough on crime, some of their own administration officials were involved in criminal behavior but were not imprisoned for their illegal deeds. While common people pay a heavy price for lesser offensives, these men were let off by their boss. This happened during the Watergate scandal and then again with the Iran-Contra Affair.

Throughout the late 1980s, crime and drugs were high-profile political issues. The Republicans and the Democrats used elections and campaigning to blame each other for the lack of successful crime-control measures. The 1988 Republican Party Platform pledged to crusade for victims' rights, toughen sentencing procedures, reestablish the federal death penalty as an option for more than 30 federal crimes (Biskupic 1990), and reform the exclusionary rule and "cumbersome" habeas corpus procedures. The Republicans also supported denying bail to those considered dangerous and likely to commit more crimes (Republican Party Platform of 1988 16 Aug 1988). In these actions, there seems to be little concern for the unintended consequences that toughening sentencing and denying bail would have on increasing the prison system.

The 1988 Democratic Party Platform warned that illegal drugs remained a threat to U.S. security. Democrats believed that law enforcement efforts should be mobilized and coordinated under the direction of a national drug czar. The platform advocated for a comprehensive educational program for children on the dangers of drug and alcohol abuse. The Democrats were also in favor of limited gun control (Democrat Party Platform of 1988).

Beginning in 1989 the Rehnquist Court began to overturn some earlier liberal precedents. In *Thornburgh v. Abbott* (1989), the Court ruled that prison officials could ban publications to maintain discipline and security. In 1990 President Bush swore in Justice David Souter to replace liberal Justice William J. Brennan, and in 1991 Judge Clarence Thomas took Justice Thurgood Marshall's seat on the Court. African American Thomas would turn out to be a strong, loyal conservative voter, as President George H. W. Bush had hoped.

However, the controversial nomination of Clarence Thomas was a watershed moment in American judicial history. Before the Senate voted on Thomas's confirmation, law professor Anita Hill alleged that Thomas had sexually harassed her while she worked with him at the Education Department and Equal Employment Opportunity Commission. The Judiciary Committee of the Senate, headed by the chair, Democrat Joe Biden, held an investigative hearing that was televised and widely viewed. Thomas, who had been against affirmative action and had always argued that race should not be taken into account, claimed that the Senate procedures were a "high tech lynching of uppity blacks" who refused to bow to an old order of politics. The U.S. Senate confirmed Clarence Thomas by the narrow margin of 52 to 48. President Bush demonstrated his conservative leadership by the appointment of this conservative African American justice (Stern 2013).

Moreover, under Chief Justice William H. Rehnquist's leadership, significant liberal precedents protecting the rights of defendants and prison inmates were overturned. In *Coleman v. Thompson* (1991), the Court decided that state inmates could not file federal habeas corpus petitions after failing to abide by state court procedural rules. In *Arizona v. Fulminante* (1991), the Court ruled that the use of coerced confessions at trial does not necessarily require reversal of a conviction if evidence amounted to "harmless error." In *Payne v. Tennessee* (1991), the Court allowed "victim impact statements" to be used against capital defendants in sentencing hearings.

George H. W. Bush's presidency was consumed by the Gulf War and foreign affairs while he continued Reagan's crime-control approach. He spoke about homelessness, crime, and drug addiction in his inaugural address. President Bush claimed that drugs were public enemy number one and supported mandatory sentencing and the death penalty for drug kingpins who committed murders (President George H. W. Bush 22 Mar 1989). He believed in strict punishment, the death penalty, strengthening law enforcement, and assisting crime victims. In an address on administration goals before a joint session of Congress, he stated:

> I mean to get tough on the drug criminals. . . . My budget asks for beefed-up prosecution, for a new attack on organized crime, and for enforcement of tough sentences—and for the worst kingpins, that means the death penalty. I also want to make sure that when a drug dealer is convicted there's a cell waiting for him. And he should not go free because prisons are too full. And so, let the word go out: If you're caught and convicted, you will do time. (President George H. W. Bush 9 Feb 1989)

Like President Reagan, President Bush increased spending for federal prisons and the courts. During the Bush administration, the prison population increased by 39 percent or by 16,946 prisoners (Gramlich 2017b). The U.S. prisons and jail system began to be overwhelmed with the upsurge of inmates that drug policies produced.

In spite of a looming incarceration situation, the George H. W. Bush administration continued to push harsher and lengthier punishment. In 1989 President Bush appointed Bill Bennett as the first director of the Office of National Drug Control Policy. The agency was created to "mobilize our moral, spiritual, and economic resources" to halt drug trafficking and drug abuse. President Bush asked for an increase of $1 billion in the budget and requested $6 billion in new funding for education, testing, interdiction, and enforcement to fight the War on Drugs (President George H. W. Bush 13 Mar 1989).

In the mid- and late 1980s, both President Reagan and then Vice President George H. W. Bush declared a War on Drugs, partly due to a powerful grassroots movement of suburban parents, which sparked the zero-tolerance stance on drug use (Gottschalk 2006, 32–33). Two parents who had discovered marijuana at a 13-year-old's birthday party formed National Families in Action, which assisted families and communities in drug prevention among children. During this time, public opinion concerning drugs spiraled upward. Responders to the "most important problem facing the country" question ranked the categories of drugs or drug abuse at a low of 18 percent in May 1989 and a high of 63 percent in July 1990 (Marion 1994, 190).

Therefore, President Bush called for "teamwork and coordination" between the government, private enterprise, and voluntary organizations to eliminate the drug problem (Marion 1994, 197). In 1989 he signed the Drug-Free

Schools and Communities Act into law. As an example of this call for civil engagement, in March 1989 President Bush enlisted the assistance of the Veterans of Foreign Wars (VFW). He asked them to volunteer in the schools and to "put the full weight of this magnificent organization behind anti-drug education" to help children resist drugs (President George H. W. Bush 6 Mar 1989). He also instructed them to contact their state and local elected officials to urge the passage of his "strong" anti-drug legislation (President George H. W. Bush 6 Mar 1989).

Furthermore, President Bush announced the creation of the anti-drug education program DARE—Drug Abuse Resistance Education—with the mission to "drug proof" America's children. This program was pioneered by the Los Angeles Police Department and the Los Angeles public school system (President George H. W. Bush 22 Mar 1989). According to DARE's website, the DARE program is implemented in "75 percent of our nation's school districts and in more than 43 countries around the world" (DARE 1996). Throughout his presidency, George H. W. Bush encouraged civil participation in the War on Drugs. He provided both symbolic and substantive support for many types of national anti-drug programs.

Moreover, Congress passed an abundance of anti-crime bills, as well as legislation on hate crimes, sex violence, child abuse, flag burning, and drunk driving. In Congress there were competing interests, with Senator Strom Thurmond (R-SC) introducing changes to President Bush's bill and Senator Joseph Biden (D-DE) introducing the Democrats' version of the legislation. President Bush's bills proposed death penalty and exclusionary rule provisions, limited habeas corpus, and pushed for stronger penalties for the illegal use of firearms (Marion 1994). President Bush urged Congress to pass his comprehensive crime bill, saying, "It is tough on criminals and supportive of police, and it has been languishing in these hallowed halls for years now. Pass it. Help your country!" (President George H. W. Bush 28 Jan 1992). As a law-and-order leader, President Bush utilized the same anti-crime rhetoric and fear tactics that former presidents had effectively used.

Though President Bush's 1990 State of the Union address was relatively absent of law-and-order rhetoric, he wanted all American schools to be drug free. And he announced his 1990 National Drug Control Strategy that included a director to coordinate police and reduce drug use (National Law Enforcement Training Week Proclamation 3 Jan 1990). Bush accused the government of being ineffectual in dealing with illegal drug use, and he called for education, treatment, and intergovernmental and international cooperation.

In 1990 immigration reform was on the president's agenda, and President George H. W. Bush took an immigrant-friendly leadership role. Instead of detainment or deportation, he issued an executive order to protect the spouses and children of individuals who were in the process of obtaining legal U.S. citizenship. In 1986 Congress had left out this group in the immigration reform legislation. Presidents Bush took the "Family Fairness" actions to avoid separating families in which one spouse or parent was eligible for legalization but the other spouse or children living in the United States were not. This group could be deported, although they would be eligible for legal status when the spouse or parent obtained legal status.

At that time, Family Fairness, which first began under Reagan, covered approximately 1.5 million family members, or 40 percent of the unauthorized population, according to the Federal Immigration commissioner, Gene McNary (Howe 1990). After Bush acted, Congress passed the Immigration Act of 1990, which protected the family members (American Immigration Council 2014). President Bush hailed the act's "support for the family as the essential unit of society" and "respect for the family unit." Family Fairness was intended to allow close family members of legalized immigrants to remain in the country under certain conditions. The president's signing statement said it preserved the "authority of the executive branch to exercise prosecutorial desecration in suitable immigration cases." The act also increased the number of visas available to spouses and minor children of those with green cards (American Immigration Council 2014).

Some officials reported that they would refrain from deporting close family members. Yet, up to that time, there was no uniform federal policy on the issue. Cecilia Muñoz of the National Council of La Raza stated: "We are very pleased with a policy that keeps families together." This advocacy group, however, warned that many would not be eligible and that applicants could be deported if they were rejected (Howe 1990). Still the Family Fairness initiative put in place by two Republican presidents, Reagan and G. H. W. Bush, ultimately protected over a third of the country's unauthorized immigrants from deportation. This is a markedly different view compared to other law-and-order leaders.

In the 1991 State of the Union Address, President Bush said freedom from the fear of crime was a fundamental civil right and promised immediate, tough crime-control legislation. He believed that crime was directly related to drugs and stated: "We will not rest until the day of the dealer is over, forever" (President George H. W. Bush 29 Jan 1991). He ordered his attorney general to convene a crime summit to help assist law enforcement officials (President George H. W. Bush 29 Jan 1991).

However, his 1992 State of the Union message contained an entire section titled "On Crime and Education." For him, crime and drugs went hand in hand, and he invoked fear that women were in special danger in the United States claiming:

> We must do something about crime and drugs. It is time for a major, renewed investment in fighting violent street crime. It saps our strength and hurts our faith in our society and in our future together. Surely a tired

woman on her way to work at 6 in the morning on a subway deserves the right to get there safely. And surely it's true that everyone who changes his or her life because of crime, from those afraid to go out at night to those afraid to walk in the parks they pay for, surely these people have been denied a basic civil right. It is time to restore it. Congress, pass my comprehensive crime bill. It is tough on criminals and supportive of police, and it has been languishing in these hallowed halls for years now. Pass it. Help your country. (On the Issues 2017c)

This tough anti-crime bill included expanding the number of federal crimes punishable by the death penalty, limiting death row appeals, and lessoning restrictions on illegally obtained evidence during criminal trials. It also contained a handgun waiting period and banned semiautomatic assault weapons and some ammunition-feeding devices (Johnston 1991).

In the second Clinton-Bush-Perot debate, Bush tried to reassure voters that he had been fighting for strong anti-crime legislation that included supporting habeas corpus reform, "So you don't have these endless appeals; so when somebody gets sentenced, hey, this is for real. I've been fighting for changes in the exclusionary rule, so if an honest cop stops somebody and makes a technical mistake, the criminal doesn't go away. I happen to think that we need stronger death penalties for those that kill police officers" (President George Bush1992). Up to this time, George Herbert Walker Bush could be accurately considered a moderate Republican. But the tide was turning, and the Republican Party would take a turn to the conservative right with very little room for moderate lawmakers.

During the Bush administration, public opinion concerning the "most important problem facing the country" question hit a high of 8 percent for crime. However, those considering drug abuse to be "the most important problem facing the country" had a high of 63 percent in September 1989 (Marion 1994, 190). Throughout 1989 and 1990 the public was especially concerned about drug abuse. The Bush administration's high level of interest and media attention to the drug issue might have contributed to this increase (Marion 1994). During this time, *Newsweek* published two cover stories, and *Time* did three cover stories concerning drugs and violence.

As with other presidents before him, President Bush expanded the criminal justice system by adding more FBI and Bureau of Alcohol, Tobacco, and Firearms agents, as well as assistant U.S. attorneys and criminal division attorneys. The expansion led law enforcement to gain funds for new programs and personnel, which meant more arrests, prosecutions, and incarceration.

In 1991 President Bush proclaimed that October was Crime Prevention Month. He signed HR 3259, which authorized federal funding for the National Diffusion Network to disseminate information to schools concerning successful drug prevention. This bill also targeted drug education and prevention to youth gangs and to runaway homeless youths (Marion 1994). In 1992 Bush initiated the Weed and Seed program, a community-based strategy sponsored by the U.S. Department of Justice (DOJ). This was a multiagency approach to law enforcement, crime prevention, and community revitalization. The initiative aimed to prevent, control, and reduce violent crime, drug abuse, and gangs in high-crime neighborhoods. The two-pronged approach was to "weed out" violent criminals and drug abusers while public agencies and private organizations were "to seed" with prevention, intervention, and treatment (Donegan 1996; Roehl 1996).

In 1992 the Democratic Platform had an entire section dedicated to combating drugs and crime. The Democrats pledged to restore government and uphold basic law and order to "crime-ravaged" communities. They claimed that under the Republicans, more than 200,000 Americans had been murdered and that violent crimes had risen by more than 16 percent since 1988. They declared that a murder was "committed every 25 minutes, a rape every six minutes, a burglary every 10 seconds" (Democratic Party Platform of 1992 13 Jul 1992). The solution to restoring law and order was to have more police on the street in the form of community police.

The 1992 Republican Party Platform stated that violent crime was "the gravest domestic threat" to the American way of life and that it had "turned our communities into battlegrounds, playgrounds into grave yards" (Democratic Party Platform of 1992 13 Jul 1992). They blamed the legacy of liberalism that elevated criminals' rights above victims' rights and that justified "soft on crime" courts, which left law enforcement "powerless" to deter crime (Democratic Party Platform of 1992 13 Jul 1992). The Republicans also held the congressional Democrats responsible for opposing legislation that would restore the severest penalties for heinous crimes. They wanted "to ensure swift and certain punishment, and to end the legal loopholes that let criminals go free" (Republican Party Platform of 1992 17 Aug 1992).

However, the president expressed disappointment that none of his original provisions were in the final Crime Control Act of 1990. This bill did include increased funding for local and federal law enforcement agencies, codified a Crime Victims' Bill of Rights in the federal justice system, made it easier to seize defendant assets, and instructed the U.S. Sentencing Commission to amend certain sentencing guidelines (O'Bryant 2003). Therefore, although the president wanted more, this important law-and-order act is considered one of the three major federal responses to crime control, as mentioned previously. No lawmaker wanted to appear soft on crime, yet Democrats and Republicans differed over issues such as the death penalty and gun control. Although President Bush did try to push through many proposals, the Democrats did not allow most to pass.

A major event kept crime and the criminal justice system on the public agenda. On March 3, 1991, an African American man named Rodney King was stopped by a group of police officers for speeding. The officers quickly decided that King was resisting, and he was shot twice with a Taser gun. This failed to subdue him, and the officers began ruthlessly beating him with their batons. A private citizen taped the arrest, and, subsequently, the video was played by the media all over the world (Gray 2007). Four officers were charged with excessive force and assault with a deadly weapon.

However, on April 29, 1992, they were acquitted of state charges. In response to what was seen as an unjust verdict, three days of rioting took place in Los Angeles, leaving 55 people dead and over 2,300 injured. Approximately 12,000 people were arrested, and over $1 billion in property damage occurred (Rodney King Wounded in Shooting 2007). Since the videotape had explicitly shown the police officers severely beating Rodney King, it was difficult for the public to understand the acquittals. However, the violence and the destruction once again placed race at the forefront of the crime issues.

In 1993 two of the officers were found guilty in federal court of violating King's civil rights and served 30 months in federal prison (Rodney King: Reluctant Symbol of Police Brutality 2001). Racial profiling by police became a controversial issue. Between April 1991 and May 1992, *Newsweek* and *Time* published one cover story each on the beating, while the *New York Times* published over 150 stories on the Rodney King beating, police brutality, the trial, the verdict, and racial violence (Lexis Nexis ProQuest Historical Newspaper, the *New York Times*, "Rodney King"). According to Melissa Hickman Barlow, "Without question, media coverage of the Rodney King beating and the riots in Los Angeles brought linkage between race and crime back into the foreground" (1998).

In 1999 a Gallup poll found that 59 percent of those surveyed believed that racial profiling was "widespread" (56 percent of whites and 77 percent of blacks), with 81 percent disapproving of the practice. The Bush administration struggled with the intersection of race, drugs, and crime, with government seemingly turning to incarceration to solve complex and lingering challenges to American society.

Doro Koch Bush, the daughter of President George H. W. Bush wrote in 2006 in a book about her father saying that Democrats and the press kept repeating false information. She claimed that it was mistakenly thought the Bush campaign used the Willie Horton story to racially divide people and not to demonstrate Dukakis's weakness on crime. She asserted that her father had sent her and her brothers a briefing paper reiterating the facts of the Horton case, because they had become so distorted over the years. Doro Koch Bush said that she had asked President Bush about the Willie Horton episode, and he had said, "'I felt we did the right thing. It was definitely a crime issue. We got on Dukakis about having this lenient furlough program where he let people out of jail, and here was the best example—a man who was a convicted rapist who went out and raped again when he was on furlough.' The crime issue was very powerful" (Koch Bush 2006). President Bush's law-and-order attitude provided him with total justification in exploiting race with little insight into collateral damage when crime was the issue.

Following President Reagan's eight years in the White House, President George H. W. Bush did not present any new approaches to the crime problem. During the 1988 and 1992 elections, both political parties blamed the other for the failure of crime-control policies. Like other Presidents before him, George H. W. Bush felt that illegal drugs were harming the country and continued to introduce initiatives, and legislation was passed that tried to address this problem. The Bush administration's Comprehensive Crime Bill of 1990 is considered to be among the major federal responses to crime control. The Rodney King beating by police officers reinforced the claims of racial discrimination in the criminal justice system. While President Bush was not the charismatic leader of the call for law and order as President Reagan had been, he certainly carried on the policies that have contributed to the United States becoming the incarceration capital of the world.

CHAPTER SEVEN

President Clinton's Three Strikes and You're Out

From the 1960s to the 1980s, the United States was in a war against crime. Presidents Johnson, Nixon, and Reagan had been the most active in the call for law and order's fight against crime, while Presidents Ford and Bush had been somewhat less active (Marion 1994). President Jimmy Carter had been the least active and did not increase incarceration. In the 1992 presidential election, the economy dominated the agenda, not crime. No one expected this Democratic president to support draconian criminal justice policies. It was the hope of many that President Clinton would take a more liberal approach to crime, which would deal with serious social and economic problems (Scheingold 1995). However, in the end, President Clinton left a legacy of tough-on-crime policies that helped filled U.S. prisons with nonviolent offenders.

Consequently, political leaders in the United States have repeatedly chosen to respond to public concern on crime by "formulating policies that punish and exclude" (Garland 2001, 202). An example of this is that, while Republicans tried to characterize Bill Clinton as soft on crime, Democrats turned out to be more conservative on crime-control (and welfare) policy. Bill Clinton was accused of being a liberal, but this law-and-order president supported the federal death penalty and increased the number of police officers. When liberal presidents are fearful of being characterized as being "soft on crime," they often take their eyes off the prize of social justice for electoral incentives. These law enforcement policies added significantly to mass incarceration in the United States.

During the 1992 presidential campaign, Bill Clinton pledged that the new Democrats would not indulge criminals (Holian 2004). The 1992 Democratic

Platform adopted the philosophy that crime and drugs were directly associated with the amount of crime-control enforcement. Both Republicans and Democrats capitalized on middle-class America's move to the right on crime and drug issues. Presidential candidate Clinton accused the Republicans of blaming the crime problems on poor non-whites—meaning he was somewhat aware of the ramification of the racial nature of these policies. However, it was President Clinton who proposed welfare reform, more federal support for prison construction, and limits on habeas corpus appeals, all of which heavily affected poor African Americans (Flamm 2005; Beckett 1997). While he was trying to balance the budget, he targeted the racially charged public welfare landscape to do his battle on the backs of the poor. Later, Clinton came to regret his law-and-order leadership, and he recognized and acknowledged his part in the United States' over-imprisonment of low-level minority offenders.

The 1992 Republican Platform accused Democrats of creating "more loopholes for vicious thugs and fewer protections for victims of crime" (Republican Party Platform of 1992 17 Aug 1992). They claimed legislation passed by Democrats crippled law enforcement "by overturning over twenty United States Supreme Court cases that have helped to reduce crime and keep violent criminal offenders off the streets" (Republican Party Platform of 1992 17 Aug 1992). However, Democrat Bill Clinton won the election with 43 percent of the vote over President George H. W. Bush and Independent Ross Perot. This provided Clinton with the opportunity to resist the pressure to appear tough on crime and bring reason and restraint to the growing criminal justice system.

In 1993 President Clinton did not give a State of the Union message, since he had just delivered an inauguration address. In April 1993 he announced his national agenda on crime, saying that the plan was not "tough" but "fair" (President William J. Clinton 15 Apr 1993). He requested $3.4 billion to fund up to 50,000 new police officers to walk the beat. He supported the Brady Bill for gun control and boot camps that gave young offenders discipline, training, and treatment for a second chance. He proposed limiting death-row inmates to a single habeas corpus appeal within a six-month time limit but guaranteeing a higher standard of legal representation. And he extended the death penalty for some federal offenses, including killing a federal law enforcement officer (President William J. Clinton 15 Apr 1993).

In 1993 President Bill Clinton took the opportunity to nominate more progressive judges to the Supreme Court. He appointed Ruth Bader Ginsburg for associate justice to replace Justice Byron White. President Clinton's appointment of Justice Ginsburg can be considered one of the most significant liberal victories in history. She had worked for the ACLU's Women Project and won confirmation from a bipartisan congress with a 96 to 3 vote. This is an amazing accomplishment, especially considering the polarization in a very partisan U.S. Senate. To highlight Justice Ginsburg's professionalism, Professor Lisa Kern Griffin states that Ginsburg's "conception of a fair criminal-justice process is infused with equality principles, and particularly with the conviction that the government should not foster inequality, and should work to remedy the effects of past injustices" (Duke University 2015). In 1994 Stephen Breyer was appointed to fill the seat previously held by Justice Harry Blackmun.

President Clinton's selection of Justice Breyer was another substantial liberal triumph. Breyer's early career was spent in Washington working in all three branches of government. He clerked for Supreme Court Justice Arthur Goldberg and worked at the Justice Department. Breyer was counsel to the Senate Judiciary Committee, which has led many to claim that the Justice defers to the legislative branch of government. Importantly, he worked for the U.S. Sentencing Commission and has experienced firsthand the difficulties with the sentencing process (Wolf 2014). Justice Breyer's more liberal leanings were revealed when writing for the dissenters declared that strip searches allowed by the majority ruling were "a serious affront to human dignity and to individual privacy" and should be used with caution (Liptak 2012). He stated that the Fourth Amendment barred strip searches for those held for "minor offenses not involving drugs or violence and without reasonable suspicion that they were using contraband" (Liptak 2012).

Moreover, violence against women remained a major problem for the Clinton administration. To protect women, the women's movement advocated for legal remedies to curtail rape and domestic violence. From the women's movement, the violence against women movement developed with an organizational base of preexisting groups and extensive communication networks. This mobilization facilitated tougher sanctions, with feminists heading the anti-rape and battered women's movements. As a result, in 1993, President Clinton signed a proclamation declaring October to be National Domestic Violence Awareness Month, and the Violence Against Women Act of 1994 was passed (President William J. Clinton 28 Oct 1993). This act provided funding for a national domestic violence hotline, increased funding for more shelters to the Family Violence Prevention and Services Act and to interstate enforcement of protective orders, and offered additional training and education for federal judges as well as anti-rape school programs (McCue 1995). Like the War on Crime, the War on Drugs, and the War on Gangs, the increased law enforcement measures to stop rape and domestic violence augmented federal powers.

Fighting crime with tougher legislation was a bipartisan effort. President Bill Clinton made sure he would not be vulnerable to being portrayed as "soft on crime," so he campaigned as a president who would be tough on crime (President William J. Clinton 24 Mar 1993). He was also an advocate of community policing and the Justice Department's Comprehensive Cities

Program, in which police and other city agencies were to work in partnership with communities to fight crime and violence (Galston and Tibbetts 1994). Clinton claimed to empower communities by hiring 100,000 more police officers in his first term (President William J. Clinton 24 Jun 1993). The unintended consequences of this tough-on-crime mentality were not only the cost in human capital of imprisonment but financial investment in the for-profit prison industry complex. The U.S. prison industry complex is

> a set of bureaucratic, political, and economic interests that encourage increased spending on imprisonment, regardless of the actual need . . . It is a confluence of special interests that has given prison construction in the United States a seemingly unstoppable momentum. It is composed of politicians, both liberal and conservative, who have used the fear of crime to gain votes; impoverished rural areas where prisons have become a cornerstone of economic development. (Scholosser 1998)

The prison industry complex is one of the sources and reasons for mass incarceration in the United States.

Les Leopold, author and director of the Labor Institute, argues that the present-day prison industrial complex not only imprisons millions of low-income people but also creates new jobs and profit opportunities (Leopold 2015). He suggests that the Better Business Climate model called for privatizing public services to generate new businesses, to reduce government, and was supposed to increase efficiency. But the Better Business Climate model fostered the collapse in manufacturing jobs that was disastrous for young people of color. Leopold claims that the failure of this Better Business model put unemployed minority youth in jail. He states: "This is a remarkable shift in America's approach to joblessness. From the New Deal to the 1980s, the government had a strategy for dealing with enormous structural unemployment and poverty: it created jobs. Now, it puts the jobless in prison" (Leopold 2015). This is a convincing explanation of how the United States' mass incarceration has occurred.

In President Clinton's 1994 State of the Union address, he urged Congress to pass federal "three strikes" legislation:

> Violent crime and the fear it provokes are crippling our society, limiting personal freedom, and fraying the ties that bind us. . . . I know what it's like to sign laws increasing penalties, to build more prison cells, to carry out the death penalty. . . . Now those who commit crimes should be punished. And those who commit repeated, violent crimes should be told, "When you commit a third violent crime, you will be put away, and put away for good." Three strikes, and you are out. (President William J. Clinton 25 Jan 1994)

Although a significant number of serious crimes were (and still are) committed by a small number of criminals, Clinton helped create the United States' mass incarceration problem. He admits that, during his eight-year reign as president, he tried to "reduce crime with a 'shotgun' approach when all that was needed was a .22" (Cohen 2014). He acknowledges that his criminal justice policies "just sent everyone to jail for too long" (Cohen 2014).

In 1994 Congress passed and President Clinton signed the Violent Crime Control and Law Enforcement Act, which embraced the law-and-order approach. This legislation increased the number of death penalty crimes and established the three-strikes provision for violent offenders (O'Bryant 2003). Three-strike laws increase the sentence of a person convicted of a felony who has been previously convicted of two or more violent crimes or serious felonies. President Ronald Reagan attempted to cut back federal protections that had been expanded under previous administrations. Notably, crime rates decreased during the 1990s, and several reasons were offered, such as innovative policing strategies, increased imprisonment, the end of the crack-cocaine epidemic, an aging population, tougher gun control laws, a stronger economy, and an increase in the number of police (Levitt 2004), as well as the legalization of abortion (Levine et al. 1999; Donohue and Levitt 2001).

As part of the Violent Crime Control and Law Enforcement Act of 1994, the Violence Against Women Act of 1994 focused on reducing domestic violence and facilitating the arrest of violent abusers. It was intended to improve law enforcement's and prosecutors' responses and to protect victims. Women could file civil lawsuits in federal court to assert that they were victims of crimes motivated by their gender. Yet Marie Gottschalk suggests that feminists should have been more cautious in this area and more critical of law enforcement's and the states' ability to deal with social problems. She argues that state involvement and the politicization of violence against women became a "contributing factor" to the success of the call for law and order and more imprisonment (2006, 159–163).

The Office of National Drug Control Policy (ONDCP) coordinated the international and domestic anti–drug abuse programs. Government funding provided over 150 federal, state, and local initiatives, which included multiagency task force operations, intelligence-sharing networks, and investigative support centers (President William J. Clinton 29 Mar 1994). Additionally, the Drug Free Media Campaign Act of 1998 directed the ONDCP to conduct a national media campaign directed at reducing and preventing drug abuse among the United States' young people.

The Violent Crime Control and Law Enforcement Act of 1994 was a $30 billion crime bill for new police and prison construction, new federal capital crimes, and mandated life sentences for several three-strike violent crimes. The bill also provided truth-in-sentencing statutes requiring offenders to serve at least 85 percent of their prison sentences and left all prisoners ineligible for educational grants (Beckett 1997, 61; Gottschalk 2006, 151). The bill appropriated $8.8 billion for the Office of Community Oriented Policing Services and $1.6 billion for the Violence Against Women Act (O'Bryant 2003). Democrats offered little criticism of mandatory sanctions and only moderate backing for preventative alternatives.

At that time, the additional 100,000 street-level police officers were a 40 percent increase in the national force of 250,000 street-level law enforcement officers (Press Briefing 29 Mar 1994). By committing this large amount of funding to crime when President Clinton signed the Violent Crime Control and Law Enforcement Act of 1994, the Democrats demonstrated that they had taken control of the crime issue.

By the time this bill passed, the surge in crime of the later 1980s and early 1990s had started to diminish, with a drop in violent crime of about 30 percent (Glazer 1996). When Democrats adopted the conservative crime and drug rhetoric, Republicans no longer held the political advantage on crime issues (Beckett 1997). In 1991, according to a *Time*/CNN poll, the Republicans had a 16 to 37 percent advantage on crime issues. However, by 1994 the Democrats had secured a 34 to 42 percent lead (Flamm 2005). The Congressional Research Service cites three omnibus crime-control bills since 1984 that extended federal jurisdiction over areas that had been considered within local and state jurisdiction, such as juvenile justice and gun control. The three bills are the Comprehensive Crime Control Act of 1984, the Crime Control Act of 1990, and the Violent Crime Control and Law Enforcement Act of 1994.

In July 1994 President Clinton urged the passing of his proposed crime legislation. He insisted that the law enforcement community and the American people wanted tougher punishment, the capacity for imprisonment, prevention funds, an assault weapon ban, a ban on teenagers owning guns, protection for women against violence, and safer schools (President William J. Clinton 28 Jul 1994). Congress passed Clinton's Violent Crime Control and Law Enforcement Act of 1994, which increased the number of crimes punishable by death and established a three-strikes provision for violent offenders (O'Bryant 2003, 1). In this bill, $9 billion was dedicated to prison expansion and led to more privatization of the penal system. The Clinton administration was warned by allies in the Congressional Black Caucus that this bipartisan harsh and retributive law could devastate communities of color, but he ignored them and signed it anyway (Cohen 2014).

In President Clinton's 1995 State of the Union address, he reminded Congress "that last year, we passed a very tough crime bill—longer sentences, three strikes and you're out, almost 60 new capital punishment offenses, more prisons, more prevention, 100,000 more police" (President William J. Clinton 25 Jan 1995). During Clinton's tenure, federal criminal justice powers were expanded, allowing him to appease the law-and-order voters. His crime bill increased federal drug seizures, established drug courts, and increased the number of FBI, DEA, and U.S. Border Patrol agents. Prosecutions also increased, more prisons were built, and stiffer penalties for federal offenses were enacted. President Clinton and Congress were wrong in their "shotgun" approach to crime and punishment and added to the mass incarceration momentum (Cohen 2014).

However, as the prisons began to fill to capacity with minority prisoners, African American leaders responded with concern over the War on Drugs and the incarceration rates for minorities. The Congressional Black Caucus tried in vain to secure more crime prevention programs in federal crime bills. Their proposed Racial Justice Act connected civil rights with social justice crime-control policies, but it failed to gain the support of the Clinton administration (Gottschalk 2006).

In November 1995 President Clinton rejected the U.S. Sentencing Commission's (USSC) proposals to equalize penalties for crack and powder cocaine distribution by reducing the penalties for crack. This was the USSC's first research report to Congress on crack cocaine, and it found that over 80 percent of crack offenders were black. Because the 100-to-1 ratio resulted in harsher penalties for minorities, this created a perception that the criminal justice system was unjust and inconsistent. When the USSC attempted to amend the guidelines to equalize the amount of crack and powder cocaine, Congress rejected the amendment (Families Against Mandatory Maximums 2013). Confronted with the evidence of racial bias in sanctions between crack cocaine mostly used by blacks and powder cocaine used by whites, President Clinton demonstrated racist law-and-order politics when he recommended increasing the sentencing for powder cocaine.

In the last days of his presidency and despite his hard-line position while in office, President Clinton proclaimed the sentencing disparities between crack and powder cocaine to be "unconscionable" and called for total reform of imprisonment policy (quoted by Gottschalk 2006, 248–60). He was willing to admit his mistakes by saying that the 1994 omnibus crime bill was "overly broad instead of appropriately tailored," which had the result of some being in prison "who shouldn't be, others are in for too long, and without a plan to educate, train, and reintegrate them into our communities," and stated that we were all suffering for this situation (Fang and Ferguson 2016).

Consequently, Ted Sorensen, former special counsel to President Kennedy, accused President Bill Clinton of failing to take the opportunity to change unjust discrimination in the law enforcement process. According to Sorensen, this included police profiling and disparate sentencing penalties, which "are populating our prisons with a large percentage of young black males" (2008). President Clinton, with his stringent get-tough policies, was a champion for the call to law and order.

The 1996 Republican Party Platform had a section on "Getting Tough on Crime." It claimed that "America has become a more fearful place, especially for the elderly and for women and children" under Bill Clinton (Republican Party Platform of 1996 12 Aug 1996). The Republicans continued to blame "the legacy of liberalism," in which judges appointed by Democrat presidents continued "their assault against the rights of law-abiding Americans" (Republican Party Platform of 1996 12 Aug 1996). They declared that the "Democrat Congresses cared more about rights of criminals than safety for Americans" (Republican Party Platform of 1996 12 Aug 1996). The Republicans took credit for the truth-in-sentencing prison grant program to provide incentives to states that enact laws requiring violent felons to serve at least 85 percent of their sentences. They promised to establish "no-frills prisons" (Republican Party Platform of 1996 12 Aug 1996).

The Republican candidate Robert Dole stated that his anti-crime bill would differ in three ways from President Clinton's: by providing as much as $12 million in resources to law enforcement, by providing more flexibility for mayors and local officials, and by targeting a portion of the funds to cities in urgent need of help and with the highest violent crime rates (Robert Dole 17 Jun 1995). In his 1996 address before a joint session of the Congress on the state of the union, President Clinton talked of reducing crime, poverty, and welfare. Like Ronald Reagan, Bill Clinton linked crime with welfare, and he made sweeping changes to the welfare system.

Importantly, Clinton directed the FBI and other federal law enforcement agencies to target gangs and began a war on gangs. While the president claimed that community policing required "bonds of trust between citizens and police" and spoke about the necessity of prevention programs, he showed his law-and-order philosophy when he sought to prosecute teenagers as adults (President William J. Clinton 23 Jan 1996). President Clinton also wanted those who took part in gang or drug behavior to be removed from public housing. Eventually, this federal policy resulted in the eviction of many families, especially single mothers and grandmothers, from public housing due to their children's drug activity (Hellegers 1999). As with the rapid expansion of the prison system, tough law-and-order policy had many unexpected and damaging outcomes.

In 1996, as part of President Clinton's "get tough on crime" agenda, he signed the Antiterrorism and Effective Death Penalty Act, which expanded grounds for detaining and deporting immigrants and for the first time authorized fast-track deportation procedures. This legislation was introduced after the domestic terrorist bombing of the Alfred P. Murrah Federal Building by Timothy McVeigh in Oklahoma City. President Clinton also signed the Illegal Immigration Reform and Immigrant Responsibility Act (IIRIRA). According to the Human Rights Watch, the IIRIRA allows the government to detain and deport immigrants, even legal permanent residents, for relatively minor, nonviolent criminal convictions (Norton 2016). The ACLU claims that these two bills were meant to keep dangerous "criminal aliens" off America's streets; however, the punishment for immigrants was out of proportion to their crimes with the result of a boom in detention (Rabinovitz 2011).

In the 1997 State of the Union Address, President Clinton continued the War on Gangs and the War on Drugs. He mounted a full-scale assault on juvenile crime that included legislation that declared "a war on gangs, with new prosecutors and tougher penalties," and extended the Brady Bill so "violent teen criminals" would not buy handguns (President William J. Clinton 4 Feb 1997). President Clinton used the threat of violence to justify the call for being tough on crime. These criminal justice policies furthered the call for law and order, expanded federal jurisdiction, and sustained the growth of the federal government into crime control.

The *Hudson v. United States* (1997) Supreme Court ruling allowed defendants to be criminally prosecuted, even after being fined in a civil enforcement action. At that time, Chief Justice Rehnquist's push toward a law-and-order agenda was hampered by Justices Sandra Day O'Connor and Anthony M. Kennedy, who tended to vote with the more liberal bloc on these issues (Jost 2005).

In 1998 President Clinton reported that violent crime, robbery, burglary, and assault had been down for five years in a row. He announced that the Brady Bill had stopped a quarter of a million criminals from buying handguns. And the murder rate was the lowest in 30 years, with crime rates dropping for 6 straight years. However, public concern about crime was going up. Therefore, President Clinton continued to support the anti-crime movement by asking Congress to add new prosecutors and tougher penalties for gang-related behavior. He also asked for a thousand new border patrol agents and sophisticated new technologies to help control the borders (President William J. Clinton 27 Jan 1998). This is evidence that this administration was a major player at the beginning of the border law enforcement buildup. In addition, because he had balanced the budget, Clinton wanted to add up to 50,000 more police in high-crime areas, equipping them with "crime-mapping computers to digital mug shots" (President William J. Clinton 19 Jan 1999).

In President Clinton's last State of the Union address in January 2000, he stated that his administration had seen the "longest decline on record" of the crime rate (President William J. Clinton 27 Jan 2000). But, because of the school shootings in Columbine and other areas, he wanted strengthened gun laws and better enforcement of existing laws. Although gun crime prosecutions were up 16 percent, he wanted to do more. President Clinton proposed to hire more prosecutors and more ATF agents and to "crack down on illegal gun traffickers and bad-apple dealers" (President William J. Clinton 27 Jan 2000). He also wanted enforcement tools that could "trace every gun and every bullet used in every gun crime in the United States" (President William J. Clinton 27 Jan 2000). Democrat Clinton was one of most ardent law-and-order presidents, in the style of Republicans Richard Nixon and Ronald

Reagan. He expanded the number of police, federalized crimes, and strengthened sentencing, which led to the United States being known as the Prison Nation. By the end of 2000, the Bureau of Prison's total inmate population had doubled to 145,125 (Federal Bureau of Prisons 2011).

Meanwhile, the anti-drug community continued to flourish during the Clinton years. The Drug-Free Communities Act of 1997, authorized by the Office of National Drug Control Policy (ONDCP), was the cornerstone of the National Drug Control Strategy. This national initiative awarded federal grants directly to community coalitions. The mission of these coalitions was to reduce substance abuse among adolescents and strengthen collaboration among private and public organizations and agencies. Government funding was provided to assist communities in identifying and responding to local substance use problems. This initiative aimed to increase citizen participation in strategic planning to reduce drug use over time (Office of the President of the United States. National Drug Control Strategy 2009). According to their website, in 2009 the Drug-Free Communities Support Program maintained over 700 drug-free community coalitions (U.S. Drug-Free Communities Support Program 2009).

In addition, the Demand Reduction Interagency Working Group (IWG) of the ONDCP included the Administrative Office of the United States Courts, Office of Probation and Pretrial Services, Department of Defense, Department of Education, Office of Safe and Drug-Free Schools, Department of Health and Human Services, Department of Homeland Security, Office of Counternarcotics Enforcement, Department of Justice, Office of Juvenile Justice and Delinquency Prevention, Department of Labor, Department of State, Department of Transportation, Department of Veterans Affairs, and the Office of Management and Budget of the Executive Branch. Most of the U.S. Demand Reduction Interagency Working Groups' mission was for government agencies to work together to "reduce the demand, availability, and consequences of illegal drug use within the United States" (Executive Office of the President 2002).

As the Clinton era began, domestic terrorism and large-scale, indiscriminate violence started to increase, and the call for law and order gained momentum. Crime events kept the administration and the public on edge. On February 26, 1993, a car bomb exploded under the World Trade Center in Manhattan, killing six people and injuring more than a thousand. Islamic militants were convicted of the crime. This bombing contributed to the added pressure to crack down on crime and aided the passage of the 1994 crime bill (Cooper 1995). *Newsweek* and *Time* published one story each on the World Trade Center bombing.

On February 28, 1993, the Clinton administration attempted to enforce gun control laws by having the U.S. Bureau of Alcohol, Tobacco, Firearms, and Explosives (ATF) execute a search warrant on David Koresh, the armed cult leader of the Branch Davidians. On the grounds of the Davidians' compound near Waco, Texas, a gun battle left four federal agents and six members of the Davidians dead. On April 19, after a 51-day siege, an FBI assault ended with 76 members of the Davidians dead, including 21 children and 2 pregnant women. This incident is known as the Waco Siege, or Waco Massacre. President Clinton, along with Attorney General Janet Reno and director of the FBI Louis Freeh, were criticized by right-wing groups for mishandling the situation and by left-wing groups for accelerated efforts to gain new federal powers under the guise of investigating domestic terrorism. However, a Harris poll showed that 71 percent of Americans blamed leader David Koresh for the standoff's tragic ending (Clark 1997). *Newsweek* ran one cover story, and *Time* ran three on David Koresh and the Waco Siege.

During the Clinton years, a string of high-profile killings and abductions kept crime on the public agenda. First, in October 1993, 12-year-old Polly Klaas was abducted from her home and murdered by a sex offender on parole. From October 1993 to December 1995, the *New York Times* published approximately 30 stories on this kidnapping, crime, and criminals (Lexis Nexis ProQuest Historical Newspaper, the *New York Times*, key words "Polly Klaas").

Next, seven-year-old Megan Kanka was sexually molested and murdered by a twice-convicted child molester, Jesse K. Timmendequas. From August 1994 to October 1997, the *New York Times* published over 150 stories on Megan's murder, on the accused and his trial, and on Megan's Law (Lexis Nexis ProQuest Historical Newspaper, the *New York Times*, key words "Megan Kanka"). As a result, Megan's Law was adopted and required government officials to notify communities when sex offenders moved into the neighborhood. The most controversial provision requires released sex offenders to register with local police (Glazer 1996).

On April 19, 1995, on the second anniversary of the Waco Siege and in retaliation for the disastrous federal raid, Timothy McVeigh parked a truck filled with explosives in front of the Alfred P. Murrah Building in Oklahoma City. The powerful blast killed 168 people, including 19 children, and prompted Congress to place anti-terrorism proposals at the top of the legislative agenda (Cooper 1995). On June 2, 1997, McVeigh was found guilty, and on June 11, 2001, he was executed by lethal injection for the bombing. Between 1995 and 2001, *Newsweek* ran five and *Time* ran six cover stories pertaining to McVeigh and the bombing. As the threat of domestic and international terrorism increased, presidents and political leaders felt more justified in their heavy-handed law-and-order responses.

During the 1997 to 1998 school year, an eruption of school shootings took place, leaving 11 students dead in Pearl, Mississippi; West Paducah, Kentucky; Jonesboro, Arkansas; Edinboro, Pennsylvania; and Springfield, Oregon. Then, in April 1999 at Columbine High School in Littleton, Colorado,

14 students and 1 teacher were killed by 2 male students who committed suicide on the scene (Koch 1998; Meserve 1999). From April 1999 to July 1, 1999, the *New York Times* published nearly 200 stories on Columbine, the shooters and their parents, the victims, gun control, and young male violence. *Newsweek* ran three and *Time* ran four stories on the school shootings. The school violence placed gun control back on the national agenda.

In response to the rash of school shootings, President Clinton held a national forum on youth violence, pushed to restore the five-day waiting period for buying a handgun, and advocated for extending the Brady Bill—named after James Brady, who was shot in the assassination attempt on President Reagan—to prevent juveniles who commit violent crimes from buying a gun. President Clinton stated:

> We must do more to keep our schools the safest places in our communities. Last year, every American was horrified and heartbroken by the tragic killings in Jonesboro, Paducah, Pearl, Edinboro, Springfield. . . . In memory of all the children who lost their lives to school violence, I ask you to strengthen the Safe and Drug-Free School Act, to pass legislation to require child trigger locks, to do everything possible to keep our children safe. (President William J. Clinton 19 Jan 1999)

Although the controversial debate about gun control continued to peak during times of random violence, gun control was not embraced by the anti-crime movement. Because of the powerful and wealthy National Rifle Association's pro-gun lobbying efforts, gun control measures were difficult to get through Congress. In 2001 Attorney General Reno stated:

> The NRA doesn't particularly care for me. But it's important for the NRA to understand what this stuff has done to America. I just think the American people are sick and fed up with what assault weapons have done. I can remember the first time I saw an assault weapon. It is deadly. It is a horrible thing. The American people have come to realize what these weapons are doing on our streets. They are saying, Enough is enough is enough. (quoted by Gibbs 2001)

However, gun control remains a complicated issue, and Second Amendment rights are heavily guarded by conservative lawmakers.

President Bill Clinton promised to be tough on crime. In the law-and-order tradition of Nixon and Reagan, President Clinton's presidential leadership fostered and supported the call for law and order by putting crime, domestic violence, and the War on Gangs on the national agenda. In the fashion of President Johnson's LEAA, President Reagan's Comprehensive Crime Act of 1984, and President George H. W. Bush's Crime Control Act of

1990, President Clinton's Violent Crime Control and Law Enforcement Act of 1994 was a historic piece of legislation. All of these tough-on-crime policies have contributed to mass incarceration.

Continually, government response to crime issues expanded federal law enforcement's authority, power, and influence. Through government support, anti-crime and anti-drug groups were maintained. Congress responded to President Clinton's crime initiative by passing a bill that supplied large amounts of crime-fighting funding. Therefore, during the Clinton years, the inmate population rose 56 percent or 38,769 prisoners—the largest increase on record (Gramlich 2017a). Like other law-and-order presidents, Bill Clinton expanded federal law enforcement powers and supported government funding to federal, local, and state criminal justice agencies and anti-crime organizations. During the Clinton years, domestic terrorism and violence, child abductions, and school shootings received intense media coverage and kept crime on the public agenda. This situation cultivated and politicized the "lock them up and throw away the key" mentality with little debate on unintended consequences to the criminal justice system or those who may be negatively affected by the harsher policies.

In 2015 former President Bill Clinton called for criminal justice reforms to address the over-imprisonment crisis that he helped create, especially for those who had not committed serious crimes. Now Clinton admits that the United States has too many people with unreasonably long sentences in prison. He claims that "we have overshot the mark" and says that after two decades:

> It's time to take a clear-eyed look at what worked, what didn't, and what produced unintended consequences. So many of these laws worked well, especially those that put more police on the streets. But too many laws were overly broad instead of appropriately tailored. A very small number of people commit a large percentage of serious crimes—and society gains when that relatively small group is behind bars. But some are in prison who shouldn't be, others are in for too long, and without a plan to reintegrate them into our communities. (Brennan Center for Justice 28 Apr 2015)

While President Clinton seems genuinely interested in correcting his misguided and overreaching law-and-order politics, the damage has been done, and sitting presidents have only contributed to the problem. On law-and-order issues, presidential power and influence has guided and enhanced the U.S. race to incarcerate.

CHAPTER EIGHT

President George W. Bush: Homeland Security and the War on Terrorism

Throughout the 1990s and early 2000s, the United States benefited from the longest period of falling crime rates since the end of World War II. The rate fell annually from 747 crimes per 100,000 people in 1993 to 463 crimes per 100,000 people in 2004 (FBI 2007). In May 2004 the United States spent $167 billion on criminal and civil justice services, and since 1982 justice expenditures average 8 percent growth annually (Bureau of Justice Statistics 2004, 2016). While the number of violent crimes fell, cities such as Atlanta, Baltimore, Dallas, New Orleans, and Miami experienced a rise in homicides. In large urban areas where handguns continued to be plentiful, youth gangs remained caught up in violence and retaliation (Katel 2008). The FBI estimated there were approximately 785,000 gang members in the United States belonging to about 26,500 different gangs in 3,400 communities (Kingsbury 2008). Accordingly, President Clinton's War on Gangs helped maintain the call for law and order's incarceration.

On the other hand, President George W. Bush's presidential legacy is defined by the 9/11 attacks, the War on Terrorism, and the PATRIOT Act. After the 9/11 attack, President George W. Bush and Congress continued to support tough law-and-order measures to combat terrorism by passing the PATRIOT Act. By using the military and creating the Department of Homeland Security, President Bush employed national executive power to wage the War on Terror and expand government power. During the Clinton era, domestic and international terrorism increased. After the 9/11 attacks, President George W. Bush altered the national crime agenda when he declared a "war on terror." New presidential initiatives and legislation increased law enforcement powers and expanded federal reach into local and state criminal justice systems. The War on Terror became an extenuation of the anti-crime call for the law-and-order movement.

President George W. Bush came into office with chief executive leadership experience as governor of Texas. He had a long record of being a law-and-order chief executive and stated that his appointees to the Board of Pardons and Paroles would reflect a no-nonsense approach to crime and punishment. The president chose people who believed that those who commit crimes against innocent Texans should pay the consequences and that sentences imposed by juries should be carried out. He claimed that the Texas prison system had become a revolving door in the early 1990s, and he was proud that Texas had "virtually eliminated parole" for violent criminals (Bush 1999). While Bush was governor, Texas executed 152 prisoners, which was more than any governor in American history (Saenz 2011). George W. Bush brought his Texas criminal justice policies to the White House.

Additionally, law-and-order Governor Bush supported stop-and-frisk policies, two-strikes penalties, as well as registration for sexual offenders. His administration also ended mandatory early release for violent offenders and approved a tough "two strikes and you're out" law for sexual predators. He proclaimed that under his leadership, it was now illegal for paroled sex offenders to live in Texas without registering. Former Governor Bush intended to extend his tough-on-crime state policies to the entire nation.

As a candidate, George Bush ran on the 2000 Republican Platform that stated Republican governors, legislators, and local leaders supported the zero-tolerance approach to crime. The platform proclaimed that a Republican Congress enacted legislation for an effective death penalty, restitution to victims, removal of criminal aliens, and vigilance against terrorism. Additionally, it stated that Republicans stopped federal judges from releasing criminals due to prison overcrowding, made it harder to file lawsuits concerning prison conditions, and with the implementation of truth-in-sentencing laws, pushed states to make sure that violent felons served actual time. They also took credit for providing billions of dollars in block grants for law enforcement agencies to hire police and acquire new equipment and technology (Republican Party Platform of 2000 31 Jul 2000).

The 2000 Democratic platform indicated that Bill Clinton and Al Gore had a tough comprehensive strategy to fight crime on every front, including more police on the streets, tougher punishments, and support for the death penalty. The platform claimed that serious crime had fallen for seven years in a row to its lowest level in a quarter-century and that violent crime was down by 24 percent. Moreover, the murder rate was down to mid-1960s levels, and the number of juveniles committing homicides with guns was down by nearly 60 percent. The Democrats declared, "We can't surrender to the right-wing Republicans who threatened funding for new police, who tried to gut crime prevention, and who would invite the NRA into the Oval Office. Nor will we go back to the old approach which was tough on the causes of crime, but not tough enough on crime itself" (Democratic Party Platform of 2000 14 Aug 2000).

Subsequently, in 2000 George W. Bush had disagreed with the Supreme Court ruling that upheld the reading of Miranda warning to suspects and said, "We should never undermine the right of a person arrested to have their rights read to them . . . I did believe, though, that voluntary confessions should be allowed without a Miranda reading. The court didn't agree with my position. I'm now going to uphold the law" (Seelye 2000). This law-and-order candidate thought that Miranda should be waived in some situations.

As U.S. president, George W. Bush was committed to continuing the War on Drugs and defending the death penalty. Even though evidence-based research shows that incarceration has a minimal effect on crime reduction or drug abuse, President George W. Bush continued supporting harsh sentencing policies. He suggested, "Our crime rate is low because we are keeping violent, repeat offenders in prison and off our streets" (Another Close Call 2004). President Bush allocated more money than ever to the dying efforts of the War on Drugs. The fight against drugs has been progressively militarized, as seen by the strong investment in the armed forces. It was President Reagan in 1986 who officially added drug trafficking as a threat to national security (Corti and Swain 2009). Presidential leadership, including that of George W. Bush, has substantially contributed to the call for law and order and the buildup of the over-militarization of U.S. civilian law enforcement.

However, in his 2001 State of the Union message, President Bush set his national agenda issues without focusing on crime. His administration focused on providing excellent schools, quality health care, a secure retirement, a cleaner environment, and a stronger defense. He only mentioned law enforcement in the attempt to "develop specific recommendations to end racial profiling" (President George W. Bush 27 Feb 2001).

Yet illegal drugs continued to present problems for President George W. Bush; therefore, he called on communities and groups to help in the fight. In 2001 he extended and expanded the Drug-Free Communities Support Program, which supported community-based efforts nationwide to reduce the demand for illegal drugs (President George W. Bush 14 Dec 2001). On National DARE Day 2001, he recognized Drug Abuse Resistance Education (DARE) as the largest and most widely known substance abuse prevention and anti-violence program in the United States. The president acknowledged DARE's partnership between the research community, educators, law enforcement, parents, and students (President George W. Bush 10 Apr 2001). At the same time, the Bush administration focused zealously on a new campaign promoting drug testing of students.

Importantly during the Bush era, there was a rapid acceleration of the militarization of domestic law enforcement. As a result, it is estimated that there are approximately 40,000 paramilitary-style Special Weapons and Tactics (SWAT) raids in the United States each year, often for misdemeanor drug offenses (Drug Policy Alliance 2016). SWAT teams are dressed as soldiers, are usually heavily armed, are unannounced, and are commonly used to serve narcotic warrants. It is reported that these raids are unnecessarily violent to the offenders, as well as to the police and bystanders (Balko 2006). President Bush's Department of Homeland Security disbursed over $35 billion in state and local grants to law enforcement between 2002 and 2011.

Moreover, the Defense Department's 1033 Program dispenses surplus military equipment, such as tanks and armed vehicles, to local counterterrorism and counter-drug agencies (J.F. 2015). The American Civil Liberties Union found that the value of military equipment used by American police departments has risen from $1 million in 1990 to nearly $450 million in 2013. Due to this militarization of U.S. domestic law enforcement beginning with the Bush administration after 9/11, the American public has grown alarmingly comfortable with civilian police dressed for war, wearing riot gear and gas masks and carrying automatic weapons and sniper rifles.

Still, after September 11, 2001, President Bush's major mission was the fight against terrorists and not domestic concerns. Like many presidents before him, George W. Bush expanded the federal government's role in law enforcement, not only with the War on Gangs but also with the War on Terror. After the 9/11 attacks, he asked Congress for sweeping new law enforcement powers. Moreover, the Bush administration sent broad-based anti-terrorism legislation to Congress that lengthened prison sentences, expanded electronic surveillance, and streamlined immigrant deportation. On September 24, 2001, Attorney General John Ashcroft, testifying before the House Judiciary Committee, claimed, "Our laws fail to make defeating terrorism a national priority" (CCN.com/Transcript. 2001). Civil libertarians warned that some of these proposals would endanger the United States' constitutional principles and freedoms. However, out of fear of another terrorist attack, Congress quickly passed the PATRIOT Act of 2001 (Masci and Jost 2001). The acronym stands for uniting and strengthening America by "Providing Appropriate Tools Required to Intercept and Obstruct Terrorism" (President George W. Bush 20 Jan 2004).

On September 20, 2001, in an address before a joint session of the Congress on the United States' response to the terrorist attacks of 9/11, President Bush announced the creation of the Office of Homeland Security. This cabinet-level department would coordinate a comprehensive national strategy to safeguard against terrorism and respond to future attacks (President George W. Bush 11 20 Sep 2001). Congress established the department in November 2002 through the Homeland Security Act (HSA) of 2002. The

HSA aimed to "organize a government that is fractured, divided and under-prepared to handle the all-important task of defending our great nation from terrorist attack" (Homeland Security Act 2002). This legislation dramatically restructured the federal government, consolidating more than 20 existing federal agencies into a single Homeland Security Department and included the Federal Emergency Management Agency (FEMA), the U.S. Secret Service, the U.S. Customs Service, the U.S. Coast Guard, and the Immigration and Naturalization Service (INS).

Civil liberty groups have strongly criticized the creation of the PATRIOT Act and the Department of Homeland Security, complaining of reduced privacy and lack of government transparency with increased secrecy. This marked a sea change transformation away from domestic criminal justice issues to a state of security focusing on terrorism that has had long-term effects. Human Rights Watch, along with the Electronic Frontier Foundation, sued the U.S. Drug Enforcement Agency for illegally collecting records as part of its secret mass surveillance and urged Congress to end bulk collection of personal data under the PATRIOT Act (Wong 2015).

Since 9/11, the ACLU claims that the U.S. government has engaged in torture, indefinite detention, warrantless mass surveillance, and religious discrimination in the effort to "keep America safe" (ACLU 2016). They argue that this law-and-order national security strategy has eroded our most cherished values of freedom, civil liberties, and human rights that are ensured in the U.S. Constitution.

President George W. Bush signed the PATRIOT Act into law on October 26, 2001. The ACLU complained that this bill was passed without adequate debate. Accordingly, "There are significant flaws in the Patriot Act, the flaws threaten your fundamental freedoms by giving the government the power to access your medical records, tax records, information about the books you buy or borrow without probable cause, and the power to break into your home and conduct secret searches without telling you for weeks, months, or indefinitely" (ACLU 2003), The legislation dramatically increased the government's power to conduct clandestine searches and surveillance in many criminal cases. Critics complained that the act impinged on the freedom from unreasonable searches and seizures due to its expansion of the government's ability to conduct wiretaps. Proponents of these methods argue that these security measures have prevented terrorism, as there were no other significant attacks during the Bush administration.

In the 2002 State of the Union message, President Bush declared that the War on Terror had just begun and that his first priority was national security. He thanked law enforcement officials for the arrest of "hundreds of terrorists" and warned that "tens of thousands of trained terrorists" remained at large and that "we must pursue them wherever they are" (President George W. Bush 29 Jan 2002). His budget supported winning the War on Terror, protecting the homeland, and reviving the economy. He identified the dangers and asserted a call to arms, while advocating his remedies to the threat.

In 2002 President Bush introduced his National Drug Control Strategy, highlighting three aspects: "One, stopping drug use before it starts; two, healing America's drug users; and three, disrupting the market" (President George W. Bush 12 Feb 2002). He gave his appreciation for the many anti-drug groups, saying that a fabulous community made up of citizens, groups, and law enforcement had acted to "do something about drug use" (President George W. Bush 12 Feb 2002). Additionally, the primary function of the DEA is to enforce the nation's federal drug laws; however, DEA special agents are assigned to communities around the nation in the Demand Reduction Program (Demand Reduction Program 2009). Demand Reduction Program coordinators work with individuals and groups, such as community coalitions, civic leaders, state and local drug prevention organizations, treatment experts, and the public to provide aid with intelligence and enforcement. From its outset in 1973, the DEA had 1,470 special agents and a budget of less than $75 million. Furthermore, in 1974 the DEA had 43 foreign offices in 31 countries.

Moreover, in 2002 the U.S. Sentencing Commission (USSC) issued their third report that continued to recommend that Congress repeal the mandatory minimum for simple possession and to increase crack cocaine quantities to 25 grams for the 5-year mandatory minimum and 250 grams for the 10-year mandatory minimum. The USSC report also found that crack penalties exaggerated the harmfulness of the substance, the penalties over-punished low-level crack offenders, and that the amount of violence associated with crack was inflated (Families Against Mandatory Minimums 2013).

In the 2003 State of the Union message, President Bush focused on his justification for invading Iraq by claiming they had weapons of mass destruction. However, he stated that he was instructing the FBI, the CIA, the Department of Homeland Security, and the Department of Defense to develop a Terrorist Threat Integration Center to merge and analyze all threat information in a single location to protect citizens (President George W. Bush 28 Jan 2003).

In the 2004 State of the Union message, President Bush claimed the government's greatest responsibility was protecting the United States from a terrorist attack. He said that key provisions of the PATRIOT Act would expire in the next year and that law enforcement needed this legislation to protect citizens (President George W. Bush 20 Jan 2004). Bush's major message was that the United States must always be on the offensive against terrorism.

Meanwhile, the Supreme Court continued ruling in favor of the law-and-order agenda. In June 2004 the Supreme Court ruled that federal sentencing guidelines were only advisory and not mandatory. Justices Sandra Day O'Connor, Anthony Kennedy, and Stephen Breyer dissented, arguing that the ruling would diminish legislature's ability to set uniform sentencing guidelines (The Oyez Project 2004). The *Blakely v. Washington* (2004) decision invalidated the federal sentencing guidelines, and the Court continued to clarify the implications of *Blakely* violations.

Between 2005 and 2006 President Bush named two new conservative justices to the bench: Chief Justice John Roberts and Associate Justice Samuel Alito. Judge Roberts was appointed to replace Justice Sandra Day O'Connor after her resignation. However, Chief Justice William Rehnquist died during the confirmation process. President Bush withdrew Roberts's nomination as Justice O'Connor's successor and nominated him for the chief justice position. On September 29, 2005, Chief Justice Roberts was confirmed by the Senate.

On January 31, 2006, U.S. Court of Appeals Judge Samuel Anthony Alito joined the U.S. Supreme Court. Judge Alito's critics complained that in a 1985 application for a Justice Department promotion, he stated that he was motivated to go to law school, in part, by conservative writings criticizing the Warren Court's decisions on criminal procedures. After a failed attempt by Senate Democrats to filibuster the nomination, the Senate confirmed Alito by a vote of 58 to 42—the closest vote in over a decade (The Oyez Project 2017).

Consequently, President Bush got what he wanted, as Chief Justice Roberts and Associate Justice Alito "have bolstered the conservative wing," joining Justices Antonin Scalia and Clarence Thomas and occasionally Justice Anthony Kennedy (Curry 2007). Marcia Greenberger, the co-president of the National Women's Law Center, which opposed the nominations of Alito and Roberts, stated, "In the past, O'Connor often made the majority and Kennedy was part of the dissent, so we have clearly seen a shift to the right, in areas from criminal law to privacy rights for women. . . . Roberts and Alito have reliably and consistently been on the conservative end with Scalia and Thomas, and that was not the case with O'Connor" (Curry 2007). Similarly to Presidents Nixon and Reagan, George W. Bush was able to leave a conservative imprint on the criminal justice system by his Supreme Court appointments. However, Chief Justice Roberts must be concerned with not only his own legacy but also the legacy of the Roberts Court. The chief justice must be aware of how he will be remembered and what will resonate about his Court throughout history. If he wants to leave a heroic imprint on the Court by restoring justice and legal fairness for millions of Americans, the Court must be willing to start building the institutional scaffolding that will bring legitimacy to the prosecuting and sentencing process.

Moreover, presidents understand that the Supreme Court can turn against them with claims of overstepping executive powers. Consequently, after the 9/11 attacks, President Bush had broad support for this War on Terror. However, when he boldly tried to exercise his commander-in-chief powers, insisting that he alone had the power to set imperatives for accused terrorists who were being detained, the high court ruled against him. Additionally, President Bush had three more Supreme Court defeats over holding Guantanamo Bay detainees without a hearing. Justice Sandra Day O'Connor, a Republican appointee, stated: "A state of war is not a blank check for the president," halting Bush's presidential power to incarcerate even accused terrorists (Savage 2014.)

The 2004 Republican Party Platform claimed that the PATRIOT Act provided the FBI with the tools to fight organized crime, drug trafficking, and terrorism. The Republicans claimed that intelligence and law enforcement were sharing information as never before. The 2004 platform's focus was the War on Terror, which had declared war on every front, including airports, seaports, and borders (Republican Party Platform of 2004 30 Aug 2004).

The Democratic Party Platform supported tough punishment on violent crime, gang violence, and drug crime. Democrats not only promised to increase drug treatment but also to increase drug courts and mandatory drug testing for parolees and probationers "so fewer crimes are committed in the first place" (Democratic Party Platform of 2004 16 Jul 2004). They supported victims' rights to be "respected, to be heard, and to be compensated" (Democratic Party Platform of 2004 16 Jul 2004). The platform stated that the cycle of domestic violence would be broken by punishing offenders and standing with victims (Democratic Party Platform of 2004 16 Jul 2004).

According to the 9/11 Commission Report, on the morning of September 11, 2001, the United States became a "nation transformed" (2004). More than 2,600 people died at the World Trade Center, 124 died at the Pentagon, and 256 perished on the four planes. *Time* and *Newsweek* published 11 stories each on 9/11 and terrorism. The 9/11 Commission found that the executive branch, the Congress, the news media, and the American public had received "clear warning that Islamic terrorists meant to kill Americans in high numbers" (2004). This historic event dominated George W. Bush's presidency. According to David L. Altheide (2006), fear is used by public officials and the media to enact certain policies. The Bush administration successfully passed stringent anti-terror criminal justice measures to ensure national security.

During the 108th Congress, a sweeping crime bill strengthened the national AMBER (America's Missing Broadcast Emergency Response) child-abduction alert system and banned Internet child pornography. The legislation mandated life sentences for twice-convicted child sex offenders, permitted electronic surveillance to investigate child pornography, suspended the statute of limitations on crimes involving sexual abuse or kidnapping of children, and limited federal judges from departing from sentencing guidelines (Law and Law Enforcement 2006).

In the 2005 State of the Union message, President Bush proposed a three-year initiative to help organizations keep young people out of gangs (President George W. Bush 2 Feb 2005). With the threat of terror somewhat relaxed and responding to criticism in 2005, Attorney General Alberto Gonzales supported changes in the PATRIOT Act concerning secret warrants for financial documents, library data, and other business records (Eggen 2005).

In the spring of 2005, Republicans in the House of Representatives, with the support of the Bush administration and the Justice Department, moved to institute tougher mandatory minimum sentences. The bill, which was introduced by Representative James Sensenbrenner (R-WI), chairperson of the House Judiciary Committee, required a mandatory two-year prison term for anyone refusing to promptly report to the police the selling of marijuana on a college campus. This draconian bill never made it out of committee. However, in May 2005 the House passed a bill focused on fighting street gangs, which increased penalties for gang-related crimes and made more of these crimes death-penalty eligible (Gottschalk 2006).

In his 2006 State of the Union message, President Bush reported that violent crime rates had fallen to their lowest levels since the 1970s and that welfare cases had dropped by more than half over the past decade. He stated that drug use among youth was down 19 percent since 2001 (President George W. Bush 31 Jan 2006). After 12 years of Reagan and Bush and 8 years of Clinton, President George W. Bush could claim a measured victory over street crime and some decrease in drug abuse.

In October 2006 the Bureau of Prisons (BOP) activated the Counter-Terrorism Unit (CTU) to identify inmates accused of terrorist activities and to provide translation services and analysis of terrorist inmate communications. In December 2006 the BOP established the Communications Management Unit, which houses inmates who, due to their offense, conduct, or other information, required enhanced custody to "ensure the safe, secure, and orderly running of BOP facilities and to protect the public" (Federal Bureau of Prisons 2011). Due to the War on Terror, government resources were shifted to homeland security and counterterrorism, and this reduced spending in traditional criminal justice areas. In 2008 the first Special Management Unit (SMU) facility was designated to operate as a "more controlled and restrictive environment for managing the most aggressive and disruptive inmates" (Federal Bureau of Prisons 2011). Later, two other SMUs were subsequently established as well.

In 2007 President Bush did not even mention domestic law enforcement or crime issues in his State of the Union messages. However, the U.S. Sentencing Commission (USSC) issued a fourth report to Congress in 2007. The report called for new legislation to increase the crack cocaine quantity that triggers the 5- and 10-year mandatory minimums, as well as to decrease, and again to repeal, the 5-year mandatory minimum for simple possession. The USSC also added an amendment to the sentencing guidelines that reduced crack sentences by an average of 15 months. Moreover, in *Kimbrough v. United States* (2007), the Supreme Court ruled that a sentencing judge could depart from the federal sentencing guideline for crack cocaine if the Court disagreed with the disparity between crack and powder cocaine sentences. In the next year, the USSC's crack guideline amendment was made retroactive, and this reduced sentences an average of 26 months for approximately 16,500 inmates in federal prisons (Families Against Mandatory Minimums 2013).

In November 2007 the White House hosted the first Prisoner Reentry Summit in Los Angeles, California. Representatives from nonprofit community organizations and leaders from the private and public sectors, including White House FBCI Director Jay Hein and Secretary of Labor Elaine Chao attended. Chao acknowledge that incarceration's "heaviest cost is the loss of human dignity when people are living lives of poverty, addiction, and despair" (White House 2004). The Bush administration believed that faith-based and community organizations had a role in prison rehabilitation.

In 2008 President Bush again did not mention domestic law enforcement or crime issues in his State of the Union message. However, his federal budget proposal slashed federal aid to state and local law enforcement agencies to $400 million, a dramatic cut from the $2.3 billion appropriated to this area by Congress. The $400 million included a new $200 million grant program for targeting violent crime and $200 million in grants for prosecuting and rehabilitating drug offenders. Bush also sought $285 million in grants to combat juvenile crime and violence against women (Katel 2008). During President George W. Bush's eight years in office, the inmate population increased by 32 percent, or 36,784 prisoners (Gramlich 2017a). By 2009 the DEA had grown to 5,235 special agents, a budget of more than $2.3 billion, and 87 foreign offices in 63 countries.

The Bush administration contributed to mass incarceration through the War on Terror and the continued War on Drugs. Therefore, decades of attention to the crime issue and punitive measures used in the drug war may have caused citizens to accept increased surveillance and law enforcement tactics that threatened civil liberties (Altheide 2006).

President George W. Bush took office with a balanced budget and the longest period of falling crime rates since the end of World War II. Bush had hopes of tackling domestic problems, such as Social Security, health care, high taxes, and education. However, with the terrorist attacks of 9/11, the Bush administration declared a War on Terror and later invaded Iraq. Street crime was no longer on the national agenda, and the public was more fearful of another terrorist attack than of crime.

The historical, political, and social context in which President George W. Bush took office indicates a growing threat of terrorism under the Clinton administration. During the election campaign, both Republicans and Democrats used tough-on-crime rhetoric to blame each other for a lack of effective crime and drug policies. Through the War on Gangs, the establishment of the Department of Homeland Security, and the introduction and passing of the PATRIOT Act, President George W. Bush and his administration vigorously pursued the call for a law-and-order agenda that continues to contribute to mass incarceration.

CHAPTER NINE

President Obama's New Law and Order: Illegal Immigration, Private Prisons, and Executive Orders

With the presidential election of Democrat Barack Obama, progressives hoped for a kinder and gentler approach to maintaining law and order. And, true to form, President Barack Obama's criminal justice legacy will be that he left the White House with a smaller federal prison population than when he took office. This is a distinction, as we learned in chapter 4, that no president since Jimmy Carter can claim (Gramlich 2017a). With U.S. crime rates down, law-and-order politics did not play a major role in the election in 2008. As a presidential candidate in 2007, Senator Obama promised to recruit more public defenders by forgiving college and law school loans, to review mandatory minimum sentences to be smarter on crime, to reduce the counterproductive warehousing of nonviolent offenders, and to eliminate the disparity between crack and powder cocaine sentencing (Merritt 2008). Many criminal justice reformers saw most of these progressive initiatives moving in the right liberal direction.

Importantly, during the 2008 primaries, candidate Obama had a hard time attracting Hispanic voters, who heavily supported their favorite, Senator Hillary Clinton. However, in the end, Obama enjoyed popularity with the Hispanic voter bloc, helping him to victory in key states such as New Mexico. Still, immigration remained a salient and controversial topic frequently discussed by presidential candidates Barack Obama and John McCain.

During the campaign, Senator McCain moved to the law-and-order right on immigration issues, and he lost most Hispanic support. Senator Barack Obama had voted for immigration reform legislation to strengthen border controls, but also to create a guest-worker program and to legalize millions of foreign workers. The future president backed the Secure Fence Act but cosponsored a bill allowing states to offer illegal immigrants in-state tuition. In addition, Senator Obama cosponsored the Citizenship Promotion Act, which would have ensured reasonable immigration application fees and supported issuing drivers' licenses to illegal immigrants. Obama claimed that his immigration policy was meant to assist business growth. However, the Republican right remained considerably hostile to immigration reform. Therefore, many unauthorized immigrants were sent to prison or deported, while businesses hiring unauthorized immigrants received lenient treatment and were encouraged to be profitable (Silva 2016, 70).

Moreover, while Americans were relieved that no major foreign terrorist attacks had occurred on U.S. soil after 9/11, civil liberty advocates had increasing anxiety over the reactionary PATRIOT Act. The legislation backed by President George Bush had bipartisan support in the 107th Congress and significantly lessened restrictions on law enforcement agencies to investigate telephone records, online communications, and medical and financial records. The PATRIOT Act also reduced limitation on U.S. foreign intelligence collection and increased the discretion of law enforcement personnel. The PATRIOT Act represents a complicated issue: while Americans want to be safe and protected from future terrorist attacks, there is substantial concern about government and criminal justice overreach—especially related to the consequences of excessive imprisonment.

The PATRIOT Act allowed immigration authorities to indefinitely detain and deport immigrants. With 11.1 million undocumented immigrants in the United States and 52 percent from Mexico, immigration was the perfect venue for the Obama administration to continue mass incarceration by detainment (Krogstad, Passel, and Cohn 2016). An example of the PATRIOT Act's thorny implications is the predicament of former contractor of the National Security Agency Edward Snowden. He disclosed classified documents revealing the massive surveillance program of Americans' phone data. Courts found that Mr. Snowden's whistle-blowing proved the U.S. government's wrong use of Section 15 of the Patriot Act. Afterward, Congress passed the 2015 USA Freedom Act, which improved transparency concerning surveillance and limited government authorization to collect certain records.

Yet Snowden was accused of potential espionage and had to flee to Russia to avoid prosecution and possible imprisonment (Ackerman 2016). While President Obama acknowledged Snowden's valuable contribution to transparency, he emphasized prosecuting him. Moreover, after his 2016 election,

President Donald J. Trump, in harsh law-and-order fashion, said, "I think he's a total traitor and I would deal with him harshly" (Roth and Shetty 2016). This demonstrates the continued tenacity of flawed presidential leadership and the U.S. government's lock-them-up and race-to-incarcerate mentality.

Even more relevant to the United States' out-of-control penal system is the government's utilization of the for-profit private prison industry. In the 1990s, the U.S. government began relying on private for-profit prisons to ease overcrowding of government facilities. The cost of the Federal Bureau of Prisons had skyrocketed 687 percent over the past 35 years, from an inflation-adjusted $950 million to nearly $7.5 billion (Reilly 2016). This crisis was mainly caused by the large numbers of drug offenders with lengthy sentences. Half of those incarcerated in federal prisons were convicted of drug crimes, while violent offenders account for just 7 percent of the federal prison population.

Therefore, American prisons are full of drug offenders and other nonviolent inmates with excessive penalties who have "squandered human potential, and sent correctional costs skyrocketing while producing only modest public safety benefits" (Reilly 2016). Incarceration is "a highly punitive, costly, and potentially harmful intervention that should be used sparingly and judiciously" (quoted by Reilly 2016). Congress and the Bureau of Prisons should take major steps to reduce incarceration and move the system toward rehabilitation. Additionally, immigration reform is essential to insure the creditability of the immigration and naturalization system.

Common sense and right-on-crime policy dictates that prison should be reserved for those convicted of the most serious crimes, instead of continuing the mass incarceration of nonviolent offenders. At the end of 2015, about 12 percent of the more than 22,000 federal inmates were housed in private facilities, according to the Justice Department (Sullivan 2016). Critics of the current system have observed that the private prison industry operates under a business model in which money is made from "warehousing people" with "tens of thousands of bodies" required to fill these facilities (Lantigua-Williams 2016). Some blame the for-profit private prison industry, including privatization of detention for detainees, as the "underlying factor" behind the "ongoing humanitarian tragedy" of our immigration policy (Cox 2014). As a result, the prison industry lobbies the government by pumping money into politics and gains profit by exploiting the crisis at the border.

In 2012 the Corrections Corporation of America (CCA), the nation's largest business of for-profit prisons, sent letters to 48 states offering to buy their prisons as a remedy for "challenging corrections budgets" (Kirkham 2012). In exchange, the company demanded a 20-year contract and reassurances that the prison population would remain at least at 90 percent capacity (Kirkham 2012). This represents a huge incentive to keep people incarcerated and detained for increasingly longer periods to make money and signifies the gross "capitalism without compassion" that is destroying social justice (Senzee 2016). Presently, efforts are being undertaken to build awareness of the "counterproductive and downright feudal nature intrinsic to the practice of transferring public funds to private companies so they can profit from incarcerating people; however, lucrative new contracts continue to be awarded to for-profit companies like Corrections Corporation of America and the GEO Group" (Senzee 2016). Shockingly, the Department of Homeland Security Appropriations Act of 2010 requires that Immigration and Customs Enforcement (ICE) fill 34,000 beds with detained immigrants every day. Additionally, ICE has a congressionally mandated quota to fill empty beds in private prisons, such as the ones owned and operated by Corrections Corporation of America (Senzee 2016). The issue of immigration enforcement was taking over the issue of domestic crime. For undocumented immigrants already in the United States, President Obama wanted a system to verify employment eligibility and supported guest-worker programs (Seelye et al. 2008). The president declared in 2007 that the time had come to fix the broken immigration system, saying, "We need stronger enforcement on the border and at the workplace. But for reform to work, we also must respond to what pulls people to America. Where we can reunite families, we should" (Debate Tracker 17 Dec 2011).

In President Obama's February 2009 Address to the Joint Session of Congress, neither crime nor law and order were even mentioned. His attention was focused on the economy, financial stability, and universal health care. The United States had gone through a terrible economic period under the Bush administration, and President Obama blamed Wall Street executives' unethical and sometime illegal behavior for the foreclosure crisis that affected many families. He explained: "Regulations were gutted for the sake of a quick profit at the expense of a healthy market. People bought homes they knew they couldn't afford from banks and lenders who pushed those bad loans anyway" (President Barack Obama 24 Feb 2009). But under his plan, "There are 57 police officers who are still on the streets of Minneapolis tonight because this plan prevented the layoffs their department was about to make" (President Barack Obama 24 Feb 2009). Keeping law and order and funding law enforcement was still a priority.

Historically, anti-immigration legislation has been the result of a long-standing national debate about immigration with more than 200 state-level immigration bills passed into law each year from 2007 to 2009 (quoted by Wilson in Wood May 2010). Many anti-immigration politicians claim that these laws are necessary because illegal immigrants take jobs away from Americans and are draining state budgets through the services they receive in public schools and hospitals. However, some human rights groups compare the anti-immigrant situation to the struggle faced by African Americans during the civil rights movement. This repressive situation has grown in a time of political fragmentation, in which liberty is elusive, with continued attempts at voter suppression and extreme religiosity that threatens basic constitutional rights.

In many places, entrenched racist, white-supremacist sentiment still exists (Gomez 2011). Immigration reform was to be one of President Obama's legacy issues, and he supported Dream Act–type legislation, which would have provided a pathway to citizenship for children who were brought to the United States by their parents. Obama wanted enforcement focused on "Felons, not families, Criminals, not children," and "Gang members, not a mom who's working hard to provide for her kids" (Berman 2014).

However, beginning in 2009 in an effort to appear strong on illegal immigration, the Obama administration directed unparalleled resources to secure the U.S.-Mexican border and increase enforcement of workplace sites. Moreover, the Obama administration's Secure Communities program has been discredited by several advocacy groups as a "dragnet that makes every cop a potential immigration agent, empowered to enforce federal laws" (Fixing the Immigration System 2011).

In May 2009 President Obama nominated federal appeals court Judge Sonia Sotomayor to the U.S. Supreme Court. Sotomayor was the first Hispanic to serve on the Court and succeeded Justice David Souter. Souter was nominated by George H. W. Bush, and it is ironic that Justice Souter was replaced by another one of senior Bush's appointees, Sonia Sotomayor. The senior Bush nominated Sotomayor to the federal bench in 1991, and she was elevated to the U.S. Court of Appeals by President Bill Clinton in 1998. George H. W. Bush's choices continue to plague Republicans, as Sotomayor is a renowned left-leaning liberal justice. President Obama demonstrated the power of the presidency to continue individual ideology and preference when he appointed Sonia Sotomayor to the Supreme Court. She has been called the "most well-known and effective member of the Court's liberal wing" (Fontana 2011).

One year later President Obama had another opportunity to cast his influence on the Supreme Court when former Harvard Law School dean and then–Solicitor General Elena Kagan was appointed by him to the Supreme Court, replacing Justice John Paul Stevens. Kagan is the fourth woman to serve on the Supreme Court, following current Justices Ruth Bader Ginsburg and Sotomayor and retired Justice Sandra Day O'Connor. With these two appointments, President Obama maintained rather than altered the Court's ideological balance. He believed that Elena Kagan was one of the nation's foremost legal minds and an acclaimed scholar, with the experience of a lifelong commitment to public service.

However, President Obama was faced with a Supreme Court led by Republican appointee Chief Justice John Roberts. While Barack Obama's administration won major cases on gay rights, affirmative action, abortion, and, of course, on health care, Obama's Supreme Court success rate was extremely low. Generally, presidents win about two-thirds of the time, but the Obama administration only won 50.5 percent of its cases (Liptak 2017). President Obama dealt with a generally conservative Court that was somewhat hostile to his more liberal policies. In their decisions, the Court was responding to the president's "expansive deployment of executive power" (Liptak 2017). After all, in our governmental system of checks and balances, oversight of power is a major function of the three branches.

In spite of the appointment of the first Hispanic Supreme Court justice, Sonya Sotomayor, an important new trend developed. Immigration offenses made Latinos the new majority in federal prisons. Immigration, which was not crime, became an important issue facing the nation. According to the Department of Homeland Security, the United States accepts more immigrants than any other country, with more than 1.13 million people becoming permanent legal residents in 2009. However, the Department of Homeland Security estimated that about 10.8 million illegal immigrants were in the United States, down from 11.6 million in 2008. Sixty-two percent of these immigrants came from Mexico (CBS News 2011).

On January 27, 2010, President Obama delivered his Address Before a Joint Session of the Congress on the State of the Union and only mentioned the elimination of hate crimes. He focused more on the economy and Wall Street. In 2010 74.5 percent of persons arrested were males, 80.5 percent were arrested for violent crime, and 62.4 percent were arrested for property crime. Of these arrests, 69.4 percent were white, 28 percent were black, and 2.6 percent were of other races (Federal Bureau of Investigation 2010).

Accordingly, jails operated at 86 percent of their rated capacity by midyear of 2010, the lowest percentage since 1984. Approximately 61 percent of jail inmates were not convicted and held pending arraignment or were awaiting trial or conviction. The remaining 39 percent were convicted and awaited sentencing, were serving a jail sentence, or were awaiting transfer to serve time in state or federal prison (Bureau of Justice Statistics 2011).

In 2010 the Fair Sentencing Act was passed, which created an 18-to-1 ratio between crack and powder cocaine. Demonstrating executive leadership, President Barack Obama signed the Fair Sentencing Act into law, which instructed the U.S. Sentencing Commission to amend the crack cocaine guidelines to reflect the law's new 18-to-1 crack-powder ratio. Under the law, 28 grams of crack and 500 grams of powder cocaine trigger the five-year mandatory minimum, and 280 grams of crack and 5 kilograms of powder cocaine trigger the 10-year mandatory minimum. The law repealed the five-year mandatory minimum sentence for simple possession of crack cocaine.

This is the first time since the Nixon Administration that a mandatory minimum had been repealed. The act had impact on approximately 3,000 crack offenders sentenced in federal prisons each year and reduces crack sentences by an average of 27 months. It was projected to save over 1,500 prison beds and $42 million in the next five years. The law does not benefit people who have already committed crack cocaine offenses (Families Against Mandatory Minimums 2013).

In April 2010 Arizona adopted the United States' harshest illegal immigration legislation, which incited a nationwide debate and a Justice Department lawsuit. After the killing of a rancher in southern Arizona by a suspected drug smuggler, Governor Brewer and other elected officials felt the need to act. Arizona SB 1070 was aimed at discouraging illegal immigrants from entering or remaining in the state. On July 28th, a day before the law was to take effect, a federal district court judge struck down controversial provisions calling for law officers to check a person's immigration status and a requirement for immigrants to carry their papers at all times. The U.S. Court of Appeals for the Ninth Circuit ruled against Arizona in April 2011, which let the lower court decision stand (Lacey 2011). Governor Brewer asked the Supreme Court to decide whether Arizona had the constitutional right to impose anti-immigration legislation. She argued that if the federal government would not deal with the immigration problem, the states had the right to do so.

Also in August 2010 public opinion polls showed support for tough state immigration laws. A Gallup poll revealed that more than three-quarters of those asked were familiar with the Arizona immigration law, and, of those, 59 percent favored the laws while 39 percent opposed. In April 2010 a Zogby Interactive poll showed that 79 percent of those asked did not feel that illegal "aliens" were entitled to the same rights and basic freedoms as U.S. citizens (Wood 30 Aug 2010). In response to the new strict anti-immigration laws, members of the Los Angeles City Council immediately called for a boycott of Arizona's businesses and conventions. The mayor of San Francisco imposed a moratorium on city travel to Arizona. These actions were intended to have an impact on Arizona's tourism (Wood 28 Apr 2010). Subsequently, there was a strong response in Mexico, as Mexicans were angered by what they saw as politically motivated actions. President Felipe Calderón and Mexico's foreign affairs secretary, Patricia Espinosa, along with many media journalists, condemned the law. Mexican lawmakers called for economic boycotts to punish Arizona. Ms. Espinosa expressed regrets that Arizona politicians failed to consider "the valuable contributions of immigrants to the economy, and society" (Llana 2010).

The new Tea Party Republicans in Congress were dedicated to tough law-and-order enforcement. Also the chairperson of the House Judiciary Committee's subcommittee on immigration, Representative Steve King (R-IA), and Representative Lamar Smith (R-TX), chairperson of the Judiciary Committee, continued to be outspoken opponents of legalization proposals. One example of continued anti-immigration legislation is that in January 2011, Representative Marsha Blackburn (R-TN) introduced the CLEAR Act (HR 100). If passed, it would authorize states and local governments to enforce immigration law; increase information sharing between state, local, and federal governments; mandate the federal government to expedite criminal aliens being detained by states and localities; and increase federal resources for local governments assisting in immigration enforcement.

On January 8, 2011, Democrat U.S. Representative Gabrielle Giffords of Arizona was shot in the head by 22-year-old Jared Lee Loughner outside a grocery store during a town meeting with constituents. The assailant killed 6 people and wounded 13 others (Gabrielle Giffords Shot 2011). Some news outlets reported that Loughner had expressed extremist political beliefs. Moreover, former Republican vice presidential candidate Sarah Palin had posted a map on her Facebook page showing areas where Democrats were running for reelection. Representative Giffords (D-AZ) was one of the Democrats noted by crosshairs, like those seen through the scope of a gun (Naiman 2011). After the shooting of Representative Giffords, the Palin camp removed the map.

Some quickly blamed the Tea Party movement and its militant rhetoric for the political violence. The remarks of Republican Sharron Angle, who failed to win the Senate race in Nevada, were also pointed out. She had advocated "second-amendment remedies" to some of the nation's problems (Somashekhar 2011). While no connection was made between the Arizona shooter and any political ideology, Democrats and Republicans acknowledge the danger of extreme political rhetoric in a toxic political environment.

On January 25, 2011, President Obama delivered his Address Before a Joint Session of the Congress on the State of the Union, but again did not mention domestic crime or incarceration. He did thank intelligence and law enforcement professionals, stating, "We're disrupting plots and securing our cities and skies. And as extremists try to inspire acts of violence within our borders, we are responding with the strength of our communities, with respect for the rule of law" (President Barack Obama 25 Jan 2011). In 2011, 7.2 million men and women were under correctional supervision, with 5 million of this number being monitored in the community on probation or parole. Approximately 2.1 million were incarcerated in prisons or jails, resulting in the United States maintaining the highest incarceration rate in the world (Porter 2010).

However, compared to 2009, two-year local arrest trends indicated that violent crime arrests declined 5.3 percent and property crime arrests decreased 4.7 percent. Most arrests were for drug abuse, driving under the influence, and larceny-theft. An estimated 6,899,000 persons were under the supervision of adult correctional systems at year-end 2013, a decline of about 41,500 from year-end 2012 (Glaze and Kaeble 2014).

According to the U.S. Sentencing Commission, for the first nine months of fiscal year 2011, Latinos comprised 50.3 percent of persons sentenced, blacks made up 19.7 percent, and whites made up 26.4 percent. Illegal crossings and smugglings accounted for most of the increase in Latinos sent to prison over the last decade (Fox News Latino 2011).

In 2011 state politicians continued to make immigration a major political issue by enacting drastic anti-immigration measures. As mentioned earlier, Arizona was the first state to pass a law targeted at illegal immigration, with Republican governor Jan Brewer blaming federal inaction and misguided policy on creating a "dangerous and unacceptable situation" (Valdes and Mears 2011). In 2011 other state lawmakers introduced some 1,600 immigration-related measures, with 42 states enacting a new law or resolution. Alabama, Georgia, Indiana, South Carolina, and Utah passed tough legislation modeled after the Arizona law (Biskupic 2011). President Obama, many Democrats, and civil rights groups objected to the state laws and claimed they would lead to harassment of Hispanic Americans. The U.S. Department of Justice challenged the Arizona state law on the grounds that the federal government has jurisdiction over immigration enforcement (Vicini and Pelofsky 2011). Governor Brewer asked for clarification from the Court on the role states have in controlling immigration.

In December 2011 the Supreme Court agreed to rule on the Arizona law, which indicated a possible decision during the 2012 presidential election campaign. In 2012 the Supreme Court handed down a split decision on the Arizona case. The Court unanimously held that state law enforcement officials can determine the immigration status of anyone they stop or arrest if they suspect the individual is an illegal immigrant. However, writing for the majority, Justice Anthony M. Kennedy stated, "Arizona may have understandable frustrations with the problems caused by illegal immigration while that process continues, but the state may not pursue policies that undermine federal law" (Liptak 2012a). This left the door open for more challenges to the law.

Under President Obama's law-and-order enforcement-first agenda, around 400,000 undocumented immigrants have been removed from the United States every year for the past three years. This represents a huge increase from fewer than 100,000 deportations in 2001. The U.S. Immigration and Customs Enforcement (ICE), with a budget of more than $6 billion, expanded programs like 287(g) agreements and Secure Communities to reach this immense number of deportations (Steigenga 2011). Offenses committed by these immigrants include being in the United States without legal status, which is a civil violation and not a crime (Preston 2011).

Understanding that the United States needs immigration reform, the Obama administration promised to review deportation policy. Their 2011 plan was to expedite deportation of those who committed felonies and misdemeanors, repeat offenders of immigration laws, and national security risks. The plan would also stop deportation of undocumented immigrants with no convictions, young students, military service members, the elderly, and those with American citizens as close family (Editorial 2011).

In December 2011 the Department of Homeland Security and the Justice Department announced a pilot project. This program focused on immigration court cases in which immigrants had been arrested for deportation but were not being detained while the cases were processed. Those who qualify for prosecutorial discretion would have their case closed but not dismissed. They could remain in the United States but have no legal immigration status. This was one way the Obama administration attempted to appease the pro-immigrant community. Republicans opposed the new deportation policy and charged the president with bypassing Congress by granting de facto amnesty to undocumented immigrants (Fixing the Immigration System 2011).

Additionally, critics accused President Obama and his administration, particularly the Department of Homeland Security, of being an "ally and enabler" of discriminatory immigration law enforcement practices through its local policing programs, 287(g) and Secure Communities (The Case against Sheriff Arpaio 16 Dec 2011). These programs have been condemned for civil rights and liberty violations, including encouraging the use of racial profiling, pre-textual stops, and abuse of detainees (U.S. Conference of Catholic Bishops May 2011).

It could be argued that President Obama's leadership on immigration has permitted the states to act more boldly. Alabama's anti-immigrant bill is one of the harshest in the nation and has attracted multiple lawsuits and pummeled the economy (in one of the poorest states in the Union), particularly farming, after immigrant workers fled. Legal experts and civil rights advocates warned that the measure violated rights for all Alabamians, criminalized routine business transactions and acts of charity, encouraged racial profiling, and cast an unconstitutional chill on school enrollment. Governor Robert Bentley confessed that the law needed adjustment and promised that this would take place in the next legislative session (Alabama Has Second Thoughts 2011).

However, some of Alabama's politicians continue to stand firm on their law-and-order stance. Alabama House of Representatives Speaker Mike Hubbard vowed, "We're not going to repeal or weaken the law, acquiescing to liberal elites' and the news media's efforts to intimidate and shame Alabama" (Alabama Has Second Thoughts 2011). Additionally, 12 other Alabama senators asked the governor not to retreat (Alabama Has Second Thoughts 2011). Yet some states like Colorado decided not to pursue these drastic immigration laws, understanding that the cost to implement and defend against lawsuits would heavily burden the citizens of their states. Civil rights organizations agree: Cecilia Wang of the ACLU Immigrants' Rights Project said that lawsuits were expensive and time consuming, and, if given a choice, civil rights organizations preferred not to have to file suit against the states (Gomez 2011).

State-elected officials asserted that they were forced to act due to the inaction of the federal government on immigration issues. However, Obama's Department of Homeland Security, under the direction of Secretary Janet Napolitano and with the support of the White House, relied heavily on law enforcement tactics. Critics reported that the Obama administration was not deporting "the worst of the worst," as Secretary Napolitano had claimed (quoted by Downes 2014). They argued that most of the 2 million deportation cases involved those who had committed minor infractions, like traffic violations, or had no criminal record (Downes 2014). The actions of both the federal and state governments reinvigorated the anti-crime movement in the direction of detention and deportation.

Furthermore, many other elected and state government officials blame violence and the illegal drug trade on the U.S. and Mexico border for the need to enact anti-immigration legislation. Yet, a *USA Today* report found that U.S. border cities were statistically safer on average than other cities in their states (Gomez, Gillum, and Johnson 2011). The analysis found that the widely held perception of an out-of-control border region has been a factor in the failure to pass a national immigration reform law. However,

> More than a decade of detailed crime data reported by more than 1,600 local law enforcement agencies in four states, federal crime statistics and interviews along the border from California to Texas found that rates of violent crime along the U.S. Mexico border have been falling for years— even before the U.S. security buildup that has included thousands of law enforcement officers and expansion of a massive fence along the border. (Gomez, Gillum, and Johnson 2011)

USA Today reports that 83 percent of Americans believe that the rate of violence along the southwestern border is higher than national rates. This situation has fueled the stringent laws that increased federal funding for more border patrol and fence building. The negative media coverage of the Mexican border and drug violence could be the cause of the United States' inaccurate perception of the border region.

Consequently, American media outlets began to recognize the importance of certain language in coverage of the immigration issue. In December 2011 the *New York Times* decided that the term "illegals" had an "unnecessarily pejorative tone" and acknowledged its use by anti-immigration groups (Uwimana 2011). The *Associated Press Stylebook* instructs journalists not to use "illegal or illegals" and warns against excluding the word "immigrant" in the phrase. The National Association of Hispanic Journalists uses "undocumented," and the Society of Professional Journalists voted earlier to stop using the term "illegal alien" and to reevaluate "illegal immigrant." However, conservative media, including the Fox Network, continue to employ the derogatory term (Uwimana 2011).

On January 24, 2012, President Obama made his State of the Union address, concentrating on financial crimes and not on common street crime. In the 2013 State of the Union Address, the president emphasized education to help reduce violent crime. He again urged the passing of comprehensive immigration reform and tougher gun laws. He stated, "Senators of both parties are working together on tough new laws to prevent anyone from buying guns for resale to criminals. Police chiefs are asking our help to get weapons of war and massive ammunition magazines off our streets, because these police chiefs, they're tired of seeing their guys and gals being outgunned." The Court unanimously sustained the best-known part of the law, which requires state law enforcement officials to determine the immigration status of anyone they stop or arrest if there is reason to suspect that the individual might be an illegal immigrant. According to the U.S. Sentencing Commission, there were 80,035 federal criminal cases reported to the commission during 2013. Consequently, out of 71,004 cases, 22,209 (31.3 percent) involved immigration offenses. Among those immigration cases, 18,498 (83.3 percent) were illegal reentry cases, constituting 26 percent of all federal criminal cases reported to the commission. The number of illegal reentry cases increased 9.3 percent from 16,921 cases in fiscal year 2009, to 18,498 cases in fiscal year 2013. The top five districts of illegal reentry cases were located along the southwestern border of the United States (U.S. Sentencing Commission 2015).

In the 2014 State of the Union Address, President Obama reiterated: "It is time to heed the call of business leaders, labor leaders, faith leaders, law enforcement and fix our broken immigration system" (President Barack Obama 28 Jan 2014). In 2014 there were nearly 8 million unauthorized immigrants working or looking for work in the United States, which makes up about 5 percent of the civilian labor force (Passel and Cohn 2016). In 2014 President Obama offered an executive order that mirrored President George H. W. Bush's Family Fairness program. Obama's plan focused on deferred action for parents of U.S. citizens and green card holders. The Bush plan protected children on behalf of their parents, while the Obama program protected parents on behalf of their children (Lind 2014).

However, the U.S. Congress at this time is much different than in the 1990s. In 2017 Republicans challenged President Obama's executive order on immigration reform, sued the Obama administration, and threatened to shut down the government and to impeach the president over this issue (Lind 2014). Notably, other law-and-order decisions made at the top involving unauthorized immigration have had significant implications for those at the bottom. The American Immigration Council reported that for almost two decades the government had been

> pursuing an enforcement-first approach to immigration control that favors mandatory detention and deportation over the traditional discretion of a judge to consider the unique circumstances of every case. The end result has been a relentless campaign of imprisonment and expulsion aimed at noncitizens—a campaign authorized by Congress and implemented by the executive branch. While this campaign precedes the Obama administration by many years, it has grown immensely during his tenure in the White House. (2014)

Under the Obama administration's implementation of the Secure Communities and the Criminal Alien programs, thousands of immigrants and their families have been funneled into detention centers. Therefore, the "drastic expansion of mandatory detention combined with a skyrocketing detention budget has created a sprawling and unaccountable system of mass detention," with a daily population of over 34,000 in 2014 (Shah, Small, and Wu 2015).

In November 2014, under pressure from the Latino community, President Obama issued a series of executive orders to temporarily delay deportation for up to 5 million people who came to the United States illegally. He demonstrated presidential leadership by announcing: "There are actions I have the legal authority to take as president—the same kinds of actions taken by Democratic and Republican presidents before me—that will help make our immigration system more fair and more just" (Debate Club 2014). Democrats who supported the president reiterated that he was within the bounds of constitutional executive power. Senate Majority Leader Harry Reid said: "President Obama is doing what he can within his well-established constitutional authority." House Minority Leader Nancy Pelosi stated: "The president's actions fall well within the clear constitutional and legal authority of his office, and the well-established precedent set by every president since Eisenhower." Former President Bill Clinton even added: "Every president in the modern era has issued some executive action on immigration. So I imagine he'll be on pretty firm legal ground" (Debate Club 2014).

Moreover, Marshall Fitz, director of immigration policy at the Center for American Progress, championed President Obama's actions and wrote that he was simply doing his job, because Republicans had blocked immigration reforms for over 10 years. He asserted that the congressional failure had resulted in "an increasingly harsh and dysfunctional immigration system that destabilizes families and communities and undermines the nation's economic and security interests" (Fitz 2014). Fitz acknowledged that only

Congress could reform the flawed system but that the president was taking a commonsense approach that was completely within his executive authority to make the process more "rational, more efficient and more humane" (Fitz 2014). Fitz emphasized that the president's actions were "grounded in ample historical precedent—similar policies have been adopted 39 times by 11 presidents over 60 years" (2014).

However, in December 2014, 24 states signed onto the legal challenge against President Barack Obama over his executive action on immigration (Killough 2014). The political right denounced President Obama's executive action as an abuse of power befitting of a "monarch or an emperor" (Savage 2014). Ilya Shapiro, of the libertarian Cato Institute, claimed that the immigration order was the "starkest example" of what he called the president's "pattern of lawlessness" (Savage 2014). On June 23, 2016, the U.S. Supreme Court, in a 4-4 decision, let the lower court of appeal decision stand that found the president's executive order to be unconstitutional (Liptak and Shear 2016).

For President Barack Obama, immigration was the issue that maintained the march to law and order, with a 2011 price tag of $19.8 billion down from $20.5 billion in 2010 (McNeill 2010). This remains an expensive public policy that has expanded government power. In 2013 the U.S. government spent $106 billion on border surveillance (quoted by Silva 2016, 64). In 2015 the Immigration and Customs Enforcement (ICE) budget request was for $5.36 billion, a reduction of $255.3 million, or 4.8 percent, below 2014 (Appropriations Committee Democrats 13 Mar 2014). Anti-immigration and conservative groups claim that the Obama administration has underfunded immigration enforcement and border security. Yet immigration offenses made Latinos the new majority in federal prisons, at 50.3 percent of persons sentenced. Illegal border crossing and alien smuggling have contributed to the increase, with huge implications for Latinos who are incarcerated for nonviolent offenses. Being in the United States without legal status is a civil violation, not a crime (Preston 2011).

According to the Migration Policy Institute, the U.S. immigration system is "marked by an intense focus on national security and border control" resulting in an "immigration machinery" (Mittelstadt et al. 2011). With approximately 400,000 undocumented persons detained or deported, the U.S. Department of Homeland Security is the new apparatus for the call for law and order. The United States has deported more immigrants under Obama's leadership than any other president in history, approximately one-fourth more than President George W. Bush. Sadly, leading migrant rights activists have labeled him the "Deporter in Chief" (Norton 2016).

In 2014 the Supreme Court held that President Obama had exceeded his power when he made temporary recess appointments during a Senate break. Chief Justice John Roberts, a George W. Bush appointee, and Justice Antonin

Scalia wrote in separate opinions that "all presidents have a high interest in expanding the powers of their office," and it is the high court's duty to keep them in check (Savage 2014). However, in 2012 Chief Justice Roberts made a surprising move when he joined the liberal justices on upholding the constitutionality of President Obama's highly controversial Patient Protection and Affordable Care Act. Justices Antonin Scalia, Anthony M. Kennedy, Clarence Thomas, and Samuel A. Alito ruled to entirely strike down the law.

Then in 2015 Chief Justice Roberts went against his conservative justices, backing President Obama's health care law in *King vs. Burwell*. Roberts stated that Congress passed the law to improve health care and that unraveling the system could "well push some states into a 'death spiral' as the health care industry had argued" (De Vogue 2015). In the same year, in the Hobby Lobby case with a 5-4 majority ruling that included the chief justice, the Court ruled that the Obama administration had overasserted its power in requiring Christian businesses to pay for female employees' contraceptives.

Accordingly, Obama's losing streak is part of a Supreme Court trend that began with Bill Clinton, with the Court siding with him 63 percent of the time and President George W. Bush on the winning side only 60 percent of the time (Liptak 2017). Arguably, presidential power is being displaced with judicial authority and capacity. This is interesting, since the framers of the U.S. Constitution believe the judicial branch should be the least dangerous branch of government.

President Obama supported the Supreme Court's decision on the constitutionality of affirmative action but was critical of the lack of a ruling on immigration reform. He stated: "For more than two decades now, our immigration system, everybody acknowledges, has been broken. And the fact that the Supreme Court wasn't able to issue a decision today doesn't just set the system back even further, it takes us further from the country that we aspire to be" (White House 2016). The unaddressed issue of immigration reform dates back to the Johnson administration and remains a national problem that many presidents and congresses have been unable to resolve. In 2009 the Southern Poverty Law Center released a report claiming that three Washington, D.C., organizations were the main opposition to comprehensive immigration reform. The report described a network of anti-immigration groups created by the white nationalist movement leader John Tanton. The report described the Federation for American Immigration Reform (FAIR), the Center for Immigration Studies (CIS), and NumbersUSA as being funded by John Tanton. The report claimed that Tanton associated with Holocaust deniers, white nationalist intellectuals, and Klan lawyers (Potok 2009). These grassroots anti-immigration organizations continue to advocate strong law enforcement measures to curb the flow of immigration. The Justice Department and Hispanic groups were also alarmed with the humanitarian concerns that enforcing harsh state laws created.

Although FAIR was designated as a hate group by the Southern Poverty Law Center in 2007, they testify frequently before Congress. FAIR boasts that it "has been called to testify on immigration bills before Congress more than any organization in America" (Anti-Defamation League 2010). According to their website, FAIR is a national nonprofit, public-interest membership organization of concerned citizens who believe that the nation's immigration policies must be reformed. The group seeks to improve border security, to stop illegal immigration, and to promote immigration levels of about 300,000 a year. They claim more than 250,000 members and supporters nationwide. FAIR's grassroots networks encourage the public to help convince Congress that U.S. immigration must be reduced. FAIR has a government relations team that concentrates on congressional committee hearings, executive orders and administrative rules, court decisions, and state actions (FAIR 2011).

Another anti-immigration group, CIS, an "independent" scholarly think tank, began its life as a FAIR program. As an organization, CIS strongly opposes the U.S. Visa Waiver Program (VWP). In December 2011 the House Subcommittee on Immigration Policy and Enforcement held a hearing to discuss the risks and benefits associated with the VWP. The VWP allows visitors from 36 countries meeting certain criteria to come and stay in the United States for tourist or business purposes for up to 90 days without obtaining a visa. During the hearing, Richard Stana, director of Homeland Security and Justice Issues for the Government Accountability Office (GAO), discussed the numerous persistent problems with the program (FAIR 2011).

Agreeing with the State Department and Homeland Security's concerns, Jessica Vaughan, director of policy at CIS, argued that overstayers of the VWP represent approximately 4 to 6 million people within the "illegal alien" population. "A few have become terrorists, some commit crimes, but in general they're costly to taxpayers. . . . between $3 billion and $5 billion every year," claimed Ms. Vaughan (FAIR 2011). She advocated for increased interior immigration law enforcement prior to any expansion of the VWP and exclaimed, "There are 2 million, roughly, criminal aliens living here [and] . . . about 7 million illegal aliens working here in jobs that we need for Americans and legal immigrants. . . . expanding the VWP too fast or irresponsibly is going to make it that much harder for ICE and the price will be paid by Americans" (FAIR 2011). Groups similar to CIS clearly believe that immigration threatens their notion of what the United States should look like.

The third significant anti-immigration group is NumbersUSA. Executive Director Roy Beck is described by Tanton as his "heir apparent" (Potok 2011). He also edited the *Immigration Invasion*, a book by Tanton and a colleague that Canadian border authorities have banned as anti-immigrant hate literature (Potok 2009). NumbersUSA reports that "illegal aliens" enter the United States in two distinct ways—approximately 60 percent cross a border illegally, with the remaining 40 percent overstaying their legal visa. Beck argues, "The chief difficulties that America faces because of current immigration are not triggered by who the immigrants are but by how many they are" (Novak 2011). The group encourages their supporters to rely on their website to "influence Congress to turn away from immigration policies," which cause "a more and more congested and regimented future for our country, our children, and our grandchildren" (Novak 2011).

However, there were Hispanic groups and other organizations that actively advocated for more immigrant-friendly solutions to immigration reform. According to the National Council of La Raza (NCLR), the current U.S. immigration system is in need of fundamental reform. NCLR is the largest national Hispanic civil rights and advocacy organization in the United States and works to improve opportunities for Hispanic Americans. In order to try to halt the march to law and order and harsh anti-immigrant sentiment and legislations, NCLR made four comprehensive immigration-reform principles. Their first principle is to develop effective enforcement policies that uphold security and the Constitution by allowing 12 million undocumented people to come forward, obtain legal status, learn English, and assume the rights and responsibilities of citizenship. The second principle is cracking down on any employer whose practices undermine conditions for all workers. The third principle is unclogging legal channels to reunite families and to offer future workers the essential rights and protections that safeguard our workforce. And the fourth principle is enacting proactive measures to advance the successful integration of new immigrants into our communities (National Council of La Raza 2011).

Furthermore, Hispanic immigrants have many other organizations supporting their cause. For example, over 39 groups and corporations gave over a million dollars in contributions to the U.S. Senate in support of the Development, Relief, and Education for Alien Minors Act of 2009, or the Dream Act (MapLight, accessed 18 Dec 2011). The Dream Act was a congressional bill that provided a path to citizenship to young migrants, or "dreamers," who came to the United States as children, completed two years of college or military service, and met other requirements, including passing a criminal background check.

With a 55 to 41 vote in favor of the bill, the anti-immigration opposition killed the Dream Act. It needed the support of 60 senators to cut off a filibuster and bring it to the floor. Senator Jeff Sessions (R-AL) led the mostly Republican opposition as the senior Republican on the Judiciary Committee. He claimed the "bill is a law that at its fundamental core is a reward for illegal activity." Roy Beck, president of NumbersUSA, who lobbied extensively against the act, exclaimed that the new Tea Party Congress "has the strongest pro-enforcement membership" in at least 15 years. "Now, we look forward to moving aggressively to offense" (Herszenhor 2010). In this battle to give young immigrants a legitimate path to citizenship instead of deportation, detainment, or incarceration, the law-and-order forces won the day.

From reforming drug sentencing to commutations, President Obama has altered the prison landscape. The president commuted terms for 1,176 people that included 395 who were serving life sentences for mostly drug offenses. He also pardoned 148 other crimes, ranging from felony firearm possession to involuntary manslaughter (Gillin 2017). As late as 2015, the Obama administration at a White House summit was encouraged to apply lessons learned from the War on Gangs to the War on Terror. Revision of strategies centered on law enforcement agencies adopting "community policing" policies instead of trying to "arrest their way" out of the problems of gang violence or terrorism (Rhodan 2015). Over the years, the notion that community policing would reduce incarceration has been supported but, unfortunately, not widely implemented by law enforcement. President Obama demonstrated more smart-on-crime policies. However, the cycle of the race to incarcerate is difficult to break.

In an open letter published in the *Washington Post* to Congress and the president, *New York Times* author Don Winslow explains how "decades of failed policies have fueled widespread violence and filled our prisons with non-violent and disproportionately black drug offenders" (Winslow 2015). Winslow claims that the U.S. drug war has increased militarization of U.S. police with dire consequences. He writes: "Police departments have become occupying armies," and asserts that a direct line can be drawn between the "War on Drugs and the recent events in Ferguson, Cleveland, Baltimore and elsewhere" (Winslow 2015).

In response to the shooting of an unarmed black suspect, Michael Brown, which took place in Missouri, SWAT teams wearing war-type uniforms were called in to clear the city's protestors from in front of the Ferguson police department (J.F. 2015). The American Civil Liberties Union (ACLU) monitors police militarization and has noticed a "more martial tone" in their recruitment and training materials (Dansky 2014). Other critics have argued that it is time to demilitarize U.S. police forces, but no legislation is in sight. Finally in 2015 President Obama issued an executive order to stem the flow of military equipment to U.S. law enforcement. Nevertheless, under the leadership of many of our presidents, the call for law and order has certainly aided how U.S. law enforcement agencies have become so heavily armed and perform more like soldiers than civilian cops.

Winslow writes that the War on Drug on the Mexican border is responsible for inappropriate law enforcement activity. He declares that police brutality and excessive force is a major issue for the U.S. Justice Department and local law enforcement agencies. Winslow writes: "A half-century of failed policy, one trillion dollars and forty-five million arrests has not reduced daily drug use—at all. . . . The U.S. still leads the world in illegal drug consumption, drugs are cheaper, more available, and more potent than ever before. . . . The answer is legalization" (2015). Winslow argues that every dollar the United States spends on prohibiting drugs raises the Mexican cartels' profits and makes them more powerful.

On January 20, 2015, President Obama delivered his Address before a Joint Session of the Congress on the State of the Union and stated, "And surely we can agree that it's a good thing that for the first time in 40 years, the crime rate and the incarceration rate have come down together, and use that as a starting point for Democrats and Republicans, community leaders and law enforcement, to reform America's criminal justice system so that it protects and serves all of us" (President Barack Obama 20 Jan 2015). Criminal justice reform is a complicated matter for election-seeking politicians. Opponents will use the soft-on-crime argument, which remains popular with conservatives. President Obama showed restrained leadership in even bringing up the issues. Due to the high financial and social cost of imprisonment, the president did have some bipartisan support in Congress and in some states for criminal justice reform. He called for a sweeping bipartisan effort to fix what Attorney General Eric Holder had called a "broken system" that "locked up too many Americans for too long, especially a whole generation of young black and Hispanic men" (Baker 2015). In 2015 there was a declining trend in the numbers.

According to the Bureau of Justice Statistics, the total number of prisoners under state and federal correctional authorities on December 31, 2015 (1,526,800) decreased by 35,500 (down more than 2 percent) from year-end 2014. The federal prison population decreased by 14,100 prisoners from 2014 to 2015 and was down almost 7 percent. This accounts for 40 percent of the total change in the U.S. prison population. The imprisonment rate decreased 3 percent, from 471 prisoners per 100,000 U.S. residents of all ages in 2014 to 458 prisoners per 100,000 in 2015 (Carson and Anderson 2016). Smart-on-crime policies should reduce the effects of mass incarceration.

On January 12, 2016, President Obama delivered his Address before a Joint Session of the Congress on the State of the Union and continued to argue for criminal justice reform. He stated, "So I hope we can work together this year on some bipartisan priorities like criminal justice reform and helping people who are battling prescription drug abuse and heroin abuse" (President Barack Obama 12 Jan 2016). The president had also sought to make it less difficult for offenders to reenter society after prison. He supported efforts to "ban the box" that asked job applicants about their past convictions and encouraged restoring the right to vote for those who serve their sentences (Baker 2015). On July 28, 2016, in his efforts to reform the criminal justice system, President Obama commuted the prison sentences of 61 drug offenders, including more than a third serving life sentences (Lederman 2016). This was a meaningful and concrete show of presidential leadership.

On August 18, 2016, U.S. Deputy Attorney General Sally Yates announced that the Obama Justice Departments would end the use of private prisons after concluding that private prisons were less safe and less effective than government-run facilities (Zapotosky and Harlan 2016). In 2016 the Obama administration instructed federal officials to reduce reliance on private prisons, declaring that they were dangerous, expensive, and did not reduce recidivism. The U.S. over-incarceration boom has resulted in billions of dollars for prison corporations, plus millions in subsidies from the federal government to many communities across the nation that are willing to have prisons in their areas (Merritt 2008). President Obama's actions were an attempt to shift away from utilizing private prisons and the social costs and financial nightmare surrounding this public policy.

For the private for-profit prison industry, however, the detention of undocumented immigrants has been a "financial boom" niche business (Silva 2016). While President Obama's Justice Department decided to phase out the use of private prisons, U.S. detention facilities are still holding illegal immigrants. These facilities are under the jurisdiction of the Department of Homeland Security. In December 2016, 73 percent of immigration detainees were still being held in private prisons, with only 10 percent in government-run facilities. The remaining are in cells in state and local prisons (Cohen 2017). The for-profit prison and detainee industry that has been forecast under the Trump administration will be addressed in the next chapter.

While less reliance on private prisons by the Obama administration was a step in the right direction, critics have charged for years that meaningful criminal justice reform is desperately needed but Congress has failed to act on most reform proposals. To make the penal system less punitive, policies—such as changes to federal and state sentencing guidelines, more benevolent pre-trial bargaining by prosecutors of low-level offenders, increased probation instead of serving time, and a more sensible application of bail practices—would do more to reduce mass incarceration (Lantigua-Williams 2016). The executive director of the Sentencing Project, Marc Mauer, blames the "unprecedented growth" of incarceration in the federal system on the privatization of prisons and jails and asserts that their use is "a stain on our democracy" (quoted by Lantigua-Williams 2016). As we have learned, this is especially true for blacks, Hispanics, and the poor. To halt U.S. mass incarceration, the United States needs to do more than just severing the Justice Department's relationship with the prison industrial complex.

Very few U.S. presidents have had the foresight or courage to acknowledge the rights of prisoners or to call for lighter sentences for nonviolent offenders. However, with $80 billion being spent yearly on mass incarceration, some on the left and right feel politically safe enough to approach the issues. Toward the end of his presidency, Barack Obama surely did.

CHAPTER TEN

President Trump: Law and Order, Politics of Fear, Alternative Facts, and the Rule of Law

President Donald Trump and his administration have embraced traditional law-and-order and War on Terror strategies. This includes populist rhetoric, strict enforcement of immigration laws, reducing legal immigration, only accepting higher skilled immigrant applications, and promoting economic nationalism by protecting U.S. business interests and investment (McKelvey 2017). On social issues Trump has made it clear that his administration will side with corporations against ecology interests and will expand the military industry complex. Most important for the purposes of this book, he is in favor of greater support for law enforcement that will intensify the prison industrial complex's mass incarceration crisis. During Trump's acceptance speech at the Republican National Convention, he used "law and order" four times: "I am the law and order candidate," "I will restore law and order in our country," "we will also be a country of law and order," and "There can be no prosperity without law and order" (Bump and Blake 2016). There is no doubt that President Trump will try to be the ultimate law-and-order leader.

President Donald Trump's law-and-order leadership is hard to reconcile with all the accusations that he is facing. With his wealth and business entanglements, it is feared that the president's decision-making will be threatened by his own corporate self-interests. Citizens for Responsibility and Ethics in Washington (CREW) is critical of him for not selling his troublesome conflict of interest businesses. They have filed suit, claiming that Trump's corporate interests violate the Emoluments Clause of the Constitution, which makes it illegal for government officials to "accept of any present, Emolument, Office, or Title, of any kind whatever, from any King, Prince, or foreign State." CREW has also filed another complaint with the General Services Administration accusing Trump of violating the lease on his Washington, D.C. hotel. This states that no U.S. government elected official "shall be admitted to any share or part of this Lease, or to any benefit that may arise therefrom." Adding to the controversy, Jeremy Venook of the *Atlantic* found over 30 business conflicts that could influence President Trump's official decision-making capability (2017).

Walter Shaub, director of the Office of Government Ethics, declared that Trump needed to sell off these questionable assets, stating: "I don't think divestiture is too high of a price to pay to be the president of the United States" (Carney 2017). Senator Elizabeth Warren and 30 other House and Senate Democrats also introduced legislation that would require President Trump and Vice President Pence to untangle themselves from any financial assets that pose a conflict of interest and place the money into a blind trust (Carney 2017). However, with a majority of Republicans in both Houses, this Democratic measure has no chance of passing.

During the campaign Donald Trump ran into trouble with his sexist and inappropriate treatment of women, which may fall under the Equal Employment Opportunity Commission's (EEOC) sexual harassment or gender discrimination guidelines. A *New York Times* article featured 50 interviews with people who witnessed Trump's inappropriate behavior with women over the course of decades (Barbaro and Twohey 2016). These women "reveal unwelcome romantic advances, unending commentary on the female form, and unsettling workplace conduct" that took place in "offices at Trump Tower, at his homes, at construction sites and backstage at beauty pageants" (Barbaro and Twohey 2016). In defending himself, Trump disputed many of the details and said he was a champion of women, took pride in hiring them, and was in awe of their work ethic. He also stated: "I have always treated women with great respect. And women will tell you that" (Barbaro and Twohey 2016). Yet Trump publically criticized candidate Carly Fiorina's face, attacked Megyn Kelly of Fox News, and claimed that Secretary of State Hillary Clinton was only getting votes because she was a woman (Timm 2016).

Furthermore, during his electoral campaign, President Donald Trump exploited race and intensified white anxieties. This is a harmful political strategy that has been used throughout American history by others, including Governor of Alabama George Wallace. In his 1968 presidential campaign, Wallace invoked law and order to attract dissatisfied whites who were angry over civil rights and urban unrest (Parton 2016). In 1988 the Willie

Horton incident was exploited by President George H. W. Bush. Likewise, Donald Trump portrayed himself as an "old school law and order" man and used racial rhetoric to cast fear, suspicion, and blame (Parton 2016).

Accordingly, some find that fear played a major role in the election of President Trump. Molly Ball of the *Atlantic* suggested that "Trump is a master of fear, invoking it in concrete and abstract ways, summoning and validating it. More than most politicians, he grasps and channels the fear coursing through the electorate" (2017). Though crime rates are down, President Trump's ominous inaugural speech was a "dark, counterfactual picture of 'American carnage': an economy in decline, communities under siege by 'the crime and the gangs and the drugs'" (quoted by MacDonald 2017). This is an example of the Trump administration's continued use of "alternative facts" instead of actuality. Malaika Jabali reported that President Trump's dark misrepresentation of "dangerous generalizations and falsehoods about crime can potentially cause damage to the entire Black community" (2017).

In February 2017 Trump falsely stated: "The murder rate in our country is the highest it's been in 47 years, right?" (Jackman 2017). This is one of Trump's "alternative facts," which is untrue, as the murder rate is comparatively down. In 2015 the murder rate was among the lowest in half a century, with 4.9 murders per 100,000 people, significantly lower from the rates in the 1970s, 1980s, and most of the 1990s (*Chicago Tribune* 2017). President Trump supports reimplementing unconstitutional stop-and-frisk procedures that allow unwarranted police searches, mostly of African Americans and Latinos. He has also declared that too much scrutiny of law enforcement is a "war on police" (Craven 2017). His distortion oversimplifies U.S. inner city crime, and Trump's solution is to expand the police state, which targets minorities.

Trump's strategy has been compared to President Richard Nixon's leadership in calling for law and order during his successful run for president. Presidential leadership matters. During Nixon's drug war, the Drug Enforcement Agency (DEA) was established through the FBI's Counter Intelligence Program. Accusations surfaced that the DEA targeted blacks, with incarceration rates increasing significantly. In 2016 Nixon's domestic policy adviser John Ehrlichman confessed during an interview that the Nixon 1968 campaign and White House

> had two enemies the antiwar left and black people . . .We knew we couldn't make it illegal to be either against the war or black, but by getting the public to associate the hippies with marijuana and blacks with heroin, and then criminalizing both heavily, we could disrupt those communities. We could arrest their leaders, raid their homes, break up their meetings, and vilify them night after night on the evening news. Did we know we were lying about the drugs? Of course we did. (Jabali 2017)

Similar to Nixon's targeting of minority populations, Trump has declared that the United States suffers from American "carnage." He references "the crime and the gangs and the drugs that have stolen too many lives and robbed our country of so much unrealized potential" (Rucker, Wagner, and Fahrenthold 2017). This nonexistent claim of carnage can lead to more civil rights suppression and oppression of minorities who are portrayed as criminals. Trump's promise to save the nation from nonexistent high crime rates is an example of his use of "alternative facts" propaganda.

Not surprisingly, Trump supporters are disproportionately fearful of crime and terror and are more leery of foreign influence and social change. This fear leads them to look for reassurance, protection, and comfort through Trump's tough and strong promises. A Gallup poll found that the fear of crime and violence was at a 15-year high in 2016, with 53 percent worried "a great deal" about crime compared to 39 percent in 2014. Also 44 percent were concerned about drug use, and this was a significant increase since 2014. Concerns about crime and violence are similar across party lines, but Democrats have worried less than Republicans and Independents since 2014 (Davis 2016). Rick Wilson, a Florida-based Republican media strategist and opinion writer, argues that candidate Trump successfully manipulated the fear of the other—"Fear of Mexicans, fear of the Chinese, fear of African Americans" (plus being anti-Muslim) and made this the centerpiece of his campaign (quoted Ball 2017). The Southern Poverty Law Center reports an increase in hate crimes targeting Muslims and other minorities (Potok 2017)[0].

Since President Trump's election, white supremacist websites and anti-Semitism traffic has spiked. This could have been predicted with his appointments of Steven Bannon, who has been criticized by many civil rights groups as being nationalistic, anti-Semitic, and misogynous, and Stephen Miller, who was communication director for controversial Alabama Senator Jeff Sessions (DeVega 2017). Another fear tactic is that the White House webpage targeted protesters and any resistance after President Trump's inauguration. Entitled, "Standing up for Our Law Enforcement Community," it stated: "Our job is not to make life more comfortable for the rioter, the looter, or the violent disrupter" (Sanburg 2017). Trump's law-and-order platform is hostile to racial justice concerns. Republicans in 11 states, including Minnesota, Washington, Iowa, Michigan, North Dakota, Indiana, Virginia, Colorado, Missouri, North Carolina, and Arizona, proposed or threatened laws making it unsafe and costly to attend protests. In spite of our constitutional right to protest, Republicans are proposing legislation that would levy drastic penalties for those who organize or participate and expand law enforcement powers to jail demonstrators and to seize assets (Bouie 2017).

On April 10, 2017, President Trump's conservative nominee Judge Neil Gorsuch was sworn in as associate justice of the Supreme Court. Justice Gorsuch was confirmed by a 54-to-45 vote, the closest margin since Justice

Thomas was confirmed over 25 years ago. Controlled by a Republican majority, the U.S. Senate did away with the filibuster in order to gain Gorsuch's appointment. Democrats consider this appointment a "stolen" seat because Republicans refused to allow President Barack Obama's nominee moderate Judge Merrick Garland a Judiciary Committee hearing (Barnes and Parker 2017). In Arkansas's first lethal injection execution since 2005, Justice Gorsuch cast his vote with the other four conservative justices, denying a stay of execution (Barnes 2017).

The most contentious aspect of Donald Trump's presidency is his appointment of the extreme law-and-order Alabama Senator Jefferson Beauregard Sessions as U.S. Attorney General. Jeff Session is a "lock 'em up and throw away the key" politician like President Richard Nixon who decided "that one way to deal with 'the racial problem' was to throw as many black Americans as he could into jail on drug charges" (Shriver 2017). We know that as more prosecutions were sought with longer and harsher sentences, the prison population increased dramatically. Then, under President Ronald Reagan's War on Drugs leadership, Congress abolished parole and the U.S. prison population continued to swell. This counterproductive public policy continues to exist. Presently, more than half of federal prisoners are doing time for drug crimes.

It is predicted that if President Donald Trump and his attorney general Jeff Sessions are successful, there are more incarcerations to come (Shriver 2017). Consequently, while many state and federal lawmakers as well as criminal justice interest groups are trying to reduce the price tag of over-imprisonment, the Trump administration led by Sessions is headed in the opposite direction. In February 2017, contrary to a bipartisan effort to diminish the harmful outcomes of mass incarceration, the newly appointed Attorney General Sessions rescinded President Obama's order to do away with for-profit private prisons holding federal inmates. This irresponsible decision reversed former Deputy Attorney General Sally Yates's August 2016 order that eliminated the Justice Department's use of for-profit private prisons that hold over 10 percent of the prison population (Wilber 2017).

In May 2017 Attorney General Jeff Sessions attempted to force federal prosecutors to pursue the toughest sentence for drug crimes, such as the discredited mandatory minimum sentences. Several Republicans have spoken out against Sessions's latest move, including GOP Senator Mike Lee, who tweeted, "To be tough on crime we have to be smart on crime . . . That is why criminal justice reform is a conservative issue." Moreover, Senator Rand Paul added: "Mandatory minimum sentences have unfairly and disproportionately incarcerated too many minorities for too long" (Laslo 2017). He told *Rolling Stone*: "Attorney General Sessions' new policy will accentuate that injustice. Instead, we should treat our nation's drug epidemic as a health crisis and less as a 'lock 'em up and throw away the key' problem" (Laslo 2017).

Furthermore, U.S. Representative Bobby Scott is revamping his efforts to reform the criminal justice system. In 2007 Scott first introduced his Youth Promise Act, designed to reduce youth violence and delinquency. In response to Sessions's recent draconian and outdated policy proposals, Scott stated, "The question is: Is the purpose of your crime policy to reduce crime and save money?—which we know how to do—or to codify simpleminded slogans and soundbites for political consumption?" (Laslo 2017). In regard to the attorney general's policy to reinstate mandatory minimums, Scott wisely claimed, "If you're trying to reduce crime and save money, it doesn't work. If you're trying to bamboozle the public, it does work" (Laslo 2017). Rep. Scott is trying to solve the mass incarceration crisis, not make it worse, like Sessions seeks to do.

According to the Brenner Center's analysis of Sessions's record, he blocked the Sentencing Reform and Corrections Act. Sessions also opposes efforts to reduce lengthy federal prison sentences for nonviolent crimes and could delay present congressional efforts to pass this legislation to reform archaic federal sentencing laws. While Sessions was U.S. attorney for the Southern District of Alabama, drug convictions made up 40 percent of his convictions, twice the rate of other Alabama federal prosecutors. Current law enforcement trends focus on violent crime and away from outdated drug war policies. But Sessions opposes all attempts to modernize criminal justice policies, such as decriminalizing marijuana and reduction in drug sentences. It is expected that he will pursue the harshest penalties possible for even low-level drug offenses.

Because of Donald Trump's flawed presidential leadership in appointing Sessions, obsolete ideas that even many conservatives and law enforcement agree do not help reduce crime will continue to affect criminal justice policy negatively. In spite of many Republicans supporting reentry programs to help former inmates better reintegrate into society, it is doubtful that Sessions will support recidivism reduction programs.

According to the Pew Research Center, federal criminal prosecutions had declined for five consecutive years and are currently at their lowest level in nearly two decades. The FBI's Crime Statistics report also showed that crime rates remain at historic lows and that violent crime is 16.5 percent lower than a decade ago. However, law-and-order Attorney General Jeff Sessions indicates that the Justice Department will seek more criminal prosecutions and reverse the trend (Gramlich 2017b). Under Trump's Justice Department, it is indicated that there will be a significant departure from an aggressive Obama Civil Rights Division, which investigated police misconduct and sought institutional law enforcement reform and accountability (Johnson 2016).

Many who support trying to enact smart-on-crime policies are concerned about the damage Trump and Sessions will do to the movement to reduce imprisonment. The director of the American Civil Liberties Union's (ACLU)

National Prison Project, David C. Fathi, issued the following statement: "Handing control of prisons over to for-profit companies is a recipe for abuse and neglect. The memo from Attorney General Sessions ignores this fact. Additionally, this memo is a further sign that under President Trump and Attorney General Sessions, the United States may be headed for a new federal prison boom, fueled in part by criminal prosecutions of immigrants for entering the country" (2017). Not surprisingly, the Trump super PAC received "hundreds of thousands of dollars" in campaign contributions from the for-profit private prison companies (ACLU 2017b). So far, President Trump has issued executive orders that will increase prosecutions of immigrants and has supported legislation that would impose harsher new mandatory minimum sentences for prosecutions. Going back to the over-sentencing of the War on Drugs, he has called for a return to these draconian sentences for most drug offenders and aggressive prosecutions of drug traffickers.

Trying to demonstrate strong law-and-order leadership, President Trump told the Major Cities Chiefs Association: "We're going to stop the drugs from pouring in . . . We're going to stop those drugs from poisoning our youth, from poisoning our people. We're going to be ruthless in that fight. We have no choice. And we're going to take that fight to the drug cartels and work to liberate our communities from their terrible grip of violence" (Smith 2017). During the campaign, Trump promoted more drug treatment for users and more access to overdose reversal drugs. However, his executive orders, which are intended to restore safety to the United States, are authoritarian responses to drugs, crime, and protest (Smith 2017).

In 2017, the U.S. Bureau of Prisons had a population of 190,000 federal inmates, with 21,000 housed in private for-profit prisons. Attorney General Sessions is ignoring the mass incarceration crisis. Wade Henderson of the Leadership Conference on Civil and Human Rights declared that relying on private prisons is "neither humane nor Budget conscious and that . . . We need a justice system that can work better for all people" (Wilber 2017). However, the Trump administration is disregarding the human toll that over-imprisonment is having on America.

Moreover, Assistant Attorney General Sally Yates's order did not affect detention of unauthorized immigrants and will not affect detained people in the country illegally. The use of private prisons is expected to surge under President Trump's promised crackdown on illegal immigration and his propensity to gain profit. His grim "factually false" vision blames immigrants as the source of "violence in our streets and the chaos in our communities" and claims that "Abroad, America is a disrespected, humiliated nation" (Editorial Board 2016). Trump signed an executive order calling for expansion of detention facilities and authorized the use of private contractors "to construct, operate, or control facilities" (Wilber 2017). His tough talk about detaining and deporting illegal immigrants and on increasing prosecutions is good news for the prison industry complex (Cohen 2017). Stocks in private prison companies have jumped on Wall Street since Trump won the presidential election and continue to rise due to Attorney General Sessions's law-and-order criminal justice mentality.

Still, there was a ray of hope as Vice President–elect Mike Pence, in one of the debates with Senator Tim Kaine, reiterated his support to divert nonviolent offenders from prison and provide treatment to addicted and mentally ill offenders as he did as governor of Indiana. Pence stated: "We have got to do a better job recognizing and correcting the errors in the system that do reflect on institutional bias in criminal justice" (Johnson 2016). Vice President Pence has actual experience with the criminal justice system at the state level, which the inexperienced President Trump does not.

Consequently, prison-reduction groups are uniting against Trump's hardline stance on crime. The Law Enforcement Leaders to Reduce Incarceration, a group of almost 200 law enforcement veterans, have criticized President Donald Trump's approach to public safety. They believe that his law-and-order policies, which focus on Jeff Sessions's arrest and prison philosophy, are harmful and will cause "more dangerous communities and a waste of federal resources" (Abadi 2017). These community leaders emphasized trying to build community relations by keeping offenders out of jail and by offering more treatment for the mentally ill. Co-chairmen Ronal Serpas and David Brown, former police chiefs in Nashville, New Orleans, and Dallas, provided a 28-page agenda to the Trump administration. The report began with the declaration: "Today's crime policies, which too often rely only on jail and prison, are simply ineffective in preserving public safety" (Abadi 2017). This group suggested that "arrest, conviction, prison should not be the result of every broken law" (Abadi 2017). Their alternatives to reduce the bloated criminal justice system include "directing mentally ill inmates toward health facilities and expanding the use of halfway homes that offer transitional support to inmates integrating back into society" (Abadi 2017). However, neither President Trump nor Attorney General Session seemed interested in expert advice.

Another interest group, Right on Crime, is made up of conservatives from the Texas Public Policy Foundation in cooperation with the American Conservative Union Foundation and the Prison Fellowship. Their mission is to use "limited resources in both the law enforcement and corrections systems to maximize further reductions in the crime rate for every taxpayer dollar spent" (Right on Crime n.d.). This group seeks to reduce excessive sentence lengths and to punish nonviolent offenders through prison alternatives. One of their central issues, along with over-criminalization, is to reduce the use of prison time for nonviolent drug-related offenses.

There are other smart-on-crime reform efforts, such as the ACLU's Campaign for Smart Justice. The ACLU warns that the 3,000 prosecutors throughout the United States are some of the most powerful but not accountable, least transparent, and unchecked criminal justice actors who can abuse power. Although prosecutors have the mandate to seek justice, many district attorneys focus on severe punishment, which has helped foster mass incarceration. According to the ACLU, President Trump and Attorney Jeff Sessions have threatened aggressive but unnecessary prosecutorial power toward people of color and the poor. The ACLU is claiming to work toward elevating and empowering a "new generation of prosecutors committed to reducing incarceration" by trying to reform "unjust federal initiatives and build a smarter and fairer criminal justice system" to reduce mass imprisonment (ACLU 2017d).

Another threat to increasing the U.S. penal crisis is President Trump's vow to build a wall on the U.S. border with Mexico, and his attempts to bar refugees speaks to a culture of fear. Many believe that Trump represents a "primal scream of white resentment, and the alarming thing is that so many are in favor of the scream" (Weinberger 2016). In 2016, along with having the world's largest prison system, the U.S. Immigration and Customs Enforcement (ICE) agency, under the U.S. Department of Homeland Security, maintains the world's largest immigration detention system. With Trump's anti-migrant threats, we can only expect more arrests and detention of unauthorized people, which will drive continued expansion of the Executive Branch's "sprawling system of unaccountable incarceration" (Shah, Small, and Wu 2015).

In addition, President Trump has made unsubstantiated claims that unauthorized immigrants are flooding our shores with crime. He has repeatedly stated "alternative facts"—that undocumented immigrants are causing crime waves and draining social service resources. The real facts are that since 2008 there has been a steady decline in immigrants. Immigrant crime rates are also lower than U.S. citizen crime rates, and most of the unauthorized population has no access to most social welfare programs (Chomsky and Dispatch 2017). In January 2017 President Donald Trump issued executive orders that will expand mass incarceration of unauthorized immigrants. The Border Security and Immigration Enforcement Improvements initiative includes the provision to build a wall on the U.S. and Mexico border. It also has a section to increase the federal government's capacity to detain immigrants, which provides greater growth to the for-profit private prison companies, such as CoreCivic (previously known as Corrections Corporation of America) and GEO Group. The Enhancing Public Safety in the Interior of the United States executive order forces sanctuary jurisdictions to comply with requests to jail immigrants past their release date with no charge or due process while Immigration and Customs Enforcement (ICE) considers federal custody and deportation proceedings (Alvarez 2017). President Trump's executive order on Border Security and Immigration Enforcement Improvements directs the

Secretary of Homeland Security to "immediately construct, operate, control, or establish contracts to construct, operate, or control facilities to detain aliens at or near the land border with Mexico" (Sonenstein 2017).

However, since unauthorized Mexican border entries have gone down 40 percent since President Trump took office, some argue that we no longer even need a wall. It seems that unauthorized immigrants fear the crackdown more than a wall and have left the United States. American taxpayers do not want to pay the $12 to $15 billion construction price of an unnecessary wall. The Trump administration can now claim victory and has scored political capital, with only threats of a wall and deportation without having to actually build the expensive wall. Therefore, President Trump changed his mind again and no longer demanded that the spending resolution to avoid a government shutdown include money for construction of the wall (Feldscher 2017).

Donald Trump is a law-and-order president following the same approach to crime as Richard Nixon and other chief executives. Here, "law and order" refers to maintaining traditional social order. In 1990 Trump first used the term "law and order" in a *Playboy* magazine interview. He had demanded the death penalty in a full-page newspaper ad for five black and Latino males charged with assault and rape of a white woman in Central Park. He had stated, "In order to bring law and order back into our cities, we need the death penalty and authority given back to the police" (Zorthian 2017). While Trump is acting like a law-and-order leader, he seems to be lacking respect for the "rule of law." Even presidents who believe they are above the law (like Richard Nixon), need to give the appearance that they have a "sense of what is right" and that their political platform is based on institutional procedures that are in place to constrain individual power and ideology. This is done by using their executive power to uphold the rule of law (Lind 2017).

Trump appointee Deputy Attorney General Rod Rosenstein is known for putting the rule of law first, while Attorney General Session is famous for this law-and-order stance. The latter is more interested in reducing crime, limiting social disorder, and assuring a safe and "loyal" public—at all costs. Adherence to the rule of law requires following proper legal and institutional processes in all cases, without favor or prejudice to where those processes might lead (Lind 2017). Sessions's directive to spend more time on low-level immigration and drug offensives with harsher punishment will surely increase mass incarceration.

For an example of Trump's misguided law-and-order zeal, DNA evidence exonerated the Central Park Five in 2002; however, Trump refused to accept their innocence. In October 2016 he was still claiming that these men were guilty. At that time, one of the Five stated, "When we hear he is going to be a 'law and order president,' a collective chill goes down the spines of those of us who have been the victims of this 'law and order'" (Pitzer 2017). Many politicians have used law and order to intimidate and instill fear and to ensure that some must pay. Even though there has been no real crime wave throughout the campaign and now as president, President Trump continues to fan the flames of resentment with his law-and-order rhetoric.

One of the first actions President Trump undertook was to enact three law-and-order executive orders. The first order requires Attorney General Jeff Sessions to investigate crimes against law enforcement. The second order directs Sessions to initiate a task force on crime reduction and public safety, with attention to unauthorized immigrants. The third order instructs cabinet members to devise strategies for prosecuting international drug cartels. In classic Nixon fashion, President Trump has played to racist fears by invoking rhetoric to induce insecurity and create chaos. This is the opposite of "soft on crime" that demands social justice and personal dignity to prevent violence along with attention to rehabilitation and bail reform (Pitzer 2017).

President Trump does not seem interested in trying to reduce U.S. mass incarceration. It appears that he and Attorney General Sessions are ignoring prison overcrowding and the financial burdens on taxpayers and federal and state governments. Their law-and-order philosophy will expand the for-profit prison industrial complex, although current evidence reveals that mass incarceration is ineffective in securing public safety. Still, Donald Trump's behavior is unpredictable, even if Attorney General Jeff Sessions's is not. To end the human, social, and financial waste of mass incarceration, we can hope that the president will be more inclined to listen to Vice President Pence's advice to help correct the institutional bias of the U.S. criminal justice system.

CHAPTER ELEVEN

Conclusion: Choices at the Top, Devastating Repercussions at the Bottom

Policy decisions made by President Johnson and Congress expanded federal intervention into crime control. From that time forward, presidents, presidential candidates, and other officials used the War on Crime, the War on Drugs, the War on Gangs, and tough-on-crime rhetoric to enact extremely punitive criminal justice policy. In 2015 former President Bill Clinton admitted that his omnibus crime bill featuring the three-strikes provision that mandated life sentences for felons after two or more prior convictions helped foster the United States' mass incarceration problem. Clearly, criminal justice choices made at the top caused the United States to be the world's "Incarceration Nation," with over 2 million people behind bars (Collier 2014). Presently, crime rates are at historic lows; therefore, federal and state lawmakers should restructure and adopt criminal justice policies that protect the public while reducing costly mass incarceration.

Over the past four decades, law-and-order politics in the United States has emerged as a full-blown criminal justice movement resulting in significant changes to the U.S. criminal justice system. This book shows how presidents, presidential candidates and other politicians, criminal justice officials, and special interests groups, aided by a fearful public and by the media, mobilized to shape and implement stringent retributive justice laws. From Lyndon Baines Johnson to Donald Trump, U.S. presidents exercised their powerful executive leadership over the government to promote and maintain the march to law and order (Table 11.1).

Table 11.1   Major Criminal Justice Legislation (1963–2017)

President	Major Legislation
Lyndon B. Johnson (1963–1969)	Law Enforcement Act (1965)
	Narcotic Addict Rehabilitation Act (1966)
	Civil Obedience Act (1968)
	Bail Reform Act (1968)
	Omnibus Crime Control and Safe Streets Act (1968)
	Omnibus Crime Control Act (1970)
Richard M. Nixon (1969–1974)	Comprehensive Drug Abuse Prevention and Control Act (1970)
	Controlled Substances Act (1970)
Gerald R. Ford (1974–1977)	Juvenile Justice and Delinquency Prevention Act (1974)
Jimmy E. Carter (1977–1981)	
Ronald W. Reagan (1981–1989)	Sentencing Reform Act (1984)
	Justice Assistance Act (1984)
	Anti-Drug Abuse Act (1986)
	Omnibus Anti-Drug Abuse Act (1988)
	Anti-Drug Abuse Act (1988)
George H. W. Bush (1989–1993)	Drug-Free Schools and Communities Act (1989)
	Crime Control Act of 1990
	Violent Crime Control and Law Enforcement Act (1994)
	Violence Against Women Act (1994)
William J. Clinton (1993–2001)	Amber Hagerman Child Protection Act (1996)
	Drug-Free Communities Act (1997)
	Media Campaign Act (1998)
George W. Bush (2001–2009)	U.S. PATRIOT Act (2001)
	Homeland Security Act (2002)
	Adam Walsh Child Protection and Safety Act (2006)
Barack Obama (2008-2016)	
Donald Trump 2017	None as of October 2017. Attorney Jeff Sessions directs federal prosecutors to charge defendants with the "most serious, readily provable" offense in nearly all cases.

Currently, Congress has failed to reform the federal prison system and is reluctant to support commonsense legislation to halt mass incarceration. In 2015, following a two-year intensive and comprehensive review of the federal criminal justice system, the Over-Criminalization Task Force, headed by Representatives Jim Sensenbrenner and Bobby Scott, introduced bipartisan, state-tested legislation targeted at safely reducing the size and cost of the federal criminal code and prison system (Sensenbrenner and Scott 2015b). The Safe, Accountable, Fair, and Effective (SAFE) Justice Act of 2015 would have improved the federal sentencing and corrections system, from front-end sentencing reform to back-end release policies. The bill also addressed the federal supervision system to ensure that probation was more effective in halting the revolving door of federal prisons. The legislation was intended to decrease recidivism, concentrate on violent and career criminals, increase the use of evidence-based alternatives to incarceration, curtail over-criminalization, reduce crime, and save money (Sensenbrenner and Scott 2015a). However, Congress failed to act on this criminal justice reform.

With the election of President Donald Trump and his long-held law-and-order commitment, reforming the U.S. criminal justice system does not look promising. However, the Coalition for Public Safety—which is composed of political groups and think tanks including the American Civil Liberties Union (ACLU), Center for American Progress, FreedomWorks, Americans for Tax Reform, and Right on Crime along with Koch Industries and the Open Society Foundation—has formed to decrease national incarceration rates (Ford 2015). Hopefully, this group with other advocates, as well as smart-on-crime lawmakers, can bring sensible justice to the irrational U.S. criminal justice system.

The U.S. criminal justice system is long overdue for reform. Over the span of more than 45 years, the call for law and order pushed the U.S. justice system toward harsher punishment and mass incarceration. This nationalization of crime resulted in stringent and more punitive procedures, including less parole and probation for offenders. Moreover, the racial bias of the criminal justice system has produced the over-imprisonment of African Americans and other minorities. The U.S. crackdown on illegal immigration has focused on unauthorized persons, and Latinos currently make up over 50 percent of the federal prison population. Therefore, due to most U.S. presidents and their administrations calling for law and order and the resulting policy decisions, the United States is the world's largest incarcerator. Accordingly, billions of dollars continue to be invested in the extremely costly, ineffectual, and ever-growing prison industrial complex. While some states are attempting to enact reforms, congressional efforts to curtail this institutionalized system of persistent mass incarceration in the United States have stalled.

Adapting more flexible, smart, and practical ways to reform the out-of-control justice system can save taxpayer money and reduce recidivism. Increasing treatment options for drug addiction and providing more opportunities for inmates to remain active parents are a few recommendations that should be embraced by prisons. In the near future, perhaps presidential leadership will focus on smart solutions that will encourage Congress to enact safe, accountable, fair, and effective justice legislation in a bipartisan effort to improve the federal sentencing and corrections system. Presidential and congressional action on reducing U.S. mass incarceration could ensure that choices made at the top would end the devastating repercussions inflicted on minority and poor people at the bottom.

Bibliography

9/11 Commission Report. 2004. *National Commission on Terrorist Attacks upon the United States,* 22 Jul. Available from http://govinfo.library.unt.edu/911/report/index.htm (accessed 19 Dec 2011).

Abadi, Mark. 2017. A Group of Nearly 200 Police Chiefs Slammed Trump's "Lawnd Order" Crime Plan. *Business Insider,* 13 Feb. Available from http://www.businessinsider.com/trump-police-crime-law-enforcement-leaders-2017-2 (accessed 30 Apr 2017).

Ackerman, Spencer. 2016. Snowden Disclosures Helped Reduce Use of Patriot Act Provision to Acquire Email Records. *The Guardian,* 29 Sep. Available from https://www.theguardian.com/us-news/2016/sep/29/edward-snowden-disclosures-patriot-act-fisa-court (accessed 13 Apr 2017).

ACLU. American Civil Liberties Union and the ACLU Foundation. 2003. USA PATRIOT Act: Safe and Free: Restore Our Constitutional Rights. *ACLU Website.* Available from http://www.aclu.org/safefree/resources/17343res20031114.html (accessed 23 Jun 2009).

ACLU. 2016. National Security, What's at Stake? *ACLU Website.* Available from https://www.aclu.org/issues/national-security (accessed 25 Sep 2016).

ACLU. 2017a. Fair Sentencing Act. *ACLU Website.* Available from https://www.aclu.org/feature/fair-sentencing-act (accessed 28 Feb 2017).

ACLU. 2017b. ACLU Statement on Trump Reversal of Policy Ending Use of Private Prisons. *ACLU Website.* Available from https://www.aclu.org/news/aclu-statement-trump-reversal-policy-ending-use-private-prisons (accessed 24 Apr 2017).

ACLU. 2017c. Mass Incarceration: What's at Stake? ACLU Website. Available from https://www.aclu.org/issues/mass-incarceration (accessed 11 Mar 2017).

ACLU. 2017d. In Effort to Significantly Reduce U.S. Jail and Prison Population, ACLU Launches New Initiative to Overhaul Prosecutorial Practices, Seeking to Establish More Accountability, Transparency in Criminal Justice System. 26 Apr. Available from https://www.aclu.org/news/effort-significantly-reduce-us-jail-and-prison-population-aclu-launches-new-initiative-overhaul

AELE (Americans for Effective Law Enforcement, Inc). 2008. *AELE Web Page.* Available from http://www.aele.org/ (accessed 15 May 2008).

Alabama Has Second Thoughts. 2011. *New York Times*, editorial, 17 Dec. Available from http://www.nytimes.com/2011/12/18/opinion/sunday/alabamas-second-thoughts.html?src=recg (accessed 19 Dec 2011).

All Politics. 1997. Brief History of Chicago's 1968 Democratic Convention. *CNN Time.* Available from http://www.cnn.com/ALLPOLITICS/1996/conventions/chicago/facts/chicago68/index.shtml (accessed 29 Jan 2017).

Alschuler, Albert W. 1984. Close Enough for Government Work: The Exclusionary Rule after Leon. *Supreme Court Review*: 309–58.

Altheide, David L. 2006. *Terrorism and the Politics of Fear.* New York: Rowman & Littlefield.

Alvarez, Riscilla. 2017. How Trump Is Changing Immigration Enforcement. *The Atlantic*, 3 Feb. Available from https://www.theatlantic.com/politics/archive/2017/02/trump-executive-order-immigration/515454/ (accessed 24 Apr 2017).

American Constitutional Society. 2009. Beware the Prison-Industrial Complex. William & Mary Law School, 3 Nov. Available from http://acs.blogs.wm.edu/2009/11/03/beware-the-prison-industrial-complex/ (accessed 27 May 2017).

American Immigration Council. 2014. Reagan-Bush Family Fairness: A Chronological History. 9 Dec. Available from https://www.americanimmigrationcouncil.org/research/reagan-bush-family-fairness-chronological-history (accessed 2 Mar 2017).

Anderson, Eric Gary. 2007. Black Atlanta: An Ecosocial Approach to Narratives of the Atlanta Child Murders. *PMLA: Publications of the Modern Language Association of America* 122 (1): 194–209.

Another Close Call. George Bush and John Kerry Comment on Key Issues in the 2004 Presidential Election. 2004. *American Bar Association (ABA) Journal* 90: 50–54, 75.

Anti-Defamation League. 2010. Immigrants Targeted: Extremist Rhetoric Moves into the Mainstream. Groups: The Federation for American Immigration Reform (FAIR) Washington, D.C. Available from http://www.adl.org/civil_ rights/ antiimmigrant/fair.asp (accessed 26 Dec 2011).

Appropriations Committee, Democrats. 13 Mar 2014. U.S. House of Representatives. Press Release: *Price Statement on Immigration and Customs Enforcement (ICE) 2015 Budget Request.* Available from http://democrats.appropriations.house.gov/news/press-releases/price-statement-on-immigration-and-customs-enforcement-ice-2015-budget-request (accessed 26 Jun 2015).

Austin, James, and John Irwin. 2001. *It's about Time: America's Imprisonment Binge.* Belmont, CA: Wadsworth Publishing Co.

Baker, Peter. 2015. Obama Calls for Effort to Fix a "Broken System" of Criminal Justice. *New York Times*, 14 Jul. Available from https://www.nytimes

.com/2015/07/15/us/politics/obama-calls-for-effort-to-fix-a-broken
-system-of-criminal-justice.html?r=0 (accessed 17 Apr 2017).

Balko, Rodney. 2006. Overkill: The Rise of Paramilitary Police Raids in America.
Cato Institute Washington, D.C. Available from http://www.cato.org/sites
/cato.org/ files/pubs/pdf/ balko_whitepaper_2006 (accessed 11 Sep 2016).

Ball, Molly. 2017. Donald Trump and the Politics of Fear: Trump's Candidacy
Relies on the Power of Fear. It Could Be the Only Way for Him to Win.
The Atlantic, 2 Sep. Available from https://www.theatlantic.com/politics
/archive/2016/09/donald-trump-and-the-politics-of-fear/498116/
(accessed 23 Apr 2017).

Barbaro, Michael, and Megan Twohey. 2016. Crossing the Line: How Donald
Trump Behaved with Women in Private: Interviews Reveal Unwelcome
Advances, a Shrewd Reliance on Ambition, and Unsettling Workplace
Conduct over Decades, *New York Times,* 14 May. Available from https://
www.nytimes.com/2016/05/15/us/politics/donald-trump-women
.html?_r=0 (accessed 29 Apr 2017).

Barker, Vanessa. 2007. The Politics of Pain: A Political Institutionalist Analysis of
Crime Victims' Moral Protests. *Law & Society Review* 41 (3).

Barlow, Melissa Hickman. 1998. Race and the Problem of Crime in *Time* and
Newsweek Cover Stories, 1946 to 1995. *Social Justice* 25 (2): 149–83.

Barnes, Robert. 2017. Gorsuch Cast Death-Penalty Vote in One of His First
Supreme Court Cases. *Washington Post,* 21 Apr. Available from https://
www.washingtonpost.com/politics/courts_law/gorsuch-casts-death-penalty
-vote-in-one-of-his-first-supreme-court-cases/2017/04/21/2d9bc5dc
-26a8-11e7-a1b3-faff0034e2de_story.html?utm_term=.ab8b30fb1859
(accessed 24 Apr 2017).

Barnes, Robert, and Ashley Parker. 2017. Neil M. Gorsuch Sworn in as 113th
Supreme Court Justice. *Washington Post*, 20 Apr. Available from https://
www.washingtonpost.compolitics/courts_law/gorsuch-to-be-sworn-in
-to-supreme-court-today-in-two-ceremonies/2017/04/10/9ac361fe-1ddb
-11e7-ad74-3a742a6e93a7_story.html?tid=a_inl&utm_term=
.f2fbb5576a05 (accessed 24 Apr 2017).

Baum, Dan. 1997. *Smoke and Mirrors: The War on Drugs and the Politics of Failure.*
New York: Little, Brown and Company.

Beckett, Katherine. 1997. *Making Crime Pay.* New York: Oxford University Press.

Beckett, Katherine, and Theodore Sasson. 2004. *The Politics of Injustice: Crime
and Punishment in America.* Thousand Oaks, CA: Sage Publications.

Benjamin, Gerald, and Stephen P. Rappaport. 1974. Attica and Prison Reform-
Governing New York State: The Rockefeller Years. *Proceedings of the Academy of Political Science,* 31 (3): 200–13.

Berman, Russell. 2014. What Obama's Immigration Action Actually Does.
The Atlantic, 21 Nov. Available from http://www.theatlantic.com/politics
/archive/2014/11/what-obamas-immigration-action-actually-does
/383037/ (accessed 28 Sep 2016).

Best, Joel. 1987. Rhetoric in Claims-making: Constructing the Missing Children Problem. *Social Problem* 34: 101–21.

Bevacqua, Maria R. 2000. *Rape on the Public Agenda: Feminism and the Politics of Sexual Assault.* Boston: Northeastern University Press.

Bills, Scott, ed. 1988. *Kent State May 4: Echoes through a Decade.* Kent, Ohio: Kent State University Press.

Biskupic, Joan. 1990. Omnibus Crime Bills Talk Tough but Need Funding Backbone. *Congressional Quarterly,* 14 Jul. Available from http://library .cqpress.com.proxyau.wrlcorg/cqweekly/WR101409832 (accessed 23 Jan 2009).

Biskupic, Joan. 2011. High Court Will Examine State Immigration Laws, States Enacting Immigration-Related Laws. *USA Today,* 12 Dec. Available from http://www.usatoday.com/news/washington/judicial/story/2011-12 -12/supreme-court-arizona-immigration/51826852/1 (accessed 22 Dec 2011).

Blum, Dan. 1997. *Smoke and Mirrors,* quoted by Merritt, Jeralyn. 2004. Reagan's Drug War Legacy, 18 Jun. *AlterNet.* Available from http://www.alternet .org/story/18990/reagan%27s_drug_war_legacy.

Bluestein, Greg. 2016. Georgia to Embark on New Phase of Criminal Justice Reform. *Atlanta Journal Constitution.com,* 4 Jan. Available from http://politics.blog .ajc.com/2016/04/27/georgia-to-embark-on-new-phase-of-criminal-justice -reform/ (accessed 4 Jan 2017).

Bouie, Jamelle. 2017. "The Meaning of 'American Carnage.'" Slate.com., 23 Jan. Available from http://www.slate.com/articles/news_and_politics/politics /2017/01/what_trump_means_when_he_talks_about_american _carnage.html (accessed 28 Apr 2017).

Bowman, Scott W. 2014. *Color behind Bars: Racism in the U.S. Prison System.* Santa Barbara, CA: ABC-CLIO.

Boyd, Gerald. 1986. Reagan Signs Anti-drug Measure; Hopes for "Drug-Free Generation." *New York Times,* 28 Oct. Available from http://www.nytimes .com/1986/10/28/us/reagan-signs-anti-drug-measure-hopes-for-drug -gree-generation.html (accessed 13 Feb 2017).

Brecher, Edward M., and the Editors of *Consumer Reports Magazine.* 1972. The Consumers Union Report on Licit and Illicit Drugs: Heroin on the Youth Drug Scene and in Vietnam. *Consumer Report Magazine.* Available from www.druglibrary.org/schaffer/Library/studies/cu/CU20.html (accessed Jan 19 2008).

Brennan, Mary C. 2003. Winning the War/Losing the Battle: The Goldwater Presidential Campaign and Its Effects on the Evolution of Modern Con- servatism. In *The Conservative Sixties,* ed. David Farber and Jeff Roche. New York: Peter Lang.

Brennan Center for Justice. 2015. In Original Essays, Political Leaders Call for End to Mass Incarceration, 28 Apr. Available from https://www.brennancenter .org/press-release/original-essays-political-leaders-call-end-mass -incarceration.

Brenner, Mark. 2005. The Long Shadow of Mass Incarceration: A Generation Imprisoned. *Solidarity*, March and April. Available from https://www.solidarity-us.org/node/63 (accessed 27 Feb 2017).

Brisbin, Richard A., Jr. 1990. The Conservatism of Antonin Scalia. *Political Science Quarterly*, 105 (1): 1–29.

Bump, Philip, and Aaron Blake. 2016. Donald Trump's Dark Speech to the Republican National Convention, Annotated. *Washington Post,* 21 Jul. Available from https://www.washingtonpost.com/news/the-fix/wp/2016/07/21/full-text-donald-trumps-prepared-remarks-accepting-the-republican-nomination/?utm_term=.d9f2f47e5840 (accessed 29 Apr 2017).

Bureau of Justice Statistics. 2004. *Justice Expenditure and Employment in the United States.* Available from http://www.bjs.gov/index.cfm?ty=pbdetail&iid=492 (accessed 10 Oct 2016).

Bureau of Justice Statistics. 2011. U.S. Jail Population Continues to Decline. *United States Department of Justice*, 15 Apr. Available from http://www corrections.com/news/article/28413-u-s-jail-population-continues-to decline (accessed 15 Dec 2011).

Bureau of Justice Statistics. 2013. Prisoners in 2012—Advance Counts. *United States Department of Justice*, 25 Jul. Available from http://www.bjs.gov/index.cfm?ty=pbdetail%iid=4737 (accessed 8 Sep 2013).

Bureau of Justice Statistics. 2014. U.S. Correctional Population Declined by Less than 1 Percent for the Second Consecutive Year. *United States Department of Justice.* Available from http:///www.bjsgov/content/pub/press/cpus13pr.cfm (accessed 8 Jul 2015).

Bureau of Justice Statistics. 2016. Correctional Population in the United States, 2015, 29 Dec. Available from https://www.bjs.gov/index.cfm?ty=pbdetail&iid=5870 (accessed 15 Mar 2017).

Bureau of Prisons. 2016. Federal Prison System: FY 2017 Budget Request at a Glance. Available from https://www.justice.gov/jmd/file/822106/download (accessed 15 Mar 2017).

Bush, George W. 1999. *A Charge to Keep.* New York: William Morrow & Company.

Caplow, Theodore, and Jonathan Simon. 1999. Understanding Prison Policy and Population Trends. In *Prisons: Crime and Justice—A Review of Research*, eds. Michael Tonry and Joan Petersilia. Chicago: Chicago University Press.

Carissimo, Justin. 2015. 24 Astounding Facts about the Private Prison Industry. *AlterNet,* 9 Mar. Available from http://www.alternet.org/civil-liberties/astounding-facts-about-private-prison-industry (accessed 27 Feb 2017).

Carney, Jordain. 2017. Warren, Dems Push Bill to Force Trump to Shed Conflicts of Interest. *The Hill*, 9 Jan. Available from http://thehill.com/blogs/floor-action/senate/313263-warren-dems-introducing-bill-to-force-trump-to-shed-conflicts-of (accessed 29 Apr 2017).

Carson, E. Ann, and Elizabeth Anderson. 2016. Prisoners in 2015. *U.S. Bureau of Justice Statistics*, 29 Dec. Available from https://www.bjs.gov/index.cfm?ty=pbdetail&iid=5869 (accessed 28 May 2017).

Carter, Jimmy. 1996. *A Government as Good as Its People.* Fayetteville: University of Arkansas Press.

Carter, Jimmy. 2005. *Our Endangered Values: America's Moral Crisis.* New York: Simon & Schuster.

The Case against Sheriff Arpaio. 2011. *New York Times,* editorial, 16 Dec. Available from http://www.nytimes.com/2011/12/17/opinion/the-case-against -sheriff-arpaio.html?_r=1&ref=opinion (accessed 17 Dec 2011).

CBS News. 2011. Latest Immigration News, 26 Dec. Available from http://www .cbsnews.com/2741-202_162-977.html (accessed 26 Dec 2011).

Chambliss, William J. 1994. Policing the Ghetto Underclass: The Politics of Law and Law Enforcement. *Social Problems,* 41 (2): 177–94.

Chambliss, William J. 1999. *Power, Politics and Crime.* Boulder, CO: Oxford.

Chemerinsky, Edwin. 2016. "Of Course Obama's Immigration Orders Are Legal." *Los Angeles Times,* 21 Jan. Available from http://www.latimes.com/opinion /op-ed/la-oe-0121-chemerinsky-obama-executive-action-immigration -20160121-story.html.

Chicago Tribune. 2017, 4 Feb. Fact Check: Trump Overstates National Murder Rate. Available from http://www.chicagotribune.com/news/nationworld /politics/factcheck/ct-fact-check-trump-murder-rate-20170207-story .html (accessed 28 Apr 2017).

Chomsky, Aviva, and Tom Dispatch. (2017). How Did We Get Here? From Bill Clinton to Donald Trump, the Immigration Debate Has Been Divisive. How Bill Clinton and Barack Obama Laid the Groundwork for Trump's Immigration Policies. *Salon,* 29 Apr. Available from http://www.salon .com/2017/04/29/tomgram-aviva-chomsky-the-criminalization-of -immigrants-from-clinton-to-trump_partner/ (accessed 30 Apr 2017).

Chua-Eoan, Howard. 2007a. Top 25 Crimes of the Century. *Time.com.* Available from http://www.time.com/time/2007/crimes/9.html (accessed 4 Aug 2008).

Chua-Eoan, Howard. 2007b. Top 25 Crimes of the Century—Richard Speck. *Time.com.* Available from http://www.time.com/time/2007/crimes/9.html (accessed 3 Feb 2009).

Clark, Charles S. 1997. The FBI under Fire. *Congressional Quarterly* 7: 313–36. Available from http://library.cqpress.com.proxyau.wrlc.org/cqresearcher /cqresrre1997041100 (accessed 8 Nov 2008).

CNN. 2005 (19 Jun). Quoted from Walsh, John. 1988. *Then & Now: John Walsh.* Available from http://www.cnn.com/2005/US/03/17/cnn25.tan.walsh/.

CCN.com/Transcript. 2001. America's New War: Attorney General Ashcroft Testifies Before House on Expanded Powers for Law Enforcement. 24 Sep. Available from http://www.cnn.com/TRANSCRIPTS/0109/24/se.25.html.

Cobb, Roger W., and Charles D. Elder. 1972. *Participation in American Politics: The Dynamics of Agenda-Building.* Boston: Allyn and Bacon.

Cohen, Andrew. 2014. Bill Clinton and Mass Incarceration. Brennan Center for Justice. New York University, New York. Available from http://www .brennancenter.org (accessed 31 Aug 2016).

Cohen, Kelly. 2017. Private Prison Industry Sees Boom Times under Trump. *Washington Examiner,* 18 Jan. Available from http://www.washington examiner.com/private-prison-industry-sees-boom-times-under-trump /article/2611154 (accessed 27 Feb 2017).

Collier, Lorna. 2014. Incarceration Nation. *American Psychology Association's Monitor* 45, 9. Available from http://www.apa.org/monitor/2014/10/incarceration .aspx.

Cooper, Mary H. 1995. Combating Terrorism. *Congressional Quarterly,* 21 Jul. Available from http://library.cqpress.com/cqresearcher/cqresrre 19950721 (accessed 2008).

Cooper, Mary H. 2000. Drug-Policy Debate. *Congressional Quarterly,* 28 Jul. Available from http:library.cqpress.com.proxyau.wrlc.org/cqresearcher /cqresrre2000072800 (accessed 11 Jul 2009).

Corti, Daniela, and Ashok Swain. 2009. War on Drugs and War on Terror: Case of Afghanistan. Peace and Conflict Review. *Peace and Conflict Review,* Spring. Available from http://www.review.upeace.org/pdf.cfm?articulo=86& ejemplar=17 (accessed 11 Sep 2016.)

Costain, Anne. 1992. *Inviting Women's Rebellion: A Political Process Interpretation of the Women's Movement.* Baltimore: Johns Hopkins University Press.

Costello, M. 1972 School Busing and Politics. *Congressional Quarterly,* 1 Mar. Available from http://library.cqpress.com.proxyau.wrlc.org/cqresearcher /cqresree1972030100 (accessed 19 Apr 2009).

Couturier, Mark. 2007. The Leadership of Richard Nixon. *The Hauenstein Center,* Grandvalley State University, 18 Dec. Available from http://hauen steincenter.org/the-leadership-of-richard-nixon/ (accessed 26 Mar 2017).

Cox, Ana Marie. 2014. Private Prisons: The GOP's Real Shame on the Border. *Guardian UK,* 22 Jul. Available at http://readersupportednews.org /opinion2/277-75/24912-private-prisons-the-gops-real-shame-on-the -border (accessed 13 Apr 2017).

Craven, Julia. 2016. Here's How Many Black People Have Been Killed by Police This Year, Too Many. *The Huffington Post,* 7 Jul. Available from http:// www.huffingtonpost.com/entry/black-people-killed-by-police-america _us_577da633e4b0c590f7e7fb17 (accessed 13 Aug 2016).

Craven, Julia. 2017. Trump Has Moved to Dismantle Criminal Justice Reform in His First 100 Days: A New Report Explains How the President's Vision of America Could Lead to Rollbacks. *Huffington Post,* 20 Apr. Available from http://www.huffingtonpost.c (accessed 3 May 2017).

Crime and Justice, 1965–1968 Overview. 1969. *Congressional Quarterly.* Available from http://65.55.133.121/1tt/GetAttachment.aspx?file=13146dd0 -0d67-432b-bf7c-33cbab4c393 (accessed Jul 28 2008).

Crutchfield, Robert, and Gregory Weeks. 2015. The Effects of Mass Incarceration on Communities of Color. *Issues in Science and Technology* 32 (1). Available from http://issues.org/32-1/the-effects-of-mass-incarceration -on-communities-of-color/ (accessed 10 Mar 2017).

Curry, Tom. 2006. Ford's Most Important Legacy: Stevens. *MSNBC.com*, 26 Dec. Available from http://www.nbcnews.com/id/16230460/ns/politics-gerald_r_ford/t/fords-most-important-legacy-stevens/#.WGvAf02V4dn (accessed 3 Jan).

Curry, Tom. 2007. Roberts, Alito Help Define New Supreme Court Frustrated on Other Front. *MSNBC.com*, 18 Jun. Available from http://www.msnbc.msn.com/id/19244921 (accessed 24 Jun 2009).

Dansky, Kara. 2014. Cops or Soldiers? America's Police Have Become Too Militarized. *The Economist,* 22 Mar. Available from http://www.economist.com/news/united-states/21599349-americas-police-have-become-too-militarised-cops-or-soldiers (accessed 24 Sep 2016).

DARE (Drug Abuse Resistance Education). 1996. About D.A.R.E. America. Available from http://www.dare.com/home/about_dare.asp (accessed 26 Jun 2009).

Davis, Alyssa. 2016. In U.S., Concern about Crime Climbs to 15-Year High. *Gallup,* 6 Apr. Available from http://www.gallup.com/poll/190475/americans-concern-crime-climbs-year-high.aspx (accessed 23 Apr).

Davis, Angela J. 1996. Benign Neglect of Racism in the Criminal Justice System. Review of M. Tonry, Malign Neglect: Race Crime and Punishment in America. *Michigan Law Review* 94 (6): 1660–89.

Davis, Angela Y. 2003. *Are Prisons Obsolete?* New York: Seven Stories Press.

Davis, Angela Y. 2012. *The Meaning of Freedom and Other Difficult Dialogues.* City Light Books.

Davis, Flora. 1991. *Moving the Mountain: The Women's Movement in America since 1960.* New York: Simon and Schuster.

Davis, R., and M. Henley. 1990. Victim Service Programs. In *Crime Victims: Problems, Programs and Policies,* eds. Arthur Lurigio, Wesley G. Skogan, and Robert C. Davis. Beverly Hills, CA: Sage Publications.

De Vogue, Ariane. 2015. How the Supreme Court Could Send Obamacare into a "Death Spiral." 23 Jun. CNN. Available from http://www.cnn.com/2015/06/18/ politics/obamacare-aca-supreme-court-exchange-state/.

Deal, Governor Nathan. 2017. Deal: Legislation "Another Meaningful Step Forward" for Criminal Justice Reform. *Office of the Governor, State of Georgia Press Release,* 9 May 2017. Available from https://gov.georgia.gov/press-releases/2017-05-09/deal-legislation-%E2%80%98another-meaningful-step-forward%E2%80%99-criminal-justice-reform (accessed 20 May 2017).

Dean, John. 2001. Should Senate Democrats Refuse to Confirm All Bush Supreme Court Nominees? Reflections on Professor Ackerman's Proposal. Available from http://writ.news.findlaw.com/dean/20010427.html (accessed 22 Jan 2009).

Debate Club. 2014. Is Obama's Immigration Executive Order Legal? *US New and World Report* 21 Nov. Available from https://www.usnews.com/debate-club/is-obamas-immigration-executive-order-legal (accessed 26 Feb 2017).

Debate Tracker: Immigration. German Marshall Fund of the United States. Available from http://www.gmfus.org/election 2008/debate_immigration .html (accessed 17 Dec 2011).

Demand Reduction Interagency Working Groups. 2009. United States Office of National Drug Control Policy (ONDCP). Available from http://www .whitehousedrugpolicy. gov/policy/demandiwg.html (accessed 28 Jun 2009).

Demand Reduction Program: Street Smart Prevention. 2009. United States Drug Enforcement Administration. Available from http://www.usdoj.gov/dea /programs/demand.htm (accessed 24 Jun 2009).

Democracy Now. 2011. 40 Years after Attica Rebellion, New Tapes Reveal Nixon, Rockefeller Praised Deadly Crackdown, 16 Sep. Available from https:// www.democracynow.org/2011/9/16/40_years_after_attica_rebellion_new (accessed 1 Feb 2017).

Democratic Party Platform of 1972. 10 Jul 1972. *American Presidency Project*. Available from http://www.presidency.ucsb.edu/ws/index.php?pid=29605 &st=crime&st 1=law+enforcement (accessed 3 Feb 2008).

Democratic Party Platform of 1976. 12 Jul 1976. *American Presidency Project*. Available from http://www.presidency. ucsb.edu/ws/index.php?pid=29606 (accessed 2 Aug 2008).

Democratic Party Platform of 1980. 11 Aug 1980. *American Presidency Project*. 11 Aug 1980. Available from http://www.presidency.ucsb.edu/ws/index.php? pid=29607&st=crime&st1=law+enforcement (accessed 9 Jun 2009).

Democratic Party Platform of 1988. 18 Jul 1988. *American Presidency Project*. Available from http://www.presidency.ucsb.edu/ws/index.php?pid=29609.

Democratic Party Platform of 1992. 13 Jul 1992. *American Presidency Project*. Available from http://www.presidency.ucsb.edu/ws/index.php?pid=29610 &st=Crime&st1=law+enforcement (accessed 12 Jun 2009).

Democratic Party Platform of 2000. 14 Aug 2000. *American Presidency Project*. Available from http://www.presidency.ucsb.edu/ws/index.php?pid=2961 2&st=crime&st1=law+enforcement (accessed 14 Aug 2009).

Democratic Party Platform of 2004. 16 Jul 2004. *American Presidency Project*. Available from http://www.presidency.ucsb.edu/ws/index.php?pid=2961 3&st=crime&st1=law+enforcement (accessed 23 Jun 2009).

Denniston, Lyle. 2006. Commentary: Gerald Ford's Impact on the Court. *SCO-TUSblog*, 27 Dec. Available from http://www.scotusblog.com/2006/12 /commentary-gerald-fords-impact-on-the-court/ (accessed 3 Feb 2017).

DeVega, Chauncey. 2017. Stop Acting Surprised America: Donald Trump Is a White Supremacist, 25 Sep. *Salon*. Available from http://www.salon .com/2017/09/17/stop-acting-surprised-america-donald-trump-is-a -white-supremacist/.

Diegelman, Robert F. 1982. Federal Financial Assistance for Crime Control: Lessons of the LEAA Experience. *Journal of Criminal Law and Criminology* 73 (3): 994–1011.

Donegan, C. 1996. Preventing Juvenile Crime. *Congressional Quarterly*, 15 Mar. Available from http://library.cqpress com.proxyau.wrlc.org/cqresearcher /cqresrre1996031500 (accessed 23 Sep 2008).

Donohue, John, and Steven Levitt. 2001. Legalized Abortion and Crime. *Quarterly Journal of Economics* 116 (2): 379–420.

Dowd, Maureen. 1988. *Bush Says Dukakis's Desperation Prompted Accusations of Racism*. New York Times, 25 Oct. Available from http://www.nytimes .com/1988/10/25/us/bush-says-dukakis-s-desperation-prompted-accu sations-of-racism.html?pagewanted=all&src=pm (accessed Jan 23 2009).

Dowler, K., T. Fleming, and S. L. Muzzatti. 2006. Constructing Crime: Media, Crime and Popular Culture. *Canadian Journal of Criminology and Criminal Justice,* 48 (6).

Downes, Lawrence. 2014. The Obama Deportation Debacle. *The New York Times*, 9 Apr . Available at http://takingnote.blogs.nytimes.com/2014/04/09/the -obama-deportation-debacle/ (accessed 26 Sep 2016).

Drug Policy Alliance. 2016. A Brief History of the Drug War: The Early Stages of Drug Prohibition. Available at http://www.drugpolicy.org/new-solutions -drug-policy/brief-history-drug-war (accessed 11 Sep 2016).

Drug Policy Alliance. 2017. A Brief History of the Drug War. Available at http:// www.drugpolicy.org/facts/new-solutions-drug-policy/brief-history -drug-war-0 (accessed 2 Apr 2017).

Drug Reform Coordination Network (DRCNet). 2004. Drug War Chronicle: The Reagan-Era Drug War Legacy, 11 Jun. Available from https://stop thedrugwar.org/chronicle-old/341/reagan.shtml.

Drug War Chronicle. 2004. The Reagan-Era Drug War Legacy. *Drug Reform Coordination Network (DRCNet)*. Available at http://stopthedrugwar.org /chronicle-old/341/reagan.shtml (accessed 13 Feb 2017).

Duke University. 2015. Considering Ginsburg's Legacy. *Duke Law News*, 28 Apr. Available from https://law.duke.edu/news/considering-ginsburgs-legacy/ (accessed 27 May 2017).

Eastland Calls Warren Pro-Red; Says His Court Decisions Favor the Communists. 1962. *New York Times*, May 2.

Editorial. 2011. An Incremental Change. *New York Times*, 18 Nov. Available from http://www.nytimes.com/2011/11/19/opinion/an-incremental-change -in-immigration-policy.html (accessed 22 Dec 2011).

Editorial Board. 2016. Donald Trump's Campaign of Fear. *New York Times*, 22 Jul. Available from https://www.nytimes.com/2016/07/22/opinion /donald-trumps-campaign-of-fear.html?_r=0 (accessed 23 Apr 2016).

Edsall, Thomas B., and Mary D. Edsall. 1991. *Chain Reaction: The Impact of Race, Rights and Taxes on American Politics*. New York: W. W. Norton.

Edwards, Alison. 1976. *Rape, Racism, and the White Women's Movement: An Answer to Susan Browmiller*. Chicago: Sojourner Truth Organization.

Eggen, Dan. 2005. Patriot Act Changes to Be Proposed Gonzales Will Seek to Respond to Critics, Get Law Renewed. *Washingtonpost.com*, 5 Apr.

Available from http://www.washingtonpost.com/wp-dyn/articles/A26235 -2005Apr4.html (accessed 24 Jun 2009).

Eisler, Kim. 1997. Eisenhower's "Mistakes." *New York Times.com,* 28 Jul. Available from mobile.nytimes.com (accessed 30 Jan 2017).

Elliott, Anthony. 1988. Celebrity and Political Psychology: Remembering Lennon. *Political Psychology* 19 (4): 833–38.

Epstein, Edward Jay. 1977. *Agency of Fear: Opiates and Political Power in America. The Story of How the Federal Drug Administration Came to Be.* New York: G. P. Putnam and Sons.

Erskine, Hazel Gaudet. 1962. The Polls: Race Relations. *Public Opinion Quarterly* 26 (1): 137–48.

Erskine, Hazel Gaudet. 1964. The Polls: Kennedy as President. *Public Opinion Quarterly* 28 (2): 334–42.

Erskine, Hazel Gaudet. 1968–1969. The Polls: Recent Opinion on Racial Problems. *Public Opinion Quarterly* 32 (4): 696–703.

Erskine, Hazel Gaudet. 1974–1975. The Polls: Politics and Law and Order. *Public Opinion Quarterly* 38 (4): 623–34.

Evans, Alona E. 1978. National Organization for Reform of Marijuana Laws (NORML) v. Drug Enforcement Administration, U.S. Department of Justice. *American Journal of International Law* 72 (1): 149–51.

Executive Office of the President of the United States. 2002. FY 2002 Annual Performance Plan and FY 2000 Annual Program Performance Report. Available from https://www.ncjrs.gov/ondcppubs/publications /pdf/fy2002pme.pdf (accessed 15 May 2017).

Executive Office of the President of the United States.2016. Economic Perspectives on Incarceration and the Criminal Justice System. Available from https://www.whitehouse.gov/sites/default/files/page/files/20160423 _cea_incarceration_criminal_justice.pdf (accessed 10 May 2017).

FAIR (Federation for American Immigration Reform). 2011a. About FAIR. Available from http://www.fairus.org/site/PageNavigator/about.html (accessed 16 Dec 2011).

FAIR (Federation for American Immigration Reform). 2011b. Immigration Issues: Abolish the Visa Waiver Program. Available from http://www .fairus.org/site/News2?page=NewsArticle&id=16907&security=1601& news_iv_ctrl=1842 (accessed 18 Dec 2011).

Fairchild, Erika S. and Vincent J. Webb, eds. 1985. *The Politics of Crime and Criminal Justice.* Beverly Hills, CA: Sage Publications.

Families Against Mandatory Minimums. 2013. A Brief History of Crack Cocaine Sentencing Laws. Available from http://famm.org/wp-content/uploads /2013/08/FS-Brief-History-of-Crack-Laws-4.13.pdf (accessed 28 Feb 2017).

Fang, Marina, and Amber Ferguson. 2016. Bill Clinton Is Sorry for a Lot of Things. *Huffington Post,* 19 Dec. Available from http://www.huffingtonpost .com/entry/bill-clinton-is-sorry us55a83397 e4b0896514d0e220 (accessed 14 May 2017).

Farber, David. 1994. *The Age of Great Dreams: America in the 1960s.* New York: Hill and Wang.

Farber, David, and Jeff Roche, eds. 2003. *The Conservative Sixties.* New York: Peter Lang Publishing.

FBI (Federal Bureau of Investigation). 2007. Crime in the United States by Volume and Rate per 100,000 Inhabitants, 1987–2006. Washington: U. S. Department of Justice.

FBI (Federal Bureau of Investigation). 2010. Uniform Crime Reports: Crime in the United States, Persons Arrested. Criminal Justice Information Services Division. Available from http://www.fbi.gov/about-us/cjis/ucr/crime -in-the-u.s/2010/crime-in-the-u.s.-2010/persons-arrested (accessed 22 Dec 2011).

FBI (Federal Bureau of Investigation). 2016. FBI Releases 2015 Crime Statistics. FBI National Press Office, 26 Sep. Available from https://www.fbi.gov /news/pressrel/press-releases/fbi-releases-2015-crime-statistics (accessed 24 Apr 2017).

Federal Bureau of Prisons. 2011. Historical Information, Timeline. Available from https://www.bop.gov/about/history/timeline.jsp (accessed 5 Feb 2017).

Federal Bureau of Prisons. 2015. Statistics: Inmate Ethnicity, 30 May. Available from http://www.bop.gov/about/statistics/statistics_inmate_ethnicity.jsp (accessed 30 Jun 2015).

Federal Prison System. 2016. Federal Bureau of Prisons (BOP). FY 2015 Budget Request At a Glance. Available from https://www.justice.gov/sites/default /files/jmd/legacy/2013/12/21/bop.pdf.

Feeley, Malcolm M., and Austin D. Sarat. 1980. *The Policy Dilemma: Federal Crime Policy and the Law Enforcement Assistance Administration.* Minneapolis: University of Minnesota Press.

Feldscher, Kyle. 2017. Trump Backs Down on Border Wall Funding. *Washington Examiner,* 25 Apr. Available from http://www.washingtonexaminer.com /trump-backs-down-on-border-wall-funding/article/2621172 (accessed 30 Apr 2017).

Feldstein, Mark. 2004. The Myth of the Media's Role in Watergate. *Washington Post,* 30 Aug. Available from http://historynewsnetwork.org/article/6813 (accessed 2 Apr 2017).

Fernandez, Alexia. 2016. Hinckley, Moore and Fromme All Tried to Kill a President. And Soon All Three Will Be Free. *Los Angeles Times,* 29 July. Available from http://www.latimes.com/nation/la-na-attempted-assassins -snap-htmlstory.html (accessed 6 Feb 2017).

Ferree, Myra Marx, and Patricia Yancey Martin, eds. 1995. *Feminist Organizations: Harvest of the New Women's Movement.* Philadelphia: Temple University.

Fitz, Marshall. 2014. Obama Is Just Doing His Job. *Debate Club, US News and Report,* 21 Nov. Available at https://www.usnews.com/debate-club/is -obamas-immigration-executive-order-legal/obama-is-just-doing-his-job (accessed 26 Feb 2017).

Fixing the Immigration System for America's 21st Century Economy. *The White House.* Available from http://www.whitehouse.gov/issues/fixing-immigration -system-america-s-21st-century-economy (accessed 24 Dec 2011).

Flamm, Michael W. 2003. The Politics of Law and Order. In *Conservative Sixties*, eds. David Faber and Jeff Roche. New York: Peter Lang.

Flamm, Michael W. 2005. *Law and Order: Street Crime, Civil Unrest, and the Crisis of Liberalism in the 1960s.* New York: Columbia University Press.

Flanary, Patrick. 2011. How the Nixon Pardon Strained a Presidential Friendship. *ProPublica,* 12 Dec. Available from https://www.propublica.org /article/presidential-pardons-how-the-nixon-pardon-strained-a -prsesidential-friendship (accessed 4 Feb 2017).

Fontana, David. 2011. New Republic: Sotomayor the Symbol of Liberal Wing. *NPR,* 29 Jun. http://www.npr.org/2011/06/29/137494039/new-republic -sotomayor-the-symbol-of-liberal-wing (accessed 20 Feb 2017).

Ford, Gerald R. 1979. *A Time to Heal: The Autobiography of Gerald R. Ford.* New York: HarperCollins Publishers.

Ford, Matt. 2015. Can Bipartisanship End Mass Incarceration? A Major Shift in Criminal Justice Is Coming, but Will It Be Enough? *The Atlantic,* 25 Feb. Available from https://www.theatlantic.com/politics/archive/2015/02/can -bipartisanship-end-mass-incarceration/386012/ (accessed 1 May 2017).

The Ford Legacy: President Gerald R. Ford. Citizen, Public Servant, Leader. 2017. Available from http://fordschool.umich.edu/ford-legacy.

Fox, John. 2017. The Court and Democracy: Biographies of the Robes, Earl Warren. *PBS.org.* Available from http://www.pbs.org/wnet/supremecourt/ rights/robes_warren.html (accessed 3 Feb 2017).

Fox News Latino. 2011. Immigration Offenses Make Latinos New Majority in Federal Prisons, 7 Sep. Available from http://latino.foxnews.com/latino /news/2011/09/07/immigration-offenses-make-latinos-new-majority-in -federal-prisons-report-says/#ixzz1hUg3ks34 (accessed 22 Dec 2011).

Frontline. 2006. Thirty Years of American's Drug War: A Chronology 1960– 1995. *PBS Online.* Available from http://www.pbs.org/wgbh/pages/front line/shows/drugs/cron (accessed 23 July 2007).

Gabrielle Giffords Shot: Congresswoman Shot in Arizona. 2011. *Huffington Post,* 8 Jan. Available from http://www.huffingtonpost.com/2011/011/08 /gabrielle-giffords-shot-c_n_806211.html (accessed 18 Dec 2011).

Galston, William A., and Geoffrey L. Tibbetts. 1994. Reinventing Federalism: The Clinton/Gore Program for a New Partnership among the Federal, State, Local, and Tribal Governments. *Publius* 3: 23–48.

Garland, David. 2001. *The Culture of Control.* Chicago: University of Chicago Press.

Garofalo, James. 1981. The Fear of Crime: Causes and Consequences. *Criminal Law & Criminology* 72 (2): 840. Available from http://scholarlycommons .law.northwestern (accessed 2 Jul 2015).

Gelb, Adam. 2015. *Criminal Justice Reform, Incarceration and Sentencing.* Washington Journal, CSPAN, Jul 1. Available from http://www.c-span.org/video /?326758-3/washington-journal-adam-gelb-incarceration-sentencing-us (accessed 2 Jul 2015).

Gelb, Joyce, and Marian Lief Palley. 1996. *Women and Public Policies.* Princeton: Princeton University Press.

Georgia Council on Criminal Justice Reform Report. Feb 2015. Available from http://www.gjp.org/wp-content/uploads/2014-2015-CJRC-Report.pdf (accessed 8 Jul 2015).

Ghandnoosh, Nazgol. 2014. Race and Punishment: Racial Perceptions of Crime and Support for Punitive Policies, September. *The Sentencing Project.* Available from http://www.sentencingproject.org/wp-content/uploads /2015/11/Race-and-Punishment.pdf (accessed 2 Apr 2017).

Gibbs, Nancy. 2001. Laying Down the Law. *Time,* 24 Jun. Available from http:// content.time.com/time/magazine/article/0,9171,1101930823-162229,00 .html (accessed 15 May 2017).

Gillin, Joshua. 2017. The Obameter: From Drug Sentencing to Commutations, Obama Altered Prison Landscape. *Tampa Bay.com,* Jan 6. Available at http://www.tampabay.com/projects/2017/politifact/obameter/drug -sentencing/?utm_source=TBT_email&utmedium=email&utm _campaign=Politifact%20Email%20Jan%2019%202017 (accessed 27 Jan 2017).

Glaze, Lauren E., and Danielle Kaeble. 2014. Correctional Populations in the United States, 2013. *U.S. Bureau of Justice Statistics.* Available from http://www.bjs.gov /content/pub/press/cpus13pr.cfm (accessed 26 Jun 2015).

Glazer, Sarah. 1996. Punishing Sex Offenders. *Congressional Quarterly,* 12 Jan. Available from http://library.cqpress.com.proxyau.wrlc.org/cqresearcher /cqresrre1996011200 (accessed 23 Sep 2008).

Gomez, Alan. 2011. Groups Target States' Illegal-Immigration Bills. *USA Today,* 18 Mar. Available from http://www.usatoday.com/news/nation/2011 -03-28-stateimmigration28_ST_N.htm (accessed 21 Dec 2011).

Gomez, Alan, Jack Gillum, and Kevin Johnson. 2011. U.S. Border Cities Prove Havens from Mexico's Drug Violence. *USA Today,* 18 Jul. Available from http://www.usatoday.com/news/washington/2011-07-15-border-violence -main_n.htm (accessed 21 Dec 2011).

Goode, Erica. 2013. U.S. Prison Population Decline, Reflecting New Approach to Crime. *New York Times,* 26 Jul. Available from http://www .nytimescom/2013/07/27/us/us-prison-Populations-decline-reflecting -new-approach-to-crime.html?nl=todaysheadlines&emc=Edit_th_2013 0726&_4=0 (accessed 26 Jul 2013).

Gottschalk, Marie. 2006. *The Prison and the Gallows: The Politics of Mass Incarceration in America.* New York: Cambridge University Press.

Gramlich, John. 2017a. Federal Prison Population Fell during Obama's Term, Reversing Recent Trend. *Pew Research Center, Factank,* 5 Jan. Available from http://www.pewresearch.org/fact-tank/2017/01/05/federal-prison -population-fell-during-obamas-term-reversing-recent-trend/ (accessed 3 Feb).

Gramlich, John. 2017b. Federal Criminal Prosecutions Fall to Lowest Level in Nearly Two Decades. Pew Research Center, 28 Mar. Available from http.//www.pewreseach.org/author/jgramlich/ (accessed 24 Apr 2017).

Gray, Madison. 2007. The L.A. Riots: 15 Years after Rodney King. *Time.com* (CNN). Available from www.time.com/time/specials/2007/a_riot/article /0,28804,1614117_ 1614084,00.html (accessed 19 Sep 2008).

Haile, Jeremy. 2015. Bogus Drug Penalty "Myths." *Daily Journal,* 24 Aug. Available from http://www.sentencingproject.org/detail/news.cfm?news_id=1952& id=107 (accessed 7 Sep 15).

Harris, Louis. 1968. Polls: An Insight. *Newsweek,* 11 Nov, Quoted in Michael W. Flamm, *Law and Order: Street Crime, Civil Unrest, and the Crisis of Liberalism in the 1960s,* 34. New York: Columbia University Press.

Hart, John. 2005. CBS Evening News. Quoted in Michael W. Flamm, *Law and Order: Street Crime, Civil Unrest, and the Crisis of Liberalism in the 1960s.* New York: Columbia University Press.

Hatfield, Mark O. 1997. *Vice Presidents of the United States, 1789–1993.* Senate Historical Office: U.S. Government Printing Office, pp. 453–461. Available from https://www.senate.gov/artandhistory/history/resources/pdf /lyndon_johnson.pdf (accessed 26 Mar 2017).

Headley, Bernard D. 1988. The "Atlanta Tragedy" and the Rule of Official Ideology. *Journal of Black Studies* 18 (4): 452–70.

Heck, Edward V. 1981. Civil Liberties Voting Patterns in the Burger Court, 1975–78. *Western Political Quarterly* 34 (2): 193–202.

Hellegers, Adam P. 1999. Reforming HUD's "One-Strike" Public Housing Evictions through Tenant Participation. *Journal of Criminal Law and Criminology,* 90.

Herszenhor, David. 2010. Senate Blocks Bill for Young Illegal Immigrants, *New York Times,* 18 Dec. Available from http://www.nytimes.com/2010/12/19 /us/politics/19immig.html (accessed 19 Dec 2011).

Hinton, Elizabeth. 2016. *From the War on Poverty to the War on Crime: The Making of Mass Incarceration in America.* Cambridge, MA: Harvard University Press.

Holian, David B. 2004. He's Stealing My Issues! Clinton's Crime Rhetoric and the Dynamics of Issue Ownership. *Political Behavior* 26 (2): 95–123.

Holland, Joshua. 2013. Land of the Free? US Has 25 Percent of the World's Prisoners. *Moyers & Company,* 16 Dec. Available from billmoyers .com/2013/12/16/lnd-of-the-free-us-has-5-of-the-worlds-population -and-25-of its-prisoners/ (accessed 14 Aug 2014).

Homeland Security Act. 2002. Legislation Predicated on the Official Story of the 9/11/01 Attack. *9-11 Research.* Available from http://911research.wtc7.net /post911/legislation/hsa.html.

Howe, Marvine. 1990. New Policy Aids Families of Aliens. *New York Times,* 5 Mar. Available from http://www.nytimes.com/1990/03/05/nyregion /new-policy-aids-families-of-aliens.html (accessed 14 May 2017).

Hurwitz, Jon, and Mark Peffley. 1997. "Public Perceptions of Race and Crime: The Role of Racial Stereotypes." *American Journal of Political Science* 41 (2): 375–40l.

Jabali, Malaika. 2017. On Trump, Nixon and the False Narrative of Lawlessness: American Citizens Are Not the Military Enemy. *Essence*, 15 Jun. Available from http://www.essence.com/news/politics/donald-trump -nixon-policies-law-and-order (accessed 28 Apr 2017.)

Jackman, Tom. 2017. Trump Makes False Statement about U.S. Murder Rate to Sheriff's Group, 7 Feb. *Washington Post.* Available from https://www .washingtonpost.com/news/true-crime/wp/2017/02/07/trump-makes -false-statement-about-u-s-murder-rate-to-sheriffs-group/?utm_term =.0c91e2680740.

Jacobs, James B. 1980. The Prisoners' Rights Movement. *Crime and Justice* 2: 429–70.

Jacobson, Michael. 2005. *Downsizing Prisons: How to Reduce Crime and End Mass Incarceration.* New York: New York University Press.

J. F. 2015. How America's Police Became so Heavily Armed. *The Economist,* 18 May. Available from http://www.economist.com/blogs/economist -explains/2015/05/economist-explains-22 (accessed 24 Sep 2016).

Johnson, Kevin. 2016. With a President Trump, an Emphasis on "Law and Order." *USA Today,* November 9. Available from http://www.usatoday .com/story/news/politics/elections/2016/11/09/donald-trump-criminal -justice/93550162/ (accessed 29 Apr 2017).

Johnson, Kirk. 1987. Goetz Judge Revises Self-Defense Definition. *New York Times,* 14 Jun. Available from http://www.nytimes.com/1987/06/14/nyregion /goetz-judge-revises-self-defense-definition.html (accessed 2 Nov 2008).

Johnson, Theodore, and Leah Wright Rigueur. 2015. Race-Baiting for the Presidency. *The Atlantic,* 18 Nov. Available from http://www.theatlantic .com/politics/archive/2015/11/racial-divisiveness-as-a-campaign-strategy /416412/ (accessed 18 Nov 2016).

Johnston, David. 1991. Bush, Pushing Crime Bill, Bends again on Gun Control. *New York Times,* 19 Apr. Available from http://www.nytimes.com/1991 /04/19/us/bush-pushing-crime-bill-bends-again-on-gun-control.html (accessed 23 Jan 2009).

Jost, Kenneth. 1996. Rethinking School Integration. *Congressional Quarterly* 6: 913–36.

Jost, Kenneth. 2005. Supreme Court's Future v.15-4. *Congressional Quarterly,* 28 Jan.

Kamisar, Yale. 2006. Miranda's Reprieve. *American Bar Association (ABA) Journal* 92 (6).

Karmen, A. 1984. *Crime Victims: An Introduction to Victimology.* Monterey, CA: Brooks.

Katel, Peter. 2008a. Fighting Crime: Can Inner-city Crime Be Significantly Reduced? *Congressional Quarterly* 18 (6). Available from http://library .cqpress.com.proxyau.wrlc.org/cqresearcher/document.php?id=cqresrre 2008020800&type=hitlist&num=0 (accessed 15 Nov 2008).

Katel, Peter. 2008b. Race and Politics. *Congressional Quarterly*, 19 July. Available from http://library.cqpress.com.proxyau.wrlc.org/cqresearcher/cqresrre 2008071 (accessed 23 Sep 2008).

Kates, Brian. 2004. The Subway Vigilante. *Daily News*, 26 Dec. Available from www.nydailynews.com/archives/news/2004/12/26/2004-12-26_the_subway _vigilante.html (accessed 17 Aug 2008).

Kent State University Libraries. 2007. *Kent State Chronology, May 1–4, 1970*. KSU Libraries and Media Services. Available from http://speccoll.library.kent .edu/4may70/exhibit/chronology /index.html (accessed Aug 7 2007).

Kernell, Samuel. 2007. *Going Public: New Strategies of Presidential Leadership*. Washington, DC: CQ Press.

Killough, Ashley. 2014. 24 States Now Suing Obama over Immigration. *CNN Politics*, 10 Dec. Available from http://www.cnn.com/2014/12/10/politics /immigration-lawsuit/index.html (accessed 26 Jun 2015.)

Kingsbury, Alex. 2008. Inside the Fed's War on Gang Violence. *US News and World Report,* 10 Dec. Available from http://www.usnews.com/news /national/articles/2008/12/10/inside-the-feds-war-on-gang-violence (accessed 24 Sep 2016).

Kirkham, Chris. 2012. Private Prison Corporation Offers Cash in Exchange for State Prisons. *The Huffington Post,* 14 Feb. Available at http://www.huffing tonpost.com/2012/02/14/private-prisons-buying-state-prisons_n_1272143 .html (accessed 27 Feb 2017).

Klarman, Michael J. 1994. *Brown,* Racial Change, and the Civil Rights Movement. *Virginia Law Review* 80 (1).

Knott, Stephen. 2017. George H. W. Bush: Campaigns and Elections. Miller Center of Public Affairs, University of Virginia. Available from http:// millercenter.org/president/biography/bush-campaigns-and-elections (accessed 20 Feb 2017).

Koch, Dorothy Bush. 2006. *My Father, My President: A Personal Account of the Life of George H. W. Bush*. New York: Warner Books.

Koch, K. 1998. School Violence. *Congressional Quarterly*, 9 Oct. Available from http://library.cqpress.com.proxyau.wrlc.org/cqresearcher/cqresrre1998 100900 (accessed 23 Sep 2008).

Krogstad, Jens Manuel, Jeffrey S. Passel, and D'Vera Cohn. 2016. 5 Facts about Illegal Immigration in the U.S. Pew Research Center, 20 Sep. Available from http://www.pewresearch.org/fact-tank/2016/09/20/5-facts-about -illegal-immigration-in-the-u-s/ (accessed 1 Oct 2016).

Lacey, Marc. 2011. Appeals Court Rules against Arizona Law. *New York Times*, 11 Apr. Available from http://www.nytimes.com/2011/04/12/us/12arizona .html.

Lamb, Charles. 1991. *Chief Justice Warren E. Burger: A Conservative Chief for Conservative Times*. The Burger Court: Political and Judicial Profiles 129, 151. Charles M. Lamb and Stephen C. Halpern, eds. University of Illinois Press.

Lanoue, David J. 1989. "The Teflon Factor": Ronald Reagan and Comparative Presidential Popularity. *Polity* 21 (3): 481–501.

Lantigua-Williams, Juleyka. 2016. Feds End Use of Private Prisons, but Questions Remain. *The Atlantic*, 18 Apr. Available at http://www.theatlantic.com/politics/archive/2016/08/end-of-private-prison-contracts-with-federal-government/496469/ (accessed 25 Sep 2016).

Laslo, Matt. 2017. Jeff Sessions' Tough-on-Crime Approach Faces Bipartisan Pushback. *Rolling Stone,* 15 May. Available from http://www.rollingstone.com/politics/features/jeff-sessions-tough-on-crime-approach-faces-bipartisan-pushback-w482327 (accessed 12 May 2017).

Lasswell, Howard D. 1936. *Politics: Who Gets What, When, How.* London: Whittlesey House.

Law and Law Enforcement, 1973–1976, Legislative Overview. 1977. *Congressional Quarterly.* Available from http://library.cqpress.com.proxyau.wrlc.org catn/document.php?id=catn73-7-6102-305958 (accessed 3 Aug 2008).

Law and Law Enforcement, 2001–2004, Legislative Overview. 2006. *Congressional Quarterly.* Available from http://library.cqpress.com/catn/catn01-426-18124-974517 (accessed 24 Oct 2008).

Lederman, Josh. 2016. Obama Commutes Sentences of 61 Drug Offenders. *U.S. News & World Report,* 30 Mar. Available from http://www.usnews.com/news/politics/articles/2016-03-30/obama-shortens-prison-sentences-for-61-drug-offenders (accessed 13 August 2016).

Leopold, Les. 2015. Runaway Inequality, Runaway Incarceration. *Huffington Post,* 21 Feb. Available from http://www.huffingtonpost.com/les-leopold/runaway-inequality-runawa_b_6362942.html.

Levine, Philip, Douglas Staiger, Thomas Kane, and David Zimmerman. 1999. *Roe v. Wade* and American Fertility. *American Journal of Public Health* 89 (2): 199–203.

Levitt, Steven D. 2004. Understanding Why Crime Fell in the 1990s: Four Factors That Explain the Decline and Six That Do Not. *Journal of Economic Perspectives* 18 (1).

Lexis Nexis ProQuest Historical Newspaper. Available from http://www.lexis-nexis.com/hottopics/lnacademic/?.

Lind, Dara. 2014. Did George H. W. Bush Really Pave the Way for Obama on Immigration? *Vox*, 20 Nov. Available from https://www.vox.com/2014/11/20/7254361/family-fairness-immigration (accessed 14 May 2017).

Lind, Dara. 2017. Donald Trump's Drive for "Law and Order" Undermines the Rule of Law. *Vox*, 16 May. Available from https://www.vox.com/policy-and-politics/2017/5/16/15641096/ trump-rule-of-law (accessed 17 May 2017).

Linder, Doug. 2000. Famous American Trials: The Trial of Orenthal James Simpson. *University of Missouri-Kansas City School of Law.* Available from http://www.law.umkc.edu/faculty/projects/trials/Simpson/simpson.htm (accessed 21 Sep 2008).

Liptak, Adam. 2012a. Blocking Parts of Arizona Law, Justices Allow Its Centerpiece. *New York Times*, 25 Jun. Available from http://www.nytimes.com/2012/06/26/us/supreme-court-rejects-part-of-arizona-immigration-law.html (accessed 26 Jun 2015).

Liptak. Adam. 2012b. Supreme Court Ruling Allows Strip-Searches for Any Arrest. *New York Times*, 3 Apr. Available from https://federalcrimesblog.com/tag/chief-justice-roberts/ (accessed 27 May 2017).

Liptak, Adam. 2017. Why Obama Struggled at Court, and Trump May Strain to Do Better, 23 Jan. *New York Times*. Available from https://www.nytimes.com/2017/01/23/us/politics/obama-supreme-court-win-rate-trump.html?mcubz=3&_r=0.

Liptak, Adam, and Michael D. Shear. 2016. Supreme Court Tie Blocks Obama Immigration Plan. *New York Times*, 23 Jun. Available from http://www.nytimes.com/2016/06/24/us/supreme-court-immigration-obama-dapa.html?_r=0 (accessed 19 Jun 2016).

Llana, Sara Miller. 2010. Mexico issues sharp rebuttal to Arizona immigration law, 26 Apr. *Christian Science Monitor*. Available from https://www.csmonitor.com/World/Americas/2010/0426/Mexico-issues-sharp-rebuttal-to-Arizona-immigration-law.

Loo, Dennis D., and Ruth-Ellen M. Grimes. 2004. Polls, Politics, and Crime: The "Law and Order" Issue of the 1960s. *Western Criminology Review* 5 (1).

Lopez, Mark Hugo, Jens Manuel Krogstad, Gustavo López, Jynnah Radford, and Antonio Flores. 2017. Latinos and the New Trump Administration Growing Share Say Situation of U.S. Hispanics Is Worsening, 23 Feb. Available from http://www.pewhispanic.org/2017/02/23/latinos-and-the-new-trump-administration/ (accessed 26 Apr 2017).

MacDonald, Heather. 2017. Trump's Truth-Telling about "American Carnage." *National Review,* 23 Jan. Available from http://www.nationalreview.com/article/444109/american-carnage-trump-truth-homicide-rate-2016 (accessed 23 Apr).

Maclin, Tracey. 2007. The Bush Administration's Terrorist Surveillance Program and the Fourth Amendment's Warrant Requirement: Lessons from Justice Powell and the Keith Case. *Law Review University of California, Davis* 41: 1277.

Maguire, Mike. 1991. The Needs and Rights of Victims of Crime. *Crime and Justice* 14: 363–433.

Mahoney, Owen. 2016. George H. W. Bush's Legacy. *New York Times,* Oct. 18. Available from https://www.nytimes.com/2016/10/19/opinion/george-hw-bushs-legacy.html?_r=0 (accessed 20 Feb 2017).

MapLight: Revealing Money's Influences on Politics. S. 729—Development, Relief, and Education for Alien Minors Act of 2009. Available from http://maplight.org/us-congress/bill/111-s-729/363139/total-contributions.table?interests-support=J7500&interests-oppose= (accessed 18 Dec 2011).

Marion, Nancy E. 1994. *A History of Federal Crime Control Initiatives, 1960–1993.* Santa Barbara, CA: Greenwood Publishing Group.

Martin, Michel. 2009. Obama: Immigration Detention System Must Change. *NPR*, 12 Oct. Available from http://www.npr.org/templates/story/story.php?storyId=111801770 (accessed 2 Oct 2016).

Masci, David and Kenneth Jost. 2001. War on Terrorism: Can the U.S. Contain the Global Terrorist Threat? *Congressional Quarterly*, 12 Oct. Available from http://library.cqpress.com.proxyau.wrlc.org/cqresearcher/document .php?id= (accessed 13 Aug 2016).

May, Lee. 1988. Reagan Signs Broad "Sword and Shield" Anti-Drug Law: Casual Users Face Stiff Fines; Kingpins Could Get the Death Penalty. *LA Times,* 19 Nov. Available from http://articles.latimes.com/1988-11-19/news/mn -388_1_death-penalty (accessed 2 Mar 2017).

McAdam, Doug. 1982. *Political Process and the Development of Black Insurgency 1930–1970.* Chicago: University of Chicago Press.

McCoy, Alfred W. 1972. *The Politics of Heroin in Southeast Asia: The Consequences of Complicity—A Generation of Junkies.* Schaffer Library of Drug Police. Available from http://www.druglibrary.org/schaffer/Library/studies/cu /CU20.html (accessed 19 Jan 2008).

McCue, Margi Laird. 1995 *Domestic Violence: A Reference Handbook.* Available from http://books.google.com/books?id_30G_awoS4DIC&pg=PA146&rl pg=PA146&dq=Bill+Clinton+and+domestic+violence&source=bl (accessed 15 Jan 2008).

McFeeley, Neil D. 1979. A Change of Direction: Habeas Corpus from Warren to Burger. *Western Political Quarterly* 32 (3): 174–88.

McGlen, Nancy, Karen O'Connor, Laura van Assendelft, and Wendy Gunther-Canada. 2011. *Women, Politics, and American Society.* New York: Longman.

McKelvey, Charles. 2017. Reflections on Trump. *Global Learning-Cuba.com,* 17 Mar. http://www.globallearning-cuba.com/blog-umlthe-view-from-the -southuml/reflections-on-trump (accessed 28 Apr 2017).

McLellan, Joseph, Richard Harrington, James LeMoyne, and James A. Miller. 1980. The Reaction. *Washington Post,* 10 Dec. Available from http:// groups.google.com/group/alt.obituaries/msg/45d1d572f5190e06 (accessed 1 Feb 2009).

McLeod, Allegra M. 2015. Mass Incarceration Is a Horrible Failure. *New York Times,* 29 Oct. Available from http://www.nytimes.com/roomfordebate /2015/10/29/will-crime-rise-if-more-people-are-kept-out-of-prison/mass -incarceration-is-a-horrible-failure (accessed 13 Aug 2016).

McNeill, Jena Baker. 2010. The FY 2011 Homeland Security Budget: Spending Doesn't Match the Missions. *Heritage Foundation,* 26 Feb. Available from http://www.heritage.org/research/reports/2010/02/the-fy-2011 -homeland-security-budget-spending-doesn-t-match-the-missions (accessed 27 Dec 2011).

Mejia, Brittny. 2016. Thinking of Family and Fearing a Wall, Latino Voters Take to the Polls in L.A. *LA Times,* 8 Nov. Available from http://www.latimes .com/local/lanow/la-me-ln-latino-voters-la-20161108-story.html (accessed 26 Apr 2017).

Melfi, Theordore, and Allison Schroeder. 2016. *Hidden Figures.* Twentieth Century Fox.

Memmott, Carol. 1989. 20 Years Later, Manson Still Chills, Fascinates. *USA Today,* 9 Aug. Available from http://pqasb.pqarchiver.com/USAToday/access

/20+Years+Later%2C+ Manson+Still+Chills%2C+Fascinates (accessed 25 July 2007).

Merica, Dan. 2015. Bill Clinton Says He Made Mass Incarceration Issue Worse. CNN, 25 Jul. Available from http://www.cnn.com/2015/07/15/politics /bill-clinton-1994-crime-bill/index.html (accessed 21 Dec 2016).

Merritt, Jeralyn. 2004. Reagan's Drug War Legacy. *AlterNet*, 18 Jun. Available from http://www.alternet.org/story/18990/reagan's_drug_war_legacy (acessed 13 Feb 2017).

Merritt, Jeralyn. 2008. Hillary vs. Obama: Who Is Trying Harder to Be "Tough on Crime"? *AlterNet*, 11 Feb. Available from http://www.alternet.org/story /76595/hillary_vs._obama%3A_who_is_trying_harder_to_be_%22tough _on_crime%22/ (accessed 26 Feb 2017).

Meserve, Jeanne. 1999. *Expulsions for Weapons in Schools down Nearly a Third.* CNN.com, 10 Aug. Available from archives.cnn.com/US/9908/1.0/guns .in.school (accessed 21Sep 2008).

Meyer, David S. and Suzanne Staggenborg. 1996. "Movements, Countermovements, and the Structure of Political Opportunity." *American Journal of Sociology* 101 (6): 1628–1660.

Mickens, Leah. 2014. R.I.P. "Law and Order" Conservatives: Why Nixon's Party Abandoned His Obsession. *Salon,* 8 Aug. Available from http://www .salon.com/2014/08/08/r_i_p_law_and_order_conservatives_why _nixons_party_abandoned_his_obsession/.

Miller, Lisa. 2004. Rethinking Bureaucrats in the Policy Process: Criminal Justice Agents and the National Crime Agenda. *Policy Studies* 32 (4): 569–89.

Miller Llana, Sara. 2010. Mexico Issues Sharp Rebuttal to Arizona Immigration Law. *Christian Science Monitor*, 26 Apr. Available at http://www.csmonitor .com/World/Americas/2010/0426/Mexico-issues-sharp-rebuttal-to -Arizona-immigration-law (accessed 2 Jan 2012).

Miskel, Ceci, and Mengli Song. 2004. Passing Reading First: Prominence and Processes in an Elite Policy Network. *Educational Evaluation and Policy Analysis* 27 (2): 89–109.

Mittelstadt, Michelle, Burke Speaker, Doris Meissner, and Muzaffar Chishti. 2011. Through the Prism of National Security: Major Immigration Policy and Program Changes in the Decade since 9/11. Migration Policy Institute, Aug. Available from http://www.migrationpolicy.org/pubs/FS23 _Post-9-11policy.pdf (accessed 27 Dec 2011).

Moore, Suzanne. 1989. Kidnapped by the Counter-Culture. *New Statesman & Society (ProQuest Social Science Journals)* 2 (45): 42.

Mothers Against Drunk Driving (MADD). 2008. News Release: New MADD Board Members Bring Valuable Expertise to MADD's Campaign to Eliminate Drunk Driving, Underage Drinking Prevention and Victim Services. Available from http://www.madd.org/./press-release/press-release/2008 /new-madd-board-members-bring-valuable-expertise-to.aspx (accessed 2 Aug 2008).

Murakawa, Naomi. 2008. The Origins of the Carceral Crisis: Racial Order as "Law and Order" in Postwar American Politics. In *Race and American Political Development*, eds. J. Lowndes, J. Novkov, and D. T. Warren. New York: Routledge.

Naiman, Robert. 2011. Is Palin's "Crosshairs" Map Relevant? Giffords Thought So. *Huffington Post*, 8 Jan. Available from http://www.huffingtonpost.com /robert-naiman/is-palins-crosshairs-map_b_806277.html (accessed 21 Dec 2011).

National Advisory Commission on Civil Disorders Report: Summary of Report. 1968. The Eisenhower Foundation. Available from www.eisenhower foundation.org/docs/kerner.pdf (accessed 5 Apr 2009).

National Council of La Raza (NCLR). 2011. Immigration Reform. Available from http://www.nclr.org/index.php/issues_and_programs/immigration /immigration_reform (accessed 18 Dec 2011).

National Law Enforcement Training Week Proclamation. 3 Jan 1990. *American Presidency Project*. Available from http://www.presidency.ucsb.edu/ws /index.php?pid=23746&st=crime&st1=law+enforcement (accessed 12 Jun 2008).

Neustadt, Richard. 1990. *Presidential Power: The Politics of Leadership*. New York: The Free Press.

Newell, Walker. 2013. The Legacy of Nixon, Reagan, and Horton: How the Tough on Crime Movement Enabled a New Regime of Race-Influenced Employment Discrimination. *Berkeley Journal of African-American Law & Policy* (15):1, 14. Available from http://scholarship.law.berkeley.edu/cgi /viewcontent.cgi?article=1014&context=bjalp (accessed 26 Mar 2017).

Newman, Tony. 2016. Nancy Reagan's Role in the Disastrous War on Drugs. *Huffington Post,* 7 Mar. Available from http://www.huffingtonpost.com /tony-newman/nancy-reagan-war-on-drugs_b_9400628.html (accessed 28 Mar 2017).

New York Times. 2017. Gun Violence on Campus. Opinion Page, 18 May. Available from https://www.nytimes.com/2017/05/18/opinion/gun-violence -on-campus.html (accessed 30 May 2017).

Norton, Ben. 2016. Bill Clinton's Shameful Legacy on Immigration: "Terrible" Laws He Signed "Rip Apart" Families and Authorize Unjust Detention, Human Rights Watch says. *Salon,* 27 April. Available from http://www .salon.com/2016/04/27/bill_clintons_shameful_legacy_on_immigration _terrible_laws_he_signed_rip_apart_families_and_authorize_unjust _detention_human_rights_watch_says/ (accessed 22 Dec 2016).

Novak, Jake. 2011a. Maybe We Don't Need a Border Wall with Mexico. *CNBC Business News*, 13 Mar. Available from NumbersUSA. 5 Jan 2011. Clear Act: Help Local Enforcement. Available from https://www.numbersusa .com/content/news/january-5-2011/help-local-enforcement.html.

Novak, Jake. 2011b. The Clear Act. Available from http://www.numbersusa.com content/node/11951 (accessed 18 Dec 2011).

Novak, Jake. 2011c. NumbersUSA for Lower Immigration Levels. NumbersUSA Action, Interior Enforcement. Available from http://www.numbersusa

.com/content/learn/attrition-through-enforcement/interior-enforcement
.html-0 (accessed 18 Dec 2011).

NPR (National Public Radio). 2010. A Reagan Legacy: Amnesty for Illegal Immigrant, 4 Jul. Available at http://www.npr.org/templates/story/story.php?
storyId=128303672 (accessed 23 Feb 2017).

O'Bryant, JoAnne. 2003. Crime Control: The Federal Response (CRS Issue Brief
for Congress). *Congressional Research Service* 1–8.

Office of the President of the United States. National Drug Control Strategy 2009
Annual Report. Available from https://www.globalsecurity.org/security
/library/policy/national/ndcs2009.pdf.

On the Issues. 1976. President Jimmy Carter. Campaign Speech in Detroit, in
"Good As Its People," 15 Oct. Available from http://www.ontheissues
.org/Celeb/Jimmy_Carter_Crime.htm.

On the Issues. 2017a. Gerald Ford on Crime President of the U.S., 1974–1977,
Republican Rep. (MI). Available from http://www.ontheissues.org/celeb
/Gerald_Ford_Crime.htm (accessed 3 Jan 2017).

On the Issues. 2017b. Clinton-Bush-Perot Presidential Debates. *On the Issues,*
Oct. 1992. Available from http://www.ontheissues.org/Clinton-Bush.htm
(accessed 3 Jan).

On the Issues. 2017c. George Bush Sr. on Crime President of the U.S., 1989–1993.
On the Issues, Available from http://www.ontheissues.org/Celeb/George
_Bush_Sr__Crime.htm (accessed 3 Jan).

The Oyez Project. 2017. Samuel A. Alito, Jr. Available from http://www.oyez.org
/justices/samuel_a_alito_jr.

Parton, Heather Digby. 2016. Donald Trump's Other Authoritarian Shtick: Why
We Should Be Paying Much More Attention to His "Law and Order"
Extremism. *Salon.* Available from http://www.salon.com/2016/03/17/donald
_trumps_other_authoritarian_htick_why_we_should_be_paying
_much_more_attention_to_his_law_and_order_extremism/ (accessed
23 Dec 2016).

Passel, Jeffrey and D'Vera Cohn. 2016. Size of U.S. Unauthorized Immigrant Workforce Stable after the Great Recession Declines in Eight States and Increases
in Seven since 2009. Pew Research Center, 3 Nov. Available from http://
www.pewhispanic.org/2016/11/03/size-of-u-s-unauthorized-immigrant
-workforce-stable-after-the-great-recession/ (accessed 13 Apr 2017).

PBS. 2012. *LBJ's "Passage of Power": The Transformation of a Legislative Genius.*
http://www.pbs.org/newshour/bb/white_house-jan-june12-lbj_05-10/
(accessed 27 May 2017).

PBS. 2016. *16 for 16: The Contenders, Michael Dukakis.* Available from http://www
.pbs.org/the-contenders/people/michael-dukakis/ (cited 4 Apr 2017).

PBS. 2017. *The Presidents: Gerald Ford. American Experience.* Available from http://
www.pbs.org/wgbh/americanexperience/features/biography/presidents
-ford/ (accessed 28 Mar 2017).

Peffley, Mark, Jon Hurwitz, and Paul M. Sniderman. 1997. "Racial Stereotypes
and White's Political Views of Blacks in Context of Welfare and Crime."
American Journal of Political Science, 41 (1): 30–60.

Peterson, Ruth D. 1985. Discriminatory Decision Making at the Legislative Level: An Analysis of the Comprehensive Drug Abuse Prevention and Control Act of 1970. *Law and Human Behavior* 9, (3): 243–69.

Pew Charitable Trusts. 2015. Fact Sheet: Federal Prison System Shows Dramatic Long-Term Growth Policy Decisions Contribute to Steep Rise in Inmate Population and Costs. 27 Feb. Available from http://www.pewtrusts.org /en/research-and-analysis/fact-sheets/2015/02/federal-prison-system -shows-dramatic-long-term-growth (accessed 2 Jul 2015).

Pitzer, Andrea. 2017. The Bitter History of Law and Order in America: It Has Stifled Suffrage, Blamed Immigrants for Chaos, and Suppressed Civil Rights. It's Also How Donald Trump Views the Entire World. *Longreads,* April. Available from https://longreads.com/2017/04/06/the-bitter-history -of-law-and-order-in-america/ (accessed 30 Apr 2016).

Porter, Nicole. 2010. The State of Sentencing 2010: Developments in Policy and Practice. Available from http://sentencingproject.org/doc/publications /publications/ Final%20State%20of%20of%20the%20Sentencing%202010 .pdf (accessed 24 Dec 2011).

Potok, Mark. 2009. The Top Three Anti-Immigration Groups Share Extremist Roots—Three D.C. Organizations That Work against Immigration Reform. *Southern Poverty Law Center,* 9 Feb. Available from http://www .alternet.org/immigration/125183/the_top_three_anti-immigration -groups_share_extremist_roots (accessed 26 Dec 2011).

Potok, Mark. 2011. The Dirty Secret behind the Nativist Lobby, 25 May. *Huffington Post Blog.* Available from http://www.huffingtonpost.com/mark-potok /the-dirty-secret-behind-t_b_163976.html.

Potok. Mark. 2017. The Year in Hate and Extremism. 15 Feb. *Southern Poverty Law Center.* Available from https://www.splcenter.org/fighting-hate /intelligence-report/2017/year-hate-and-extremism.

President Barack Obama. Address before a Joint Session of Congress on the State of the Union, 9 Feb 2009. *American Presidency Project.* Available from http://www.presidency.ucsb.edu/ws/?pid=85753 (accessed 7 Apr 2017).

President Barack Obama. Address Before a Joint Session of the Congress, 24 Feb 2009. *American Presidency Project.* Available from http://www.presidency .ucsb.edu/ws/index.php?pid=85753.

President Barack Obama. Address before a Joint Session of Congress on the State of the Union 27 Jan 2010. *American Presidency Project.* Available from http://www.presidency.ucsb.edu/ws/index.php?pid=87433 (accessed 14 Apr 2017).

President Barack Obama. Address before a Joint Session of Congress on the State of the Union 25 Jan 2011. *American Presidency Project.* Available from http://www.presidency.ucsb.edu/ws/index.php?pid=88928 (accessed 14 Apr 2017).

President Barack Obama. Address before a Joint Session of Congress on the State of the Union 24 Jan 2012. *American Presidency Project.* Available from http://www.presidency.ucsb.edu/ws/index.php?pid=99000 (accessed 14 Apr 2017).

President Barack Obama. Address before a Joint Session of Congress on the State of the Union 12 Feb 2013. *American Presidency Project.* Available from http://www.presidency.ucsb.edu/ws/index.php?pid=102826 (accessed 14 Apr 2017).

President Barack Obama. Address before a Joint Session of Congress on the State of the Union, 28 Jan 2014. *American Presidency Project.* Available from http://www.presidency.ucsb.edu/ws/index.php?pid=104596 (accessed 14 Apr 2017).

President Barack Obama. Address before a Joint Session of Congress on the State of the Union, 20 Jan 2015. *American Presidency Project.* Available from http://www.presidency.ucsb.edu/ws/index.php?pid=108031 (accessed 14 Apr 2017).

President Barack Obama. Address before a Joint Session of Congress on the State of the Union, 12 Jan 2016. *American Presidency Project.* Available from http://www.presidency.ucsb.edu/ws/index.php?pid=111174 (accessed 14 Apr 2017).

President Dwight D. Eisenhower. President's News Conference. 8 Feb 1956. *American Presidency Project.* Available from http://www.presidency.ucsb .edu/ws/index.php?pid=10742 (accessed 8 Feb 2008).

President Dwight D. Eisenhower. Regarding Occurrences at Central High School in Little Rock. 23 Sep 1957. *American Presidency Project.* Available from http://www.presidency.ucsb.edu/ws/?pid=10908 (accessed 8 Feb 2008).

President George H. W. Bush. Address on Administration Goals before a Joint Session of Congress. 9 Feb 1989. *American Presidency Project.* Available from http://www.presidency.ucsb.edu/ws/index.php?pid=16660&st=cri me&st1+law+enforcement (accessed 12 Jun 2008).

President George H. W. Bush. Remarks at the Annual Conference of the Veterans of Foreign Wars. 6 Mar 1989. *American Presidency Project.* Available from http://www.presidency.ucsb.edu/ws/index.php?pid=16727&st=drug&st1 =drug+abuse (accessed 11 Feb 2009).

President George H. W. Bush. Remarks Following the Swearing-in Ceremony for William J. Bennett as Director of National Drug Control Policy. 13 Mar 1989. *American Presidency Project.* Available from http://www.presidency .ucsb.edu/ws/index.php?pid=16769&st=Crime&st1=law+enforcement (accessed 12 Jun 2009).

President George H. W. Bush. Remarks to Students at Conestoga Valley High School in Lancaster, Pennsylvania. 22 Mar 1989. *American Presidency Project.* Available from http://www.presidency.ucsb.edu/ws/index.php?pi d=16823&st=drug&st1=drug+abuse (accessed 11 Feb 2009).

President George H. W. Bush. Address before a Joint Session of the Congress on the State of the Union. 29 Jan 1991. *American Presidency Project.* Available from http://www.presidency.ucsb.edu/ws/index.php?pid=19253&st=cri me&st1=law+enforcement (accessed 12 Jun 2008).

President George H. W. Bush. Address before a Joint Session of the Congress on the State of the Union. 28 Jan 1992. *American Presidency Project.* Available from http://www.presidency.ucsb.edu/ws/index.php?pid=20544&st=crime&st1=law+enforcement (accessed 8 Feb 2009).

President George W. Bush. Address before a Joint Session of the Congress on the State of the Union. 29 Jan 2001. *American Presidency Project.* Available from http://www.presidency.ucsb.edu/ws/index.php?pid=29644 (accessed 8 Feb 2009).

President George W. Bush. Address before a Joint Session of the Congress on Administration Goals. 27 Feb 2001. *American Presidency Project.* Available from http://www.presidency.ucsb.edu/ws/?pid=29643.

President George W. Bush. Proclamation 7425—National D.A.R.E. Day, 2001. 10 Apr 2001. *American Presidency Project.* Available from http://www.presidency.ucsb.edu/ws/index.php?pid=61722&st=drugs&st1=drug+abus (accessed 24 Jun 2009).

President George W. Bush. Address before a Joint Session of the Congress on the United States Response to the Terrorist Attacks of September 11. 20 Sep 2001. *American Presidency Project.* Available from http://www.presidency.ucsb.edu/ws/?pid=64731# axzz1tFyUdhjx (accessed 24 Jun 2009).

President George W. Bush. Fact Sheet: President Empowers Communities in the Fight against Illegal Drug Abuse. 14 Dec 2001. *American Presidency Project.* Available from http://www.presidency.ucsb.edu/ws/index.php?pid=79274 (accessed 24 Jun 2009).

President George W. Bush. Address before a Joint Session of the Congress on the State of the Union. 29 Jan 2002. *American Presidency Project.* Available from http://www.presidency.ucsb.edu/ws/index.php?pid=29644 (accessed 8 Feb 2009).

President George W. Bush. Remarks on the 2002 National Drug Control Strategy. 12 Feb 2002. *American Presidency Project.* Available from http://www.presidency.ucsb.edu/ws/index.php?pid=72976&st=crime&st1=law+enforcement (accessed 23 Jun 2009).

President George W. Bush. Statement on the Signing of the Homeland Security Act of 2002. 25 Nov 2002. *American Presidency Project.* Available from http://www.presidency.ucsb.edu/ws/index.php?pid=64224 (accessed 8 Feb 2008).

President George W. Bush. Address before a Joint Session of the Congress on the State of the Union. 28 Jan 2003. *American Presidency Project.* Available from http://www.presidency.ucsb.edu/ws/index.php?pid=29645 (accessed 23 Jan 2009).

President George W. Bush. Address before a Joint Session of the Congress on the State of the Union. 20 Jan 2004. *American Presidency Project.* Available from http://www.presidency.ucsb.edu/ws/index.php?pid=29646 (accessed 23 Jun 2009).

President George W. Bush. Address before a Joint Session of the Congress on the State of the Union. 2 Feb 2005. *American Presidency Project.* Available from http://www.presidency.ucsb.edu/ws/index.php?pid=58746 (accessed 23 Jun 2009).

President George W. Bush. Address before a Joint Session of the Congress on the State of the Union. 31 Jan 2006. *American Presidency Project.* Available from http://www.presidency.ucsb.edu/ws/index.php?pid=65090 (accessed 23 Jun 2009).

President Gerald R. Ford. President's News Conference. 3 Apr 1974. *American Presidency Project.* Available from http://www.presidency.ucsb.edu/ws/index.php?pid=4812 (accessed 3 Feb 2008).

President Gerald R. Ford. Statement on Signing the Juvenile Justice and Delinquency Prevention Act of 1974. 8 Sep 1974. *American Presidency Project.* Available from http://www.presidency.ucsb.edu/ws/index.php?pid=4697&st=crime&st1= (accessed 9 Jun 2009).

President Gerald R. Ford. Remarks to the Annual Convention of the International Association of Chiefs of Police. 24 Sep 1974. *American Presidency Project.* Available from http://www.presidency.ucsb.edu/ws/index.php?pid=4734&st=crime&st1=law+enforcement (accessed 8 Feb 2009).

President Gerald R. Ford. Address at the Yale University Law School Sesquicentennial Convocation Dinner. 25 Apr 1975. *American Presidency Project.* Available from http://www.presidency.ucsb.edu/ws/index.php?pid=4869&st=law&st1=order (accessed 8 Feb 2008).

President Gerald R. Ford. 166—The President's News Conference. 3 Apr 1975. *American Presidency Project.* Available from http://www.presidency.ucsb.edu/ws/index.php?pid=4812.

President Gerald R. Ford. Special Message to the Congress on Crime. 19 Jun 1975. *American Presidency Project.* Available from http://www.presidency.ucsb.edu/ws/index.php?pid= (accessed 8 Feb 2009).

President Gerald R. Ford. Remarks at the Career Criminal Conference of the Law Enforcement Assistance Administration. 26 Sep 1975. *American Presidency Project.* Available from http://www.presidency.ucsb.edu/ws/index.php?pid=5283&st=crime&st1=law+enforcement (accessed 8 Feb 2008).

President Gerald R. Ford. President Ford '76 Fact Book. 1976. President Ford's Leadership. *Gerald R. Ford Library.* Available from https://fordlibrarymuseum.gov/LIBRARY/document/factbook/accompli.htm (accessed 4 Feb 2017).

President Gerald R. Ford. Annual Message to the Congress on the State of the Union. 19 Jan 1976. *American Presidency Project.* Available from http://www.presidency. ucsb.edu/ws/index.php?pid=5677 (accessed 3 Jan 2017).

President Gerald R. Ford. Address before a Joint Session of the Congress Reporting on the State of the Union. 19 Jan 1976. *American Presidency Project.* Available from http://www.presidency.ucsb.edu/ws/?pid=5677 (accessed 2 Aug 2008).

President Gerald R. Ford. Remarks at Federal Bar Association Dinner in Miami, Florid. 14 Feb 1976. *American Presidency Project.* Available from http://www.presidency .ucsb.edu/ws/?pid=6542 (accessed 3 Feb 2017).

President Gerald Ford's Radio Address on Crime. 29 Oct 1976. *American Presidency Project*. Available from http://www.presidency.ucsb.edu/ws/index .php?pid= 6562&st=official+corruption&st1= (accessed 8 Feb 2008).

President Jimmy Carter. Report to the American People. 2 Feb 1977. *American Presidency Project*. Available from http://www.presidency.ucsb.edu.ws /index.php?pid+7455&st+crime&&st1=law+enforcement (accessed 14 Mar 2009).

President Jimmy Carter. News Conference. 24 Mar 1977. *American Presidency Project*. Available from http://www.presidency.ucsb.edu/ws/index.php?pid =7229&st=crime&st1=law+enforcement (accessed 14 Mar 2009).

President Jimmy Carter. Interview with the National Black Network Question-and-Answer Session with Representatives of the Network. 18 Jul 1977. *American Presidency Project*. Available from http://www.presidency.ucsb .edu/ws/index.php?pid=7857&st=crime&st1=law+enforcement (accessed 9 Feb 2009).

President Jimmy Carter. Drug Abuse Message to the Congress. 2 Aug 1977. *American Presidency Project*. Available from http://www.presidency.ucsb .edu/ws/index.php?pid=7908&st=drugs&st1=drug+abuse (accessed 9 Jun 2009).

President Jimmy Carter. State of the Union Annual Message to the Congress. 19 Jan 1978. *American Presidency Project*. Available from http://www.presi dency.ucsb.edu/ws/index.php?pid=30867&st=crime&st1=law+enforcem ent (accessed 8 Feb 2009).

President Jimmy Carter. State of the Union Annual Message to the Congress. 25 Jan 1979. *American Presidency Project*. Available from http://www .president.ucsb.edu/ws/index.php??pid=32735&st=crime&st1=law +enforcement (accessed 9 Feb 2009).

President Jimmy Carter. State of the Union Annual Message to the Congress. 23 Jan 1980. *American Presidency Project*. Available from http://www .presidency.ucsb.edu/ ws/index.php?pid=33079 (accessed 9 Feb 2009).

President Jimmy Carter. Baltimore, Maryland Remarks at the Opening Session of the White House Conference on Families. 5 Jun 1980. *American Presidency Project*. Available from http://www.presidency.ucsb.edu/ws/index .php?pid=45200&st=drugs&st1= (accessed 3 Apr 2017).

President Jimmy Carter. State of the Union Annual Message to the Congress. 16 Jan 1981. *American Presidency Project*. Available from http://www.presidency .ucsb.edu/ws/index.php?pid-44541&st=crime&st1=law+enforcement (accessed 13 Mar 2009).

President John F. Kennedy. Address to Congress on the State of the Union, 14 Jan 1963.

President Lyndon B. Johnson. Remarks in New York City before the 50th Anniversary Convention of the Amalgamated Clothing Workers. 9 May 1964. *American Presidency Project*. Available from http://www.presidency.ucsb .edu/ws/index.php?pid=26237&st=crime&st1=poverty (accessed 4 Dec 2009).

President Lyndon B. Johnson. Remarks to the United States Marshals. 18 Aug 1964. *American Presidency Project.* Available from http://www.presidency.ucsb.edu/ws/index.php?pid=26447&st=crime&st1=law+enforcement (accessed 11 Nov 2008).

President Lyndon B. Johnson. Remarks upon Signing the Economic Opportunity Act. 20 Aug 1964. *American Presidency Project.* Available from http://www.presidency.ucsb.edu./ws/index.php?pid=26452 (accessed 11 Nov 2008).

President Lyndon B. Johnson. Annual Message to the Congress on the State of the Union. 4 Jan 1965. *American Presidency Project.* Available from http://www.presidency.ucsb.edu/ws/index.php?pid=26907&st=crime&st1 (accessed 12 Nov 2008).

President Lyndon B. Johnson. Special Message to the Congress on Law Enforcement and the Administration of Justice. 8 Mar 1965. *American Presidency Project.* Available from http://www.presidency.ucsb.edu/ws/?pid-26800 (accessed 17 Mar 2008).

President Lyndon B. Johnson. Remarks on Crime Control at the Signing of the District of Columbia Appropriations Bill. 16 Jul 1965. *American Presidency Project.* Available from http://www.presidency.ucsb.edu/ws/index.php?pid=27092&st=crime&st1=law+enforcement (accessed 11 Nov 2008).

President Lyndon B. Johnson. Remarks to the Members of the President's Commission on Law Enforcement and Administration of Justice. 8 Sep 1965. *American Presidency Project.* Available from http://www.presidency.ucsb.edu/ws/index.php?pid=27242&st=crimest1=law+enforcement (accessed 2 Feb 2009).

President Lyndon B. Johnson. Annual Message to the Congress on the State of the Union. 12 Jan 1966. *American Presidency Project.* Available from http://www.presidency.ucsb.edu/ws/index.php?pid=28015 (accessed 5 Feb 2009).

President Lyndon B. Johnson. Special Message to the Congress on Crime and Law Enforcement. 9 Mar 1966. *American Presidency Project.* Available from http://www.presidencyucsb.edu/ws/index.php?pid=27478&st=crime&st1=law+enforcement (accessed 2 Feb 2009).

President Lyndon B. Johnson. Remarks at a Meeting with Federal Enforcement Officials to Deal with the Problem of Organized Crime. 5 May 1966. *American Presidency Project.* Available from http://www.presidency.ucsb.edu/ws/index.php?pid=27576&st=crime&st1=law+enforcement (accessed 2 Feb 2009).

President Lyndon B. Johnson. Remarks to the Delegates to the Conference of State Committees on Criminal Administration. 15 Oct 1966. *American Presidency Project.* Available from http://www.presidency.ucsb.edu/ws/index.php?pid=27933&st=crime&st1=law+enforcement (accessed 11 Nov 2008).

President Lyndon B. Johnson. Statement by the President upon Signing Bills to Aid in the Crusade against Crime. 8 Nov 1966. *American Presidency*

Project. Available from http://www.presidency.ucsb.edu/ws/index.php?pid =28013&st=crime&stl=law+enforcement (accessed 2 Feb 2009).

President Lyndon B. Johnson. Annual Message to the Congress on the State of the Union. 10 Jan 1967. *American Presidency Project*. Available from http:// www.presidency.ucsb.edu/ws/index.php?pid=28338&st=crime&stl=law +enforcement (accessed 2 Feb 2009).

President Lyndon B. Johnson. Special Message to the Congress on Crime in America. 6 Feb 1967. *American Presidency Project*. Available from http:// www.presidency.ucsb.edu/ws/index.php?pid=28394&st=crime&stl=la w+enforcement (accessed 11 Nov 2008).

President Lyndon B. Johnson. Meeting of the International Association of Chiefs of Police. 14 Sep 1967. *American Presidency Project*. Available from.edu /ws/index.php?pid=28430&st=crime&stl=law+enforcement (accessed 2 Feb 2009).

President Lyndon B. Johnson. President Johnson's Program for Crime Prevention 1968. 1969. *Congressional Quarterly*. Available from http://library.cqpress .com/catn/catn65-5-6043-303981 (accessed Jul 28 2008).

President Richard M. Nixon. Address Accepting the Presidential Nomination at the Republican National Convention in Miami Beach, FL. 8 Aug 1968. *American Presidency Project*. Available from http://www.presidency. ucsb.edu/ws /index.php?pid=25968&st=law+and+order&stl= (accessed 6 Jun 2009).

President Richard M. Nixon. Statement Outlining Actions and Recommenda-tions for the District of Columbia. 31 Jan 1969. *American Presidency Project*. Available from http://www.presidency.ucsb.edu/ws/Index.php?pi d=2053&st=crime&stl=law+enforcement (accessed 5 Feb 2009).

President Richard M. Nixon. Memorandum on the Narcotic and Dangerous Drug Traffic in the District of Columbia. 22 Feb 1969. *American Presi-dency Project*. Available from http://www.presidency.ucsb.edu/ws/index .php?pid=2406&st=crime&stl=law+enforcement (accessed 6 Feb 2009).

President Richard M. Nixon. Special Message to the Congress on Forthcoming Leg-islative Proposals Concerning Domestic Programs. 14 Apr 1969. *American Presidency Project*. Available from http//ww.presidency.ucsb.edu/ws/index. php?pid=1998&st=crime&stl=law+enforcement (accessed 6 Feb 2009).

President Richard M. Nixon. Conversation with Newsmen on the Nomination of the Chief Justice of the United States. 22 May 1969. *American Presidency Project*. Available from http://www.presidency.ucsb.edu/ws/index.php?pi d=2065&st=Burger&stl=Chief+Justice (accessed 17 Jul 2009).

President Richard M. Nixon. Remarks at a Bipartisan Leadership Meeting on Narcotics and Dangerous Drugs. 23 Oct 1969. *American Presidency Proj-ect*. Available from http://www.presidency.ucsb.edu/ws/index.php?pid=2 280&st=crime&stl=law+enforcement (accessed 7 Feb 2009).

President Richard M. Nixon. Annual Message to the Congress on the State of the Union. 22 Jan 1970. *American Presidency Project*. Available from http:// www.presidency.ucsb.edu/ws/index.php?pid=2921&st=crime&stl=law+ enforcement (accessed 7 Feb 2009).

President Richard M. Nixon. Remarks to Delegates Attending the Annual United States Attorneys' Conference. 11 Jun 1970. *American Presidency Project.* Available from http://www.presidency.ucsb.edu/ws/index.php?pid=2541& st=crime&stl (accessed 7 Feb 2009).

President Richard M. Nixon. Statement on Establishing the President's Commission on Campus Unrest. 13 Jun 1970. *American Presidency Project.* Available from http://www.presidency.ucsb.edu/ws/index.hp?id=2544&st=Ca mpus&stl=Unrest (accessed 11 Feb 2008).

President Richard M. Nixon. Remarks at the 50th Anniversary Convention of the United States Jaycees in St. Louis, Missouri. 24 Jun 1970. *American Presidency Project.* Available http://www.presidency.ucsb.edu/ws/index .php?pid=2560&st=crime&stl=law+enforcement (accessed 7 Feb 2009).

President Richard M. Nixon. Remarks on Arrival at Denver, Colorado. 3 Aug 1970. *American Presidency Project.* Available http://www.presidency.ucsb .edu/ws/index.php?pid =606&st=crime&stl=law+enforcement (accessed 7 Feb 2009).

President Richard M. Nixon. 297—Letter to Educators and University Officials on Campus Violence. 22 Sep 1970. *American Presidency Project.* Available from http://www.presidency.ucsb.edu/ws/index.php?pid=2665 (accessed 2 Jun 2017).

President Richard M. Nixon. Remarks on Signing the Comprehensive Drug Abuse Prevention and Control Act of 1970. 27 Oct 1970. *American Presidency Project.* Available from http://www.presidency.ucsb.edu/ws/?pid =2767 (accessed 1 Feb 2017).

President Richard M. Nixon. Statement on Signing the Omnibus Crime Control Act. 2 Jan 1971. *American Presidency Project.* Available from http://www .presidency.ucsb.edu/ws/index.php?pid=3043 (accessed 7 Feb 2009).

President Richard M. Nixon. Annual Message to the Congress on the State of the Union. 22 Jan 1971. *American Presidency Project.* Available from http:// www.presidency.ucsb.edu/ws/index.php?pid=3110&st=crime&stl=law+ enforcement (accessed 7 Feb 2009).

President Richard M. Nixon. Remarks at the Opening Session of the National Conference on the Judiciary in Williamsburg, Virginia. 11 Mar 1971. *American Presidency Project.* Available http://www.presidency.ucsb.edu /ws/index.php?pid=3344&st=crime&stl (accessed 7 Feb 2009).

President Richard M. Nixon. Special Message to the Congress on Drug Abuse Prevention and Control. 17 Jun 1971. *American Presidency Project.* Available from http://www.presidency.ucsbedu/ws/index.php?pid=3048&st= drugs &stl=crime (accessed 7 Feb 2009).

President Richard M. Nixon. Telephone Remarks to Students and Educators Attending a Drug Education Seminar in Monroe, Louisiana, 4 Oct 1971. *American Presidency Project.* Available from http://www.presidency.ucsb .edu/ws/?pid=3179 (accessed 1 Aug 2008).

President Richard M. Nixon. Address to the Nation Announcing Intention to Nominate Lewis F. Powell, Jr., and William H. Rehnquist to Be Associate

Justices of the Supreme Court of the United States. 21 Oct 1971. *American Presidency Project*. Available from http://www.presidency.ucsb.edu/ws /index.php?pid=3196 (accessed 6 Jun 2009).

President Richard M. Nixon. Address on the State of the Union Delivered before a Joint Session of the Congress. 20 Jan 1972. *American Presidency Project*. Available from http://www.presidency.ucsb.edu/ws/index.php?pid=3396 &st=crime&st1=law+enforcement (accessed 11 Feb 2008).

President Richard M. Nixon. Statement on Establishing the Office for Drug Abuse Law Enforcement. 28 Jan 1972. *American Presidency Project*. Available from http://www.presidency.ucsb.edu/ws/?pid=3552 (accessed 1 Aug 2008).

President Richard M. Nixon. State of the Union Message to the Congress on Law Enforcement and Drug Abuse Prevention. 14 Mar 1973. *American Presidency Project*. Available from http://www.presidency.ucsb.edu/ws/index .php?pid=4140&st=crime&st1=law+enforcement (accessed 3 Feb 2008).

President Richard M. Nixon. Message to the Congress Transmitting Reorganization Plan 2 of 1973 Establishing the Drug Enforcement Administration. 28 Mar 1973. *American Presidency Project*. Available from http://www .presidency.ucsb.edu/ws/?pid=4159 (accessed 1 Aug 2008).

President Ronald Reagan. Statement Announcing Additional Federal Aid for Programs Relating to the Murdered and Missing Youth in Atlanta, Georgia. 5 Mar 1981. *American Presidency Project*. Available from http://www .presidency.ucsb.edu/ws/index.php?pid=43503&st=crime&st1=law+enf orcement (accessed 1 Feb 2009).

President Ronald Reagan. Proclamation 4831—Victims Rights Week. 8 Apr 1981. *American Presidency Project*. Available from http://www.presidency .ucsb.edu/ws/index.php? (accessed 1 Feb 2009).

President Ronald Reagan. Remarks in New Orleans, Louisiana, at the Annual Meeting of the International Association of Chiefs of Police. 28 Sep 1981. *American Presidency Project*. Available from http://www.presidency.ucsb .edu/ws/index.php?pid=44300&st=crime&st1=law+enforcement (accessed 8 Feb 2009).

President Ronald Reagan. Address before a Joint Session of the Congress on the State of the Union. 26 Jan 1982. *American Presidency Project*. Available from http://www.presidency.ucsb.edu/ws/index.php?pid=42687 (accessed 1 Feb 2009).

President Ronald Reagan. Statement on Proposed Anticrime Legislation. 26 May 1982. *American Presidency Project*. Available from http://www.presidency .ucsbedu/ws/index.php?pid=42568&st=crime&st1=law+enforcement (accessed 1 Feb 2009).

President Ronald Reagan. Remarks to Reporters Announcing Proposed Criminal Justice Reform Legislation. 13 Sep 1982. *American Presidency Project*. Available from http://www.presidency.ucsb.edu/ws/index.php?pid=4295 5&st=crime&st1=drug (accessed 11 Feb 2009).

President Ronald Reagan. Address before a Joint Session of the Congress on the State of the Union. 25 Jan 1983. *American Presidency Project.* Available from http://www.presidency.ucsb.edu/ws/index.php?pid=41698 (accessed 1 Feb 2009).

President Ronald Reagan. Proclamation 5064—Missing Children Day. 25 May 1983. *American Presidency Project.* Available from http://www.presidency.ucsb.edu/ws/index.php?pid=41374&st=crime&st1=law+enforcement (accessed 1 Feb 2009).

President Ronald Reagan. Address before a Joint Session of the Congress on the State of the Union. 25 Jan 1984. *American Presidency Project.* Available from http://www.presidency.ucsb.edu/ws/index.php?pid=40205 (accessed 1 Feb 2009).

President Ronald Reagan. Remarks at a White House Ceremony Marking the Observance of National Crime Prevention Week. 15 Feb 1984. *American Presidency Project.* Available from http://www.presidency.ucsb.edu/ws/index.php?pid=39525&st=Neighborhood+Watch+Program&st1= (acessed 2 Feb 2009).

President Ronald Reagan. Remarks at the Annual Conference of the National Sheriff's Association in Hartford, Connecticut. 20 Jun 1984. *American Presidency Project.* Available from http://www.presidency.ucsb.edu/ws/index.php?pid=40074.

President Ronald Reagan. Radio Address to the Nation on Law Enforcement and Crime. 7 Jul 1984. *American Presidency Project.* Available from http://www.presidency.ucsb.edu/ws/index.php?pid=40135&st=crime&st1=law+enforcement (accessed Feb 2009).

President Ronald Reagan. President's News Conference. 9 Jan 1985. *American Presidency Project.* Available http://www.presidency.ucsb.edu/ws/index.php?pid=38344&st=crime&st1=law+enforcement (accessed 1 Feb 2009).

President Ronald Reagan. Address before a Joint Session of the Congress on the State of the Union. 6 Feb 1985. *American Presidency Project.* Available from http://www.presidency.ucsb.edu/ws/index.php?pid=38069 (accessed 1 Feb 2009).

President Ronald Reagan. Address before a Joint Session of Congress on the State of the Union. 4 Feb 1986. *American Presidency Project.* Available from http://www.presidency.ucsb.edu/ws/?pid=36646 (accessed 17 Aug 2008).

President Ronald Reagan. Remarks on Signing the Anti-Drug Abuse Act of 1986. 27 Oct 1986. *American Presidency Project.* Available from http://www.presidency.ucsb.edu/ws/index.php?pid=36654&st=Anti-Drug+Abuse+Act&st1= (accessed 2 Feb 2009).

President Ronald Reagan. Address before a Joint Session of Congress on the State of the Union. 27 Jan 1987. *American Presidency Project.* Available from http://www.presidency.ucsb.edu/ws/index.php?pid=34430 (accessed 17 Aug 2008).

President Ronald Reagan. Address Concerning the Iran Contra Affair. 4 Mar 1987. Ronald Reagan Foundation. Available from http://millercenter.org

/ridingthetiger/this-day-in-history-reagan-addresses-the-nation-on-iran
-contra (accessed 9 Sep 2016).

President Ronald Reagan. Remarks at a White House Briefing on the Nomination
of Robert H. Bork to Be an Associate Justice of the Supreme Court of the
United State. 30 Sep 1987. *American Presidency Project*. Available from
http://www.presidency.ucsb.edu/ws/index.php?pid=33475&st =crime&st1
(accessed 2 Feb 2009).

President Ronald Reagan. Address to the Nation on the Supreme Court Nomination of Robert H. Bork. 14 Oct 1987. *American Presidency Project*. Available from http://www.presidency.ucsb.edu/ws/index.php?pid=33548&st
=crime&st1=law+enforcement (accessed 2 Feb 2009).

President Ronald Reagan. Remarks on Signing the Anti-Drug Abuse Act of 1988.
18 Jan 1988. *American Presidency Project*. Available from http://www
.presidency.ucsb.edu/ws/index.php?pid=35182.

President Ronald Reagan. Address before a Joint Session of Congress on the State
of the Union. 27 Jan 1988. *American Presidency Project*. Available from
http://www.presidency.ucsb.edu/ws/index.php?pid=36035 (accessed 17
Aug 2008).

President Ronald Reagan. Remarks to Media Executives at a White House Briefing on Drug Abuse. *American Presidency Project*. 8 Mar 1988. Available
from http://www.presidency.ucsb.edu/ws/index.php?pid=35521&st=dru
gs&st1=law+enforcement (accessed 1 Feb 2009).

President William J. Clinton. Interview with Dan Rather of CBS News. 24 Mar
1993. *American Presidency Project*. Available from http://www.presidency
.ucsb.edu/ws/index.php?pid=46370&st=crime&st1=law+enforcement
(accessed 13 Jun 2009).

President William J. Clinton. Proclamation 6619—National Domestic Violence
Awareness Month, 1993 and 1994. 28 Oct 1993. *American Presidency
Project*. Available from http://www.presidency.ucsb.edu/ws/index.php?
pid=62453 (accessed 15 Mar 2009).

President William J. Clinton. Remarks to Law Enforcement Organizations and
an Exchange with Reporters. 15 Apr 1993. *American Presidency Project*.
Available from http://www.presidency.ucsb.edu/ws/indix.php?pid=4643
5&st=crime&st1=lawenforcement (accessed 13 Jun 2009).

President William J. Clinton. Remarks to the National Association of Police
Organizations and an Exchange with Reporters. 24 Jun 1993. *American
Presidency Project*. Available at http://www.presidency.ucsb.edu/ws/index
.php?pid=46747&st=crime&st1=law+enforcement (accessed 13 Jun 2009).

President William J. Clinton. Address before a Joint Session of the Congress
on the State of the Union. 25 Jan 1994. *American Presidency Project*.
Available from http://www.presidency.ucsb.edu/ws/index.php?pid=50409
(accessed 20 Sep 2008).

President William J. Clinton. Press Briefing by Attorney General Janet Reno,
Secretary of H.U.D. Henry Cisneros, Director of the Office of National
Drug Control Policy Lee Brown, and Assistant Secretary of Treasury Ron

Noble. 29 Mar 1994. *American Presidency Project*. Available from http://www.presidency.ucsb.edu/ws/index.php?pid=59891.

President William J. Clinton. Remarks on Proposed Crime Legislation at the Department of Justice. 28 Jul 1994. *American Presidency Project*. Available from http://www.presidency.ucsb.edu/ws/index.php?pid=50560&st=crime&st1=law+enforcement (accessed 13 Jun 2009).

President William J. Clinton. Address before a Joint Session of the Congress on the State of the Union. 25 Jan 1995. *American Presidency Project*. Available from http://www.presidency.ucsb.edu/ws/index.php?pid=51634 (accessed 20 Sep 2008).

President William J. Clinton. Address before a Joint Session of the Congress on the State of the Union. 23 Jan 1996. *American Presidency Project*. Available from http://www.presidency.ucsb.edu/ws/index.php?pid=53091 (accessed 20 Sep 2008).

President William J. Clinton. Address before a Joint Session of the Congress on the State of the Union. 4 Feb 1997. *American Presidency Project*. Available from http://www.presidency.ucsb.edu/ws/index.php?pid=53358&st=State+of+the+Union&st1= (accessed 19 Jun 2009).

President William J. Clinton. Address before a Joint Session of the Congress on the State of the Union. 27 Jan 1998. *American Presidency Project*. Available from http://www.presidency.ucsb.edu/ws/index.php?pid=56280 (accessed 20 Sep 2008).

President William J. Clinton. Address before a Joint Session of the Congress on the State of the Union. 19 Jan 1999. *American Presidency Project*. Available from http://www.presidency.ucsb.edu/ws/index.php?pid=57577 (accessed 19 Jun 2009).

President William J. Clinton. Address before a Joint Session of the Congress on the State of the Union. 27 Jan 2000. *American Presidency Project*. Available from http://www.presidency.ucsbedu/ws/index.php?pid=58708&st=guns&st1= (accessed 20 Jun 2009).

President's Commission on Law Enforcement and Administration of Justice. 1967. *The Challenge of Crime in a Free Society*. Washington, D.C.: U.S. Government Printing Office.

Press Briefing by Attorney General Janet Reno, Secretary of H.U.D. Henry Cisneros, Director of the Office of National Drug Control Policy Lee Brown, and Assistant Secretary of Treasury Ron Noble. 29 Mar 1994. *American Presidency Project*. Available from http://www.presidency.ucsb.edu/ws/index.php?pid=59891&st=crime&st1=law+enforcement (accessed 13 Jun 2009).

Preston, Julia. 2011. U.S. to Review Cases Seeking Deportations. *New York Times*, 17 Nov. Available from http://www.nytimes.com/2011/11/17/us/deportation-cases-of-illegal-immigrants-to-bereviewed.html (accessed 24 Dec 2011).

Pye, Kenneth A. 1968. "The Warren Court and Criminal Procedure." *Michigan Law Review* 7: 249–268. Available from http://scholarship.law.duke.edu/cgi/viewcontent.cgi?article=5627 &context=faculty_scholarship.

Pye, Kenneth A., and Cym H. Lowell. 1975. The Criminal Process during Civil Disorders. Part II. Permissible Powers in Serious Civil Disorders. *Duke Law Journal* 5: 1021–101.

Pyle, G. F. 1980. Systematic Sociospatial Variation in Perceptions of Crime Location and Severity. *Crime: A Spatial Perspective*, eds D. E. Georges-Abeyie and K. D. Harris. Columbia University Press, New York.

Rabinovitz, Judy. 2011. Ending the Laws That Fuel Mass Detention and Deportation. American Civil Liberties Union (ACLU), 20 Oct. Available from https://www.aclu.org/blog/ending-laws-fuel-mass-detention-and-depor tation (accessed 22 Dec 2016).

Reagan, Nancy. 2009. *First Lady Biography: Nancy Reagan.* The National First Ladies' Library. Available from http://www.firstladies.org/biographies/firstladies .aspx?biography=41 (accessed 22 Jan 2009).

Reilly, Ryan J. 2016. Federal Prisons Are in Crisis. Congress and the President Need to Step Up, 26 Jan. Available from http://www.huffingtonpost.com /entry/federal-prisons-colson-report-drug-war_us_56a66df4e4b0d8cc10 9ae9c9 (acessed 27 Jan 2017).

Republican Party Platform of 1968. 15 Aug 1968. *American Presidency Project.* Available from http://www.presidency.ucsb.edu/ws/index.php?pid=25841 (accessed 29 May 2008).

Republican Party Platform of 1972. 21 Aug 1972. *American Presidency Project.* Available from http://www.presidency.ucsb.edu/ws/index.php?pid=2584 2&st=crime&st1=law+enforcement (accessed 3 Feb 2008).

Republican Party Platform of 1976. 18 Aug 1976. *American Presidency Project.* Available from http://www.presidency.ucsb.edu/ws/?pid=25843.

Republican Party Platform of 1980. 15 July 1980. *American Presidency Project.* Available from http://www.presidency.ucsb.edu/ws/index.php?pid=2584 4&st=crime&st1=law+enforcement (accessed 9 Jun 2009).

Republican Party Platform of 1984. 20 Aug 1984. *American Presidency Project.* Available from http://www.presidency.ucsb.edu/ws/index.php?pid=25845 (accessed 19 Sept 2008).

Republican Party Platform of 1988. 16 Aug 1988. *American Presidency Project.* Available from http://www.presidency.ucsb.edu/ws/index.php?pid=2584 6&st=Crime&st1=law+enforcement (accessed 12 Jun 2009).

Republican Party Platform of 1992. 17 Aug 1992. *American Presidency Project.* Available from http://www.presidency.ucsb.edu/ws/index.php?pid=2584 7&st=Crime&st1=law+enforcement (accessed 12 Jun 2009).

Republican Party Platform of 1996. 12 Aug 1996. *American Presidency Project.* Available from http://www.presidency.ucsb.edu/ws/index.php?pid=25847& st=Crime&st1=law+enforcement (accessed 12 Jun 2009).

Republican Party Platform of 2000. 31 Jul 2000. *American Presidency Project.* Available from http://www.presidency.ucsb.edu/ws/index.php?pid=2584 9&st=crime&st1=law+enforcement (accessed 23 Jun 2009).

Republican Party Platform of 2004. 30 Aug 2004. *American Presidency Project.* Available from http://www.presidency.ucsb.edu/ws/index.php?pid=2585 0&st=crime&st1=law+enforcement (accessed 23 Jun 2009).

Rhodan, Maya. 2015. What the War on Terrorism Can Learn from the War on Gangs, White House Summit, 20 Feb. Available from http://time.com/3716160/terrorism-gangs-white-house-summit/ (accessed 27 Jan 2017).

Right on Crime. 2017a. About Right on Crime. Available from http://rightoncrime.com/about/ (accessed 30 Apr 2017).

Right on Crime. 2017b. Priority Issues. Right on Crime. Available from http://rightoncrime.com/priority-issues/ (accessed 30 Apr 2017).

Right on Crime. n.d. Conservative Case for Reform. Available fromhttp://rightoncrime.com/the-conservative-case-for-reform/.

Rioting, 1965–1968 Overview. 1969. *Congressional Quarterly*. Available from http://library.cqpress.com.proxau.wrlc.org/catn/document.php?id=catn65-510025-645830 (accessed 9 May 2008).

Robert Dole: Remarks to the United States Conference of Mayors in Miami. 17 Jun 1995. *American Presidency Project*. Available from http://www.presidency.ucsb.edu/ws/index.php?pid=85194&st=crime&st1=law+enforcement (accessed 28 Jun 2008).

Robnett, Belinda. 1997. *How Long? How Long? African-American Women in the Struggle for Civil Rights*. New York: Oxford University Press.

Roche, Jeff. 2003. Cowboy Conservatism. In *The Conservative Sixties*, eds. David Farber and Jeff Roche. New York: Peter Lang.

Rodney King: Reluctant Symbol of Police Brutality. 2001. CNN/Law Center, 3 Mar. Available from http://archives.cnn.com/2001/LAW/03/02/beating.anniversity.king.02 (accessed 19 Sep 2008).

Rodney King Wounded in Shooting. 2007. CNN/US, 29 Nov. Available from http://www.cnn.com/2007/US/11/29/rodney.king.shot (accessed 19 Sep 2008).

Roehl, Janice A., Robert Huitt, Mary Ann Wycoff, Antony Pate, Donald Rebovich, and Ken Coyle. 1996. National Process Evaluation of Operation Weed and Seed. *National Institute of Justice,* Oct. Available from https://www.ncjrs.gov/pdffiles/weedseed.pdf.

Roth, Kenneth and Salil Shetty. 2016. Pardon Edward Snowden. *New York Times,* 15 Sep. Available from https://www.nytimes.com/2016/09/15/opinion/pardon-edward-snowden.html?_r=0 (accessed 13 Apr 2017).

Rourke, Francis. 1984. *Bureaucratic Power in Public Politics.* Reading, MA: Addison-Wesley.

Rucker, Philip, John Wagner, and David Fahrenthold. 2017. Trump Takes Office, Vows an End to "American Carnage." *Washington Post*, 20 Jan. Available from https://www.washingtonpost.com/politics/trump-takes-office-vows-an-end-to-american-carnage/2017/01/20/4b2677d8-df4e-11e6-acdf-14da832ae861_story.html?utm_term=.6ca21d02cf45 (accessed 15 May 2017).

Saenz, Arlette. 2011. George Bush Executed Texans at Faster Rate than Rick Perry. ABC News, 22 Sep. Available from http://abcnews.go.com/blogs/politics/2011/09/george-bush-executed-texans-at-faster-rate-than-rick-perry/ (accessed 17 May 2017).

Sanburn, Josh. 2017. President Trump Just Signaled Some Dramatic Changes for Police and Criminal Justice. 20 Jan. *Time*. Available from http://time .com/4641374/trump-inuaguration-police-protestors-justice/.

Savage, David G. 2014. With Executive Action, Obama Risks Losing Chief Justice John Roberts. *Los Angeles Times*, 1 Dec. Available from http://www .latimes.com/nation/la-na-obama-roberts-20141201-story.html (accessed 26 Feb 2017).

Schechter, Susan. 1982. *Women and Male Violence*. Boston: South End.

Scheingold, Stuart A. 1984. *The Politics of Law and Order: Street Crime and Public Policy*. New York: Longman.

Scheingold, Stuart A. 1995. Politics, Public Policy, and Street Crime. *Annals of the American Academy of Political and Social Science 539, Reactions to Crime and Violence*: 155–68.

Schlanger, Margo. 1999. Beyond the Hero Judge: Institutional Reform Litigation as Litigation. *Michigan Law Review* 97 (6): 1994–2036.

Schlosser, Eric. 1998. Prison Industry Complex. *The Atlantic*, Dec. Available from https://www.theatlantic.com/magazine/archive/1998/12/the-prison -industrial-complex/304669/.

Schneider, A., and P. Schneider. 1981. Victim Assistance Programs: An Overview. In *Perspectives on Crime Victims*, eds. B. Galaway and J. Hudson. St. Louis: Mosby.

Schram, Sanford, and Joe Soss Jacobin. 2015. America Demonizes Its Poor: Ronald Reagan, Sam Brownback, and the Myth of the "Welfare Queen." *Salon*, 8 Sep. Available from http://www.salon.com/2015/09/08/how_welfare _restrictions_demonize_the_poor_partner/ (accessed 31 Mar 2017).

Schuparra, Kurt. 2003. A Great White Light: The Political Emergence of Ronald Reagan. In *The Conservative Sixties*, eds. David Faber and Jeff Roche. New York: Peter Lang.

Scott, Bobby. 2015. Bipartisan Summit on Criminal Justice Reform. Washington, D.C. 26 Mar. Available from https://bobbyscott.house.gov/scott-speaks-at -bipartisan-criminal-justice-reform-summit.

Seelye, Katharine Q. 2000. The 2000 Campaign: The Texas Governor; Bush Would Use Power of Persuasion to Raise Oil Supply. *New York Times*. Available from http://www.nytimes.com/2000/06/28/us/2000-campaign -texas-governor-bush-would-use-power-persuasion-raise-oil-supply .html (accessed 4 Jan 2017).

Seelye, Katharine Q., Shan Carter, Jonathan Ellis, Farhana Hossain, and Alan McLean. 2008. On the Issues: Social Issues, Barack Obama and John McCain. *New York Times*. Available from http://elections.nytimes.com /2008/president/issues/abortion.html (accessed 22 Dec 2011).

Segura, Liliana. 2013. With 2.3 Million People Incarcerated in the U.S., Prisons Are Big Business. *The Nation*, 1 Oct. Available at http://www.thenation .com/prison-profiteers (accessed Apr 2017).

Sensenbrenner, Jim. U.S. Representative (R-WI) and Bobby Scott, U.S. Representative (D-VA). 2015a. Sensenbrenner and Scott to Introduce SAFE Justice Act Press Release, 23 Jun. Available at http://bobbyscott.house.gov/media

-center/press-releases/sensenbrenner-scott-to-introduce-safe-justice-act (accessed 16 Jul 2015).

Sensenbrenner, Jim. 2015b. Sensenbrenner, Scott Introduce Bipartisan, State-tested Criminal Justice Reform Legislation. Available at http://bobbyscott .house.gov/media-center/press-releases/sensenbrenner-scott-introduce -bipartisan-state-tested-criminal-.justice (accessed 25 Jun 2015).

Sentencing Project. 2013 (Aug). *Report of the Sentencing Project to the United Nations Human Rights Committee Regarding Racial Disparities in the United States Criminal Justice System.* Available from http://sentencingproject.org /doc/publications/rd_ICCPR%20Race%20and%20Justice%20Shadow %20Report.pdf (accessed 30 Jun 2015).

Sentencing Project. 2015. *Incarceration.* Available from http://www.sentencing project.org /template/page.cfm?id=107 (accessed 6 Jun 2015).

Sentencing Project. 2016. *Felony Disenfranchisement.* Available from http://www .sentencingprojectorg/IssueAreaHome.Aspx?IssueID=4 (accessed 21 Dec 16).

Senzee, Thom. 2016. Private Prisons Capitalism without Compassion: Aloe Blacc. *The Huffington Post,* 18 Apr. Available at http://www.huffingtonpost .com/thom-senzee/private-prisons-capitalism_b_9703140.html (accessed 13 Apr 2017).

Shah, Silky, Mary Small, and Carol Wu. (2015). Banking on Detention: Local Lockup Quotas and the Immigrant Dragnet. *Detention Watch Network.* Available from https://www.detentionwatchnetwork.org/sites/default/files /reports/DWN%20CCR%20Banking%20on%20Detention%20Report .pdf (accessed 22 Dec 2016).

Shales, Tom. 1994. The Gruesome Twosome and Diane Sawyer: Turning Point Premieres with Manson Family Reunion. *Washington Post,* 9 Mar. Available from Lexis Nexus (accessed 25 Jul 2007).

Shargel, Gerald. 2004. No Mercy: Ronald Reagan's Tough Legal Legacy. *Slate,* 14 Jun. Available from http://www.slate.com/articles/news_and_politics /jurisprudence /2004/06/no_mercy.html (accessed 10 May 2017).

Shipp, E. R. 1987. Gauging Reasonability in Goetz Case. *New York Times,* 31 May. Available from http://query.nytimes.com/gst/fullpage.html?res=9B0DE3 DA1438F932A05756C0A961948260&scp=2&sq=Bernhard%20H.%20 Goetz&st=cse (accessed 19 Aug 2008).

Shootings at Jackson State University: Thirty Years Later. 2000. *The Journal of Blacks in Higher Education* (28): 42–43.

Shriver, Donald. 2017. Crimes and Punishments. *Moyers and Company,* 31 Mar. Available from http://billmoyers.com/story/condensed-crimes-and-punishments/ (accessed 18 Apr 2017).

Shull, Steven A. 1999. *American Civil Rights Policy from Truman to Clinton: The Role of Presidential Leadership.* Armonk, NY: M.E. Sharpe.

Silva, Andrea. 2016. Neoliberalism Confronts Latinos: Paradigmatic Shifts in Immigration Practices. *Latino Studies* 14 (1): 59–79.

Simon, Jonathan. 2008. *Governing through Crime: How the War on Crime Transformed American Democracy and Created a Culture of Fear.* Oxford, England. Oxford University Press.

Simon, Jonathan. 2014. *Mass Incarceration on Trial: A Remarkable Court Decision and the Future of Prisons in America.* New York: New Press.

Smith, Phillip. 2017. Trump Goes Full Nixon on Law-and-Order Executive Orders, Vows "Ruthless" War on Drugs and Crime. *AlterNet,* 11 Feb. Available from http://www.alternet.org/drugs/trump-goes-full-nixon-law-and-order-executive-order-vows-ruthless-war-drugs-crime (accessed 30 Apr 2017).

Smith, Craig Allen, and Kathy B. Smith. 1994. *The White House Speaks: Presidential Leadership as Persuasion.* Westport, CT: Praeger.

Smith, Jackie, John D. McCarthy, Clark McPhail, and Boguslaw Augustyn. 2001. From Protest to Agenda Building: Description Bias in Media Coverage of Protest Events in Washington, D.C. *Social Forces* 79 (4): 1397–423.

Snow, David A., and Robert D. Benford. 2002. Framing Processes and Social Movements: *Annual Review of Sociology* 26: 611–639.

Somashekhar, Sandhya. 2011. Gabrielle Giffords Shooting in Tucson: Did It Stem from State of Political Discourse? *Washington Post,* 9 Jan. Available from http://www.washingtonpost.com/wp-dyn/content/article/2011/01/08/AR201101 0803652.html (accessed 21 Dec 2011).

Sonenstein, Brian. 2017. Trump Executive Orders Expand Mass Incarceration of Immigrants. *Shadow Proof,* 2 Feb. Available from https://shadowproof.com/2017/02/02/trump-orders-expand-incarceration-immigrants/ (accessed 24 Apr 2017).

Sorensen, Ted. 2008. Sorensen on Bill Clinton's Legacy. *Big Think New York Global Online Forum,* 31 Jan. Available from http://bigthink.com/tedsorensen/bill-clintons-legacy (accessed 21 Jun 2009).

Spence, Clark C. 1993. Reviewed: No Duty to Retreat: Violence and Values in American History and Society by Richard Maxwell Brown. *The Pacific Historical Review* 62 (2): 237–38.

Squier, Bob. 1968. *"Law and Order Democrat,"* Citizens for Humphrey-Muskie. Minnesota Historical Society. From Museum of the Moving Image, *The Living Room Candidate: Presidential Campaign Commercials 1952–2008.* Available from www.livingroomcadidate.org/commercials/1968/law-and-order-democrat (accessed 7 Feb 2009).

Steigenga, Timothy J. 2011. Commentary: U.S. Immigrant Detention System Is Costly, Inhumane and Undemocratic. *Palm Beach Post,* 14 Nov. Available at http://www.palmbeachpost.com/opinion/commentary/commentary-u-s-immigrant-detention-system-is-costly-1968738.html (accessed 22 Dec 2011).

Stern, Mark J. 2013. Clarence Thomas, Liberal. *Salon,* 18 Jun. Available at http://www.slate.com/articles/news_and_politics/jurisprudence/2013/06/clarence_thomas_s_liberal_rulings_how_the_supreme_court_justice_s_originalism.html (accessed 31 Aug 2016).

Sullivan, Eileen. 2016. Obama Administration to End Use of Private Prisons. *PBS News Hour,* 18 Aug. Available at http://www.pbs.org/newshour

/rundown/obama-administration-end-use-private-prisons/ (accessed 25 Sep 2016).

Taylor, Michael. 2008. Sara Jane Moore, Who Tried to Kill Ford in '75, Freed on Parole. *SF Gate*, 1 Jan. Available from http://www.sfgate.com/cgi-bin/article.cgi?f=/c/a/2008/01/01/MN2UU7JA4.DTL (accessed Feb 2009).

Tierney, John. 2012. For Lesser Crimes, Rethinking Life Behind Bars. *New York Times*, 11 Dec. Available from http://www.nytimes.com/2012/12/12/cience/mandatory-prison-face-growing-skeptcism.html (accessed Jul 2015).

Time Magazine. 1968. Lurching off to a Shaky Start. 92 (12), Sep. 20. Available at http://content.time.com/time/magazine/0,9263,7601680920,00.html.

Timm, Jane. 2016. Key Source Disputes Times Story on Trump's Behavior with Women. *NBC News*, 16 May. Available from http://www.nbcnews.com/politics/2016-election/key-source-disputes-times-story-trump-s-behavior-women-n574741 (accessed 29 Apr 2016).

Tolan, Casey. 2016. The Bold Step President Obama Could Take to Let Thousands of Federal Inmates Go Free. *Fusion*, 4 May. Available from http://fusion.net/story/298158/obama-clemency-board-gerald-ford/ (accessed Feb 2017).

Two Nights of Butchery. 1992. *The Advertiser*. Available from Lexis Nexis (accessed 25 July 2007).

U.S. Conference of Catholic Bishops, Migration and Refugee Services/Office of Migration Policy and Public Affairs. May 2011. *Secure Communities: The Facts about Local Immigration Law Enforcement*. Available from http://www.justiceforimmigrants.org/documents/2011-05-06-State-and-Local-Immigration-Enforcement-issue-brief.pdf (accessed 18 Dec 2011).

U.S. Demand Reduction Interagency Working Groups. 2009. Available from https://www.ncjrs.gov/pdffiles1/ondcp/ONDCP_brochure.pdf (accessed 11 Sep 2016).

U.S. Department of Justice, Office of Justice Programs. 2010. *Weed and Seed*. Available from http://www.ojp.usdoj.gov/ccdo/wswelcome.html (accessed 23 Jan 2009).

U.S. Drug Free Communities Support Program. 2009. *The Drug Free Communities Support Program*. Office of National Drug Control Policy, Executive Office of the President. Available from http://www.ondcp.gov/DFC (accessed 28 Jun 2009).

U.S. Office of Justice Programs, Bureau of Justice Statistics. 2009. *Number of State Prisoners Declined by Almost 3,000 during 2009; Federal Prison Population Increases by 6,800*. Available from http://bjs.ojp.usdoj.gov/content/pub/press/pim09stpy09acpr.cfm (accessed 8 Jun 2011).

U.S. Office of National Drug Control Policy (ONDCP). 2012. *National Drug Control Strategy*. Available from http://usgovinfo.about.com/gi/dynamic/offsite.htm?site= http:/www.whitehousedrugpolicy.gov (accessed Jun 2012).

U.S. Sentencing Commission. Apr 2015. *Illegal Reentry Offenses*. Available at http://www.ussc.gov/sites/default/files/pdf/research-and-publications

/research-projects-and-surveys/immigration/2015_Illegal-Reentry-Report
.pdf (accessed 26 Jun 2015).

Uwimana, Solange. 2011. NY Times Drops "Illegals," as Fox Continues to
Cling to Slur. *Media Matters for America,* 14 Dec. Available from http://
mediamatters.org/blog/201112140009 (accessed 27 Dec 2011).

Valdes, Gustavo, and Bill Mears. 2011. States Ask Courts to Halt Appeals in
Immigration Law Cases. CNN, 15 Dec. Available from http://www.cnn
.com/2011/12/15/us/state-immigration-laws/index.html (accessed 22
Dec 2011).

Venook, Jeremy. 2017. Donald Trump's Conflicts of Interest: A Crib Sheet: A
Semi-Comprehensive List of the Business Concerns That May Influence
the President during His Time in Office. *The Atlantic,* 24 Apr. Available
https://www.theatlantic.com/business/archive/2017/04/donald-trump
-conflicts-of-interests/508382/ (accessed 29 Apr 2017).

Vicini, James, and Jeremy Pelofsky. 2011. Alabama Immigration Law: Obama
Administration Files Lawsuit to Block Measure. *Huffington Post Politics,*
1 Aug. Available from http://www.huffingtonpost.com/2011/08/01
/alabama-immigration-law-lawsuit_n_915460.html (accessed 22 Dec 2011).

Vulliamy, Ed, and John Arlidge. 2001. Clinton Grants Full Pardon to Patty
Hearst. *The Guardian,* 20 Jan. Available from https://www.theguardian
.com/world/2001/jan/21/edvulliamy.johnarlidge (accessed 3 Feb).

Waldron, Jeremy. 2008. The Concept and the Rule of Law. *Georgia Law Review,* 5
Mar. Available from http://digitalcommons.law.uga.edu/lectures_pre_arch
_lectures_sibley/29/ (accessed 22 May 2017).

Weaver, Vesla M. 2007. Frontlash: Race and the Development of Punitive Crime
Policy. *Studies in American Political Development,* 21. Available from http://
www.ebonterr.com/site_editor/assets/EBONTERR_41.pdf (accessed 11
Mar 2017).

Weinberger, Matt. 2016. Donald Trump Exploited the Politics of Fear and We've
Seen Where That Leads. *Business Insider,* 9 Nov. Available at http://www
.businessinsider.com/donald-trump-policies-fear-and-hate-2016-11
(accessed 23 Apr 2017).

Wheaton, Sarah. 2008. Clinton's Civil Rights Lesson. *New York Times,* 7 Jan.
Available from http://thecaucus.blogs.nytimes.com/2008/01/07/civilrights
/comment-page-23/?_r=0 (accessed 27 Dec 2016).

Whitehead, John W. 2012. Jailing Americans for Profit: The Rise of the Prison
Industrial Complex, *Huffington Post,* 10 Jun. Available from http://www
.huffingtonpost.com/john-w-whitehead/prison-privatization_b_1414467
.html (accessed 12 Mar 2017).

White House. Press Release. 5 May 1987. Appointment of Lois Haight Herrington as Chairman and Executive Director of the White House Conference for a Drug Free America. University of Texas: Reagan Archives.
Available from http://www.reagan.utexas.edu/archives/speeches/1987
/050587f.htm (accessed 1 Feb 2009).

White House. 2004. Prisoner Re-Entry Initiative. Available from https:// georgewbush-whitehouse.archives.gov/government/fbci/pri.html (accessed 24 Jan 2017).

White House. 2016. Remarks by the President on the Supreme Court Decision on U.S. Versus Texas, 23 Jun. Available from https://obamawhitehouse .archives.gov/the-press-office/2016/06/23/remarks-president-supreme -court-decision-us-versus-texas (accessed 29 Jan 2017).

Wilber, Del Quentin. 2017. Justice Department Rescinds Order Phasing out Use of Private Prisons, Feb 23. Available from http://www.latimes.com/politics /washington/la-na-essential-washington-updates-justice-department -rescinds-order-1487893081-htmlstory.html (accessed 18 Apr 2017).

Winslow, Dan. 2015. It's Time to Legalize Drugs: An Open Letter to Congress and the President. *The Daily Beast,* 28 Jun. Available at http://www.thedaily beast.com/articles/2015/06/28/it-s-time-to-legalize-drugs-an-open-letter -to-congress-and-the-president.html (accessed 12 Aug 15).

Wolf, Richard. 2014. After 20 Years, Breyer Is High Court's Raging Pragmatist. *USA Today,* 7 Aug. Available from https://www.usatoday.com/story/news /politics/2014/08/07/justice-stephen-breyer-supreme-court-20-years /13269445/ (accessed 27 May 2017).

Wood, Daniel B. 2010. Arizona Immigration Law: California Leads Call for Boycotts. *Christian Science Monitor,* 28 Apr. Available at http://www .csmonitor.com/USA/Society/2010/0428/Arizona-immigration-law -California-leads-call-for-boycotts (cited 2 Jan 2012).

Wood, Daniel B. After Arizona, 2010. Why Are 10 States Considering Immigration Bills? *Christian Science Monitor,* 10 May. Available from http://www .csmonitor.com/USA/Society/2010/0510/After-Arizona-why-are -10-states-considering-immigration-bills (cited 19 Dec 2011).

Wood, Daniel B. 2010. Opinion Polls Show Broad Support for Tough Arizona Immigration Law. *Christian Science Monitor,* 30 Aug. Available at http:// www.csmonitor.com/USA/Society/ 2010/0430/Opinion-polls-show-broad -support-for-tough-Arizona-immigration-law (accessed 2 Jan 2012).

Wong, Cynthia M. 2015. Dispatches: No More Excuses on Patriot Act Surveillance Reform. *Human Rights Watch,* 9 Apr. Available from https:// www.hrw.org/news/2015/04/09/dispatches-no-more-excuses-patriot-act -surveillance-reform (accessed 25 Sep 2016).

Woolley, John T., and Gerhard Peters. *American Presidency Project.* Santa Barbara, CA: University of California. Available from http://www.presidency.ucsb .edu.

Yates, Jeff, and Richard Fording. Nov 2005. Politics and State Punitiveness in Black and White. *Journal of Politics.* 67 (4): 1099–112 (accessed 4 Jan 2017).

Young, Peter, and David Garland. 1983. Towards a Social Analysis of Penalty. In *The Power to Punish: Contemporary Penalty and Social Analysis,* eds. David Garland and Peter Young, 1–36. Atlantic Highlands, NJ: Humanities Press.

Zapotosky, Matt, and Chico Harlan. 2016. Justice Department Says It Will End Use of Private Prisons. *Washington Post*, 18 Aug. Available from https://www.washingtonpost.com/news/post-nation/wp/2016/08/18/justice-department-says-it-will-end-use-of-private-prisons/?tid=sm_fb&utm_term=.1d7ce91fb76f (accessed 19 Aug 2016).

Zion, Sidney E. 1965. Attack on Court Heard by Warren. *New York Times*, 10 Sep, Front Page. Available from http://www.nytimes.com/1973/05/07/archives/warren-attacks-plan-to-screen-supreme-court-cases-caseload-held.html?_r=0 (accessed 19 Aug 2016).

Zorthian, Julia. 2017. Here's Roughly Every Controversial Thing Donald Trump Has Ever Said Out Loud. 7 Aug. *Time*. Available from http://time.com/3988886/donald-trump-controversy/.

Index

Page numbers followed by *t* indicate tables.

About the Author

Linda K. Mancillas, PhD, is assistant professor of political science at Georgia Gwinnett College (GGC) near Atlanta, GA. She is co-author of "Born Digital: Integrating Media Technology in the Political Science Classroom," published in the *Journal of Political Science Education* (2015). She serves as chair of the American Political Science Association's Committee on the Status of Latinos y Latinas in the Profession. In 2015 Dr. Mancillas was nominated for the GGC Outstanding Teaching Award and the Outstanding Student Engagement Award. In 2011 she was awarded the American Political Science Association's Latino/a Caucus' Adaljiza Sosa-Riddell Mentoring Award. She was a Women's Research and Education Institute Congressional fellow for 2010, working on education policy issues in the Washington, D.C., office of Representative Bobby Scott (D-VA 3rd). Mancillas received the American University campus-wide 2008 Alice Paul Award and the 2005 Women & Politics Institute's Outstanding Graduate Student Award.